Enterprise Agility

Being Agile in a Changing World

Sunil Mundra

BIRMINGHAM - MUMBAI

Enterprise Agility

Acquisition Editors: Ben Renow-Clarke, Suresh M Jain
Project Editor: Radhika Atitkar
Content Development Editor: Joanne Lovell
Technical Editor: Bhagyashree Rai
Proofreader: Tom Jacob
Indexer: Priyanka Dhadke
Graphics: Tom Scaria
Production Coordinator: Sandip Tadge

First published: June 2018

Production reference: 1270618

Published by Packt Publishing Ltd.
Livery Place
35 Livery Street
Birmingham B3 2PB, UK.
ISBN 978-1-78899-064-6
www.packtpub.com

I dedicate this book to my wife Samta for her unconditional support and for the sacrifices she has made for the sake of my career.

`mapt.io`

Mapt is an online digital library that gives you full access to over 5,000 books and videos, as well as industry leading tools to help you plan your personal development and advance your career. For more information, please visit our website.

Why subscribe?

♦ Spend less time learning and more time coding with practical eBooks and Videos from over 4,000 industry professionals

♦ Learn better with Skill Plans built especially for you

♦ Get a free eBook or video every month

♦ Mapt is fully searchable

♦ Copy and paste, print, and bookmark content

PacktPub.com

Did you know that Packt offers eBook versions of every book published, with PDF and ePub files available? You can upgrade to the eBook version at `www.PacktPub.com` and as a print book customer, you are entitled to a discount on the eBook copy. Get in touch with us at `service@packtpub.com` for more details.

At `www.PacktPub.com`, you can also read a collection of free technical articles, sign up for a range of free newsletters, and receive exclusive discounts and offers on Packt books and eBooks.

Forewords

I'm a complex adaptive system. So are you. Every organization we have ever been a part of, including our families, are also complex adaptive systems. I have been talking about the properties of complex adaptive systems for years, and I have been yearning for a reference that would not only bring out the considerable theory of these fascinating systems but would also tie it to agile development. Now, I am happy to be able to point you, dear reader, and everyone else, who wants to know the bigger, broader story of agile, to this book that Sunil Mundra has written. He has done an excellent job of making what could be a difficult subject easy for all of us to understand and apply.

It's so easy to fall into the trap of believing that we can understand both ourselves and the environments in which we function. This is why I'm always suspicious of anyone who tries to explain the history of anything in a neat story. The truth is, we have been sold a bill of goods by teachers and philosophers. The pig in a poke we bought without hesitation is that things are modular, made up of pieces with clean interfaces, easily identified, easily extracted, and easily combined. Understanding these components leads to an understanding of the whole. It seems so obvious. It seems so right. But it was so wrong. It led us to take a simplistic view of change—both personal and organizational. We thought we could simply apply enough force and voila the result would appear. If we only had enough power, we could literally move mountains. No wonder all our change efforts failed!

Part of the reason for this mechanistic thinking that we now struggle to undo is the work of Frederick Taylor and his "scientific management." His contribution is often denigrated, but I believe we should celebrate his efforts. He was a well-intentioned, intelligent thinker who tried to bring what was at that time a new methodical approach to the workplace. He experimented. He measured. He learned. Sounds agile to me! I have the same reaction to those who disparage "waterfall." First, the current, incorrect, linear interpretation of Royce's original paper has caused the same disparaging of his work. For those careful readers of his article, the true meaning, an iterative solution to the then chaos that surrounded software development, will unfold.

It wasn't that far removed from where we are today and was certainly a very good step in the right direction. A dose of humility, realizing that we all are products of our environments and can only see what we can see, would serve us well. It's too easy to see the problems of the past and too difficult to see our current dilemmas. An ancient text admonishes, "How can you say to your brother or sister, 'Brother, Sister, let me take the splinter out of your eye,' when you don't see the log in your own eye?"

Fortunately for you, dear reader, Sunil doesn't take the high ground but, step by step, leads us forward, building on the great contributions of the past. And so on to what I consider the "heart" of the book—the discussion of complex adaptive systems. CAS for the rest of us! A CAS is well-named. There is nothing simple about it. The components, their interactions, the resulting, emergent behavior. It may be too much for our limited understanding, but the direction is clear, we have to begin to adopt this model if we are to survive.

As Sunil points out, this notion has been with us, in some form, from the beginning. We may not have applied it consciously, but it has been the key to our survival in a changing world. It is the answer to many of the big questions. How did we get here? How can we face our current reality? How can we get better? The answer is close to miraculous. It's exactly what we need. It's not prescriptive, it's adaptive. It's not stuck in the past, it's always about learning and improving. It's not about reaching a goal and relaxing, it's about always, always, always reaching and moving forward. The label "agile" insists on being applied.

The image of butterflies, so delicate and beautiful, helps us understand this. I'm a musician and occasionally play in a small ensemble for our local hospice organization. In the spring, a very special event honors those who have passed on during the previous year. It's a butterfly release. Families who have lost loved ones are given a small box that contains a butterfly. They stand with heads bowed, shoulders down, holding each other, deep in sad remembering. After a short service (with music from my group), each family opens its box and holds a drowsy butterfly briefly before it opens its wings and soars upward. The metaphor is stunning. What seems to be dead is alive. Regardless of your religious beliefs (and hospice espouses none), we all crave that feeling of hope in a time of despair. The feelings spread throughout the crowd as the butterflies appear overhead. The system has changed. People are now looking up, raising their hands, smiling, chattering to each other. What caused this? The butterflies? Some deep instinct in all of us for survival in difficult times? The beautiful spring morning and our love of being outside with flowers and others close to us? It's a system. It's a complex adaptive system that responds to small changes in the environment.

Those small changes change everything. It's wonderful to see that shift. This is the essence of our story, so we should pay attention. The larger system is sensitive to even the slightest probe. If we stand back, nudge, observe, and learn, that will lead us home.

This "probe, sense, respond" framework is often called "small experiments" by the agile community. Small, simple, fast, frugal, safe-to-fail "lever points" are the stepping stones in a fearless change journey. As Sunil points out (he has probably read *Fearless Change* and *More Fearless Change*) this is the secret to any kind of change—technical, organizational, cultural—small steps based on safe-to-fail experiments. I don't know how many times I have heard an intelligent, thoughtful executive declare: our organization will be agile by June! This sense that we can shove systems around, that all it takes is determination and incentives, is an unfortunate, widespread misunderstanding of systems theory. We often consider upheaval in the past as being a single event. It doesn't matter whether it's an uprising or an invasion, we somehow see it as an overnight phenomenon, when it took years of baby steps. Close examination of any significant historical event will reveal an intricate pattern of small efforts, some failures, with overall progress in a direction that eventually led to the attention-getting occurrence.

What can we learn from all this? In his instructive section *Implications for enterprises*, Sunil offers us concrete suggestions that we can all use to better understand how we and our organizations change, learn, and grow. The key is resilience, a technical term in psychology that refers to the ability we all have, to some degree, to recover from difficult times. It seems to be the defining characteristic, more so than the actual circumstances or genetic qualities of an individual. For those who are resilient, the world is less daunting. The good news is that, like many other important attributes, it can be learned. That's not only true for individuals, it's also true for organizations. That's the good news. And for you, dear reader, that's hope. We are lucky to have discovered Sunil's handbook. We are lucky that he has taken the time to document his wisdom, and, finally, we are lucky that we have resolved to apply it and get better.

Dr Linda Rising
Co-author of Fearless Change and More Fearless Change

As I pored over the manuscript of this book at a coffee shop near my home, I could see the big "Going Out of Business" banner in the window of the store across the road—Carson's. This American chain of department stores was established 160 years ago, not so long after the first industrial revolution. It survived two world wars, the big depression, mass automation and scaling in manufacturing. But it couldn't survive the information age; it recently filed for bankruptcy.

Carson's story is depressingly familiar. Its 50 stores are but a small fraction of the estimated 2,500 stores being shuttered across the US retail sector this year. And that's on the back of 5,000 stores closed in 2017. The shift to e-commerce and online retail has resulted in a perilous decline in foot traffic at malls up and down the country.

Reflecting on the closing sign, as I sipped my coffee, I wondered if the leadership team at Carson's would echo what the Nokia CEO said, as he announced his firm was being acquired by Microsoft: "We didn't do anything wrong, but somehow, we lost." Such sentiments would probably resonate with Kodak, Borders, Blockbusters and other companies crushed by the digital age.

Like it or not, we live in an age of rapid changes, and the pace of change is still accelerating.

Take a look at what's happening at our biggest companies. According to a 2016 study, in 1965 the average tenure of companies on the S&P 500 was 33 years; by 1990, it was 20 years. By 2026, it's forecast to be just 14 years. To put that in context, it means around half of the current S&P 500 will be replaced over the next 10 years.

At the heart of this disruption are digital technologies. The rapidly decreasing cost of computing, storage and data transfer are creating network effects driving the growth of even more exciting technologies like artificial intelligence, virtual/augmented reality, voice/facial recognition, natural language processing, and self-driving vehicles, just to name a few.

But we are not fine-tuned to deal with accelerating changes. The majority of the human history has been defined by linear and incremental changes. Even today, our organizational designs and management theories are based on a relatively stable and consistent environment, where certain competitive advantages can be protected for decades.

That's not to say that our preferred state is complete stasis. Every enterprise has some level of agility and can deal with gradual changes. But in an era of accelerating change, enterprises need to be more agile than ever before: agility is becoming as important as, if not more than, vision and strategy.

There have been some successful attempts bring more agility to various industries—notably Lean Manufacturing and Agile Software Development. But scaling Agile to the entire enterprise, regardless of function, unit and geography, remains the business world's greatest challenge.

Many books have tried to address enterprise agility at scale, mostly from a component perspective—technology, process, people, culture, and so on. But in trying to encapsulate Agile practices, some of these titles given the mistaken impression that there can be a one-size-fit-all solution. The danger of such an approach is that enterprises jump on the Agile adoption bandwagon without truly understanding how to derive value from Agile.

This book brings a fresh perspective to scaling Agile at the enterprise level. Sunil's favorite metaphor compares an organization with a human body, and agility with health. The first implication is that it's not about "doing" Agile (as doing health), but more about "being" Agile (as being healthy). Being Agile stems from the organization's mindset, culture and leadership behaviors, rather than anything mechanistic.

The second implication is that Agile is less about transformation from state X to state Y; it's about continuous improvement, becoming a learning organization. Every organization is unique in certain ways. Agility also means something different from organization to organization. Sunil distilled his observations on Agile teams (both successful ones and unsuccessful ones) in different context into patterns (enablers to agility) and anti-patterns (inhibitors to agility). While they are organized through six different categories—organizational structure, process, people, technology, governance, and customer—for easier navigation and mental model building, they are never meant to be a catalog of tools to be applied separately.

If you want a cookie-cutter style roadmap for Agile, this is not the book for you. Instead, what Sunil's provided is a framework to enable you to create your own roadmap, one that's tailored to your own unique organization and situation. This book guides you through assessments you can undertake to identify the inhibitors to agility, as well as enablers you can introduce to enhance agility. It helps you plan for change based on your own business context, to prioritize and execute. Working with CEOs and senior business leaders, I am often asked questions like: "Should I copy the Spotify Squad framework?" (or whichever the latest "success story"). I am glad that I can now offer Sunil's book illustrating the path to a customized roadmap through understanding patterns and anti-patterns.

Sunil has years of experience of working closely with Agile teams in large organizations, and he's used that wealth of knowledge and learning from the coalface to produce a book that offers practical advice and encouragement.

We all know that the next two decades promise to be more challenging than ever, as the pace of technological advance increases. And we can't promise that Carson's, Nokia and Kodak will be the last companies to be caught out by the pace of change. But I wholeheartedly believe that those business leaders that follow the advice laid out in Sunil's book—and embrace *Enterprise Agility* as a core competence—will be well placed to thrive in this hyper-competitive environment.

Guo Xiao
CEO, ThoughtWorks

Endorsements

Sunil Mundra's book displays his deep practitioner experience in developing agility in organizations across the world. It highlights the many challenges we face in organizations today in a systematic approach and then helps you develop a strategy for agility with an organic and human approach. Sunil is a master in change and one of the brightest minds I've worked with. It takes years of experience and great mastery to distil complex knowledge in this way. This is a must-read book if you want to learn about real world agility.

João Cardoso
Head of Digital, GroupM Portugal

With this book, Sunil Mundra has created *the* must have handbook for enterprise leaders today. He has elegantly articulated what it means for an enterprise to truly anticipate, adapt and respond to change. One of the smartest and most humble consultants I've worked with.

Christopher Carydias
Founder & CEO, Lexicon Digital

I found myself continually nodding throughout reading this book, recognizing many of the behaviors or characteristics in the organizations I've worked through within my career. What I found most useful was the clear and rounded descriptions of why that was the case and clear suggestions of how to address them. The book offers a comprehensive view of how an Agile organization should operate and through the use of examples and diagrams guides you through how these elements come together. A must read for anyone involved in or starting a digital transformation. I would suspect even if you are "transformed" you will take some valuable tips from reading this book.

Kathryn Chase
Head of Digital Agility, Shop Direct

We are at the precipice of a digitization revolution and can assume that anything procedural will be automated and what would be left for humans to do would require a higher degree of creative and analytical input. Each knowledge worker of tomorrow would be a "craftsman."

Through this well compiled work of his, Sunil has highlighted the need for agility to be treated at par with the need for having a sound business vision. The treatment of an enterprise like a human body rather than a machine and the need for focus on "being agile" versus "doing agile," helps bring out a very fundamental need of transformation initiatives to be much more intrinsic and holistic rather than following a cookie cutter approach. Based on his extensive delivery and consulting experience, he has been able to substantiate his ideas using simple but effective terms like "T-shaped skills" and watermelon metrics.

This book approaches the complex topic of enterprise agility in a refreshing way – looking at the concept top down, provide a framework for implementation with a set of cross functional ideas across industries but stops short of providing dogmatic recommendations.

All in all, a must read for all "thinking" leaders who are driving or are about to drive large scale transformation initiatives!

Ashwin Dugar

**Director – Information Technology
of a leading European Bank**

Sunil provides clarity and insight in how to embrace enterprise agility in a pragmatic and thoughtful way. In fact, I'd go as far to say I've never met anyone so passionate about enterprise agility in all my travels! In *Enterprise Agility: Being Agile in a Changing World* there is an emphasis on what it means "being" agile rather than just "doing" agile based on years of hard-learned lessons and diverse experience across numerous organizations and geographies. This is an important book that goes to the heart of what enterprise agility means from an organizational culture and leadership perspective, not just how to follow an agile process.

What I found really useful is that Sunil provides practical and principled advice and perspectives on how to take action to succeed in enterprise agility adoption from lessons learnt over many years. This is based on a foundation of real-world experience dealing with the enterprise as a living system, the importance of mindsets and culture, and the critical role that leadership has to play.

Peter How

Co-Founder & Director at Decida Digital Pty Ltd

I have known Sunil over the last 19 years and can attest that he delves deep into the founding principles of the domain he is engaged with. This book is an important marker reflecting his ability to connect the dots of his rich and varied experiences with a rigorous theoretical analysis.

Business history is replete with examples of successful companies thinking about problems differently, reasoning out solutions and then defining the process for delivering efficiently the solution. But with time, the process gains more importance and soon the form gets confused with function.

Sunil expertly differentiates between Being Agile and Doing Agile. He draws out this distinction with his own experience in product companies in highly dynamic markets, his grounding in agile methodologies and rich consulting experience in guiding teams to adapt.

We could read this book and restrict ourselves to understanding the need for an organization to be agile, but that would be our failing. Sunil is alerting us to a world in which organization mortality is rapidly increasing due to the inability to truly understand the changes and the actions required to cope and meet it. This book reinforces Descartes's "I think therefore I am" existential challenge for the 21st century world.

Ramaswamy Iyer
Founder and CEO, Vayana Network

An invaluable source for leaders on a quest to transform their enterprises to stay relevant and lead the charge during the bleeding edge of fourth industrial revolution where ability to change at break neck speed is the new currency for success. Sunil skillfully illustrated how to transition from Agile to agility at scale and sustain it to continuously delight customers.

Rash Khan
Global Leader, Digital Sales & Marketing Platforms, IBM CIO

Enterprise Agility provides key insights in a clear, structured and thorough way into the various aspects of facilitating a higher level of agility across the enterprise, and why this is key. Organizational change is complex. This book based on the vast field experience of the author helps executives better understand the barriers in important and complex domains such as mindset and culture, leadership, organization, governance. It also helps bridge the knowledge gap we too often see in the agile coaching practice and thereby forms an important contribution to the agile literature.

Adrian Lander
Lead Agile Enterprise Transformation Coach and
Executive Coach, AgiLive Asia
Co-founder of Agnostic Agile

In *Enterprise Agility: Being Agile in a Changing World*, Sunil Mudra has collected his wide breadth and depth of research and knowledge with his experiences of applying what he's learned into a comprehensive compendium of what it takes to gain true enterprise agility. He challenges the mechanistic, compartmentalized view of organizations seeking predictability and stability, with a more clear-eyed view of the organic, complexity-ridden organizational organism made of living parts. And gives us the leavening of humor along the way.

Sunil sees and describes the inhibitors that lead to enterprise destruction as well as offering the enablers that lead to a successful, productive future. Simultaneously providing practical (and difficult) steps to custom fit for purpose, he also offers readers the hope of true enterprise agility—where learning leads to resilience, diligent attention leads to high performance, and people at every level of the enterprise thrive along with the business outcomes.

Diana Larsen

Co-founder, Agile Fluency Project LLC

Co-founder, Futureworks Consulting LLCCo-author, Agile Retrospectives: Making Good Teams Great; Liftoff: Start and Sustain Successful Agile Teams; Five Rules for Accelerated Learning; and The Agile Fluency Model: A Brief Guide to Success with Agile.

By changing the metaphor for business structure, from mechanistic to organic, Sunil provides the reader with a clear vision of how an agile organization operates and thrives in an unpredictable market. The practical tips, clear case studies, and transformation guidance are a great addition to the wider enterprise agile body of knowledge. Drawing on his personal experiences and the history of software agility, this book is a must read for anyone looking to expand agile from their IT functions across the enterprise.

Evan Leybourn

Founder and CEO, Business Agility Institute

Sunil brings his wealth of experience in a series of thought provoking ideas on enterprise wide agility. His primary message is agility is urgent and is a mandate, not an option. He drives this hard with multiple examples. He defines agile transformation versus agility and insightfully shows that transformation has a destination while agility is a journey.

With this introduction, he forays into the way of getting this on the ground. Aptly he starts with the organizational design and shows how the knowledge economy is structured as complex adaptive systems (CAS). He illustrates that CAS is a feedback driven, self-learning setup at its core. These organizations work as living organisms where the overall system works as a unit. He goes to show that these have an altogether different mindset, culture and leadership. He defines these terms which makes the reader think and apply to their own context.

Having laid the foundation, he lays down various components like process, people, governance and technology, and some finer points on managing change. Across the book he deals how each component inhibits agility and how to overcome. Each chapter has significant experiential aspects inbuilt that makes a reader compare with reality and reflect.

It is one of the fine balanced book on agility. It is neither too skewed on people, nor on methodology, nor on processes. For any serious learner on agile who would like to get a 360 view of agile transformation, I would recommend this book

R. Mosesraj
CIO and Head of Excellence, Brillio

This book highlights a point that is often made but seldom internalized by those who lead transformation efforts: that organizations are living systems, not machines. Therefore, transformation plans need to account for feedback during the process. One can only paint a vague outline of phase two before phase one concludes. From this starting point, Sunil goes on to provide a useful compendium of recent thinking on various dimensions of enterprise agility.

Sriram Narayan

Author of Agile IT Organization Design, ThoughtWorks

Sunil Mundra's book is not so much a roadmap for business leaders as it is a real-time, interactive GPS that will guide them around traffic jams and onto the fastest routes to their destinations.

To accomplish that, he provides a sophisticated and insightful review of the vast literature on organizational agility, brings it to life with well-chosen case examples, and, most importantly, provides a thoughtful, well-developed framework for leaders. His use of the Complex Adaptive Systems model as the basic building block for his analysis allows him to employ the best findings from the literature of organization theory and change to elaborate a comprehensive model of effective organizational functioning.

Any CEO, division manager or entrepreneur working in a fast-paced industry environment who ignores the inhibitors and enablers to agility embedded in Sunil's analysis does so at their own peril.

Edward J. Ottensmeyer, Ph.D.

Dean Emeritus, Graduate School of Management, Clark University, USA

Sunil Mundra's *Enterprise Agility* is one of the best books to guide professionals through the process of enhancing agility—with his extensive personal experience in the field, Sunil shares his knowledge while taking into consideration the complexity of organizations due to the human element which plays such an integral role in any transition and transformation in a simple and easy-to-understand manner.

This book is a treasure which encompasses all we need to know about agility.

Chiranya Prachaseri
Chief Executive Officer -
Southeast Asia Cryoviva (Thailand) Ltd.
(An Indorama Ventures/RJ Corp promoted Company)

Sunil Mundra has raised a question which exists in deep subconsciousness of all leaders of large enterprises—how to transform our organizations in order to be able to compete in modern day society; a society characterized by high information availability, fast spread of information, fickle minded customers demanding personalization and ready to switch loyalties quickly. The cycle time needed to respond to market dynamics is decreasing rapidly and large enterprises are finding extremely difficult to complete in this market place. The problem is real for now and is staring at our faces. This book creates an intellectual curiosity about this issue and forces us to think. The book is very timely as all big and small enterprise leaders, CEO's and visionaries must tackle this question in the next 5 years. The author has further extended the concepts of Agile software development to be applied to deal with this situation.

Madhur Saxena
Vice President, A large multinational technology
company

This book is a distilled synthesis of Sunil' practical experience across domains and his build-up and exploration of the theoretical constructs of a very contemporary discourse. This "labor-of-love" work from Sunil forces contemplation and introspection, and hopefully can help you challenge the set fundamentals of your business operations.

Raj Swaminathan
CEO, Indus Software Technologies

Sunil Mundra has written a must-read book about profound challenges enterprises are facing today. Sunil shares his knowledge, practical experience and convictions. Comprehensive, focused and inspiring. Learn from one of the best consultants, I have ever worked with.

Thierry Thibault
CEO, Societe Generale Insurance Germany

Sunil has done a fabulous job of putting together a compelling case for Enterprise Agility. Unlike dozens of books that simply latch on to commercial frameworks to argue their case, Sunil's approach is practically devoid of prescriptive frameworks, and comes as fresh air. He gradually and systematically builds his case. Starting with why do we need it in the first place, he goes on to deconstruct its foundational elements of enterprises as living systems, mindset and culture, and finally the leadership. It is critical that business leaders understand that their organization's lack of agility is not simply because of not having the latest agile process but because of more fundamental organizational challenges, most of which happen to be self-inflicted, with the leadership being rightly held responsible for all such ills!

Tathagat Varma
Country Head and General Manager,
ChinaSoft International

If you feel it is time to re-inject agility into your organization ... it is time to read this book. Sunil penned down thought-provoking facts that have long swirled around the minds of those involved in leadership and transformational roles. How do we continue down the complexities of a continuous improvement path while at the same time influence the minds and hearts of our broader audience?

Every reader will find much to stimulate their thinking in this book. The encouraging nature of Sunil's arguments and the variety of angles explored will provoke both thought and emotion.

Sunil homes in on personal traits and behavioral capabilities of leaders. Understanding the significance of mindset and culture is critical to influencing a workforce to see a new future. Maybe one of the most missed opportunities in our understanding of agility at the enterprise level is the courage and convictions of our leaders.

This book will have an impressive impact and become an important source for fundamentalists, novices and executives alike, gaining greater understanding and support for agility in transforming organizations.

Marianne Vosloo
CIO and National Manager for Technology &
Innovation, Australian Federal Police

Contributors

About the author

 **Sunil Mundra** is a Principal Consultant at ThoughtWorks with decades of experience consulting, working with some of the world's largest enterprises. He has helped organizations tackle their most urgent business challenges and has worked with senior executives to shape and execute their roadmap for change.

ThoughtWorks (www.thoughtworks.com) is a global software company and a community of passionate, purpose-led individuals. Our teams think disruptively to deliver empowering technology that addresses clients' toughest challenges, all while seeking to revolutionize the IT industry and create positive social change.

I have a lot of people to thank for their role in the highly fulfilling but tough initiative of writing this book. First, I want to thank my entire family, especially my parents, my wife Samta and my daughter Shreya for their constant encouragement and support. It means a lot to me to see the pride in their eyes, as I became a publishing author.

Next, I wish to thank the leadership and my colleagues at ThoughtWorks in India and across the globe. It is only due to their wholehearted help, encouragement, and support that I gained the courage to think about writing a book and then take it to completion. The number of people who have helped me, directly and indirectly, are far too many to name specifically. However, a few names stand out as first among equals. Neal Ford played a key role in inspiring me, as he was the first to suggest that I write a book, about six years ago. Jean-Marc (JM) Domaingue, was a solid pillar of support right from the time I put pen to paper and always made time to give feedback on raw content. Gary O'Brien gave me candid advice on how I should go about building the narrative of the book. I also wish to thank Guo Xiao for graciously agreeing to write one of the two forewords for the book.

I wish to thank Dr. Linda Rising, a globally renowned thought leader, for writing an insightful foreword, and for agreeing to do so despite having an extremely busy calendar.

I am grateful to all those who wrote the endorsements for the book. These people are senior corporate and thought leaders and they have spared their valuable time to read the imperfect manuscript and write the endorsements. Thank you, João Cardoso, Christopher Carydias, Kathryn Chase, Ashwin Dugar, Peter How, Ramaswamy Iyer, Rash Khan, Adrian Lander, Diana Larsen, Evan Leybourn, R. Mosesraj, Edward J. Ottensmeyer, Chiranya Prachaseri, Sriram Narayan, Madhur Saxena, Raj Swaminathan, Thierry Thibault, Tathagat Varma and Marianne Vosloo. Your endorsements have enhanced the credibility of the book.

I wish to thank Chandra Srivastava for the important role she played in shaping the contents of the book. She was the first person to review each chapter, leveraging her Agile expertise and experience. Her validation and feedback gave me the confidence that the content was ready to be submitted to the publisher. I also owe my thanks to my friends and ex-colleagues, for providing critiques, which helped to improve the contents of the book.

My sincere thanks to Packt Publishing for partnering with me to make this book a reality. I was pleasantly surprised that they work in an Agile way: they had me deliver the content incrementally and iteratively, which helped me to constantly remain focused on my deliverables. My special thanks to Ben Renow-Clarke, Acquisitions Managing Editor, Radhika Atitkar and her predecessor Savvy Sequeira, Project Editor, Joanne Lovell, Development Editor and Bhagyashree Rai, Technical Editor for their responsiveness and support. I also wish thank Allan Kelly, whom Packt engaged as the Technical Reviewer for the book. His reviews were very helpful as he pointed out a few "blind spots" in the content.

Lastly, I wish to thank all my friends and well-wishers for keeping me inspired throughout this exciting journey to becoming an author.

About the reviewer

Allan Kelly inspires, educates, and advises teams and executives creating digital products. He helps companies large and small enhance their agility and boost their digital offering. He has over 20 years software engineering experience and has spent the last 10 years advising companies and teams on agile and digital strategy. Clients include: Virgin Atlantic, Qualcomm, The Bank of England, lastminue.com, Reed Elsevier, Fugro N.V. and West Midland Fire Service.

He is the originator of Value Poker, Time-Value Profiles and Retrospective Dialogue Sheets. Allan is the author of the perennial essay: *Dear Customer: The Truth about IT Projects* and several books, including: *Xanpan: Team Centric Agile Software Development* and *Business Patterns for Software Developers*. His latest book is *Continuous Digital: An agile alternative to projects for digital business*. His blog is at https:// www.allankellyassociates.co.uk/blog/ and on Twitter he is @allankellynet.

Packt is searching for authors like you

If you're interested in becoming an author for Packt, please visit authors.packtpub.com and apply today. We have worked with thousands of developers and tech professionals, just like you, to help them share their insight with the global tech community. You can make a general application, apply for a specific hot topic that we are recruiting an author for, or submit your own idea.

TABLE OF CONTENTS

Part Three

Part Four

Part Five

Preface

The challenge of fast-paced change

One of the biggest challenge enterprises are facing today is how to deal with disruptions arising from fast-paced change. This change is largely driven by technological innovations, to the extent that it's forcing enterprises in every sector to put technology at the core of their respective businesses. The change is so disruptive and fast that no enterprise—regardless of its age or size—can take its survival for granted.

My hypothesis is that enterprises are struggling to deal with change as they are modeled as mechanistic systems, that is, to optimize predictability and stability. An enterprise that is modeled for this will inevitably struggle to deal with fast-paced change. I believe that enterprises must be infused with "life" in order to not just deal but also leverage the changing environment for their benefit.

Agility is a necessity

I am a passionate believer in the need for agility (the use of non-capital "a"; in agility is deliberate as it's a capability and not a noun) at the enterprise level. Being an evangelist for enterprise agility, I believe that it's the only agility that will enable enterprises not only to deal with a fast changing environment, but more importantly to leverage change for competitive advantage and customer delight. The reason I say this with full conviction is that, in my opinion, this is the common attribute of enterprises that are successfully dealing with and/or leveraging change, be it large corporations such as Google and Amazon or newer start-ups such as Uber and Tesla, which are causing widespread disruptions. My conviction is validated not only by the virtue of me being a part of an organization—ThoughtWorks—which has achieved a mature and sustainable level of agility across the globe.

My sentiment about agility is aligned with what Jim Highsmith, one of the signatories of the Agile Manifesto, has said: "Agility is the ability to both create and respond to change in order to profit in a turbulent business environment." (http://jimhighsmith. com/what-is-agility/)

It is an indisputable fact that the Agile Manifesto and its twelve Principles were abstracted from the methodologies such as Scrum, XP, and DSDM, which were being used to overcome software-delivery-related problems. However, I am very sure that the Agile Manifesto signatories intended the outcome to be agility, and not just following Agile as a methodology. This difference is extremely significant and goes beyond nuances of grammar. It's about "being" Agile: having agility versus "doing" Agile.

While I will deal with the issue of Agile versus agility at length in the core of the book, my hypothesis is that most Agile Transformations initiated—by adopting Agile at enterprise level—have met with limited success because the focus has been on "doing" rather than on "being" Agile. Compared with Agile, agility is a very different ballgame. This is because it's intrinsic in nature and so applies to the whole and not to just one or more parts of the whole. To give an analogy, "doing" Agile is akin to mechanically lifting weights to strengthen the arms, and "being" Agile is about aligning the physical body, mind, and emotions to improve the holistic health of a person. Sure, it may need to include lifting weights to strengthen the arms, but it may also include overarching things such as giving up smoking, practicing meditation, and improving work-life balance.

My experience and reading suggests that leaders who have taken their enterprises down the Agile Transformation path have often found that achieving enterprise agility is hard, scary, and painful. Moreover, the illusion that agility can be achieved merely based on scaling Agile practices and processes across teams is not helping the cause at all. Unless the enterprise achieves real agility, the benefits gained from "doing" Agile will at best be very limited and will most likely regress the concerned parts of the enterprise to their original dysfunctional state.

It's therefore not surprising that leaders of such enterprises are unable to see the full potential of agility, and at times, have actually lost faith in it. On the other hand, leaders who have had the courage, conviction, and persistence to transform the enterprise and themselves as well, have experienced incredible outcomes.

Goal of the book

My goal through this book is to highlight that the approach to enterprise agility must be based on treating the enterprise like a living system, say a human body, rather than treating it like a machine, such as a car. When a machine slows down or breaks, the relevant part the machine can be fixed or even replaced. However, if the overall health of a human being is not good, it can rarely be cured by just fixing a specific part or parts of the body.

This book is about improving the enterprise's health and is not just about fixing something which is broken and localized, say a fractured leg. The key message that I wish to convey is that enterprise agility is not about making the parts Agile and then adding it up—working on each part separately. The human body analogy will be to improve agility in hands, legs, head, eyes, and so on, to hope that the overall health will improve. It may also involve diet, exercise, and stress management, which result in the holistic wellbeing of a person.

Optimal functioning of human organs does not imply overall good health, but at the same time good health needs all organs to function well. Similarly, to achieve optimal agility at the enterprise level, the components of the enterprise—people, processes, structure, governance, technology, and customers (yes, I consider the customer to be an integral component of the enterprise!)— must be enabled and leveraged for greater agility. Hence, in the book I have approached enterprise agility from both holistic and component level perspectives.

Moreover, just like the meaning of good health is specific to an individual, what "good" agility is will be specific to the enterprise. Hence, enterprises must create an action plan to enhance and sustain agility based on their respective context. As in case of health, there are patterns that are known to inhibit and enhance agility. I have shared some patterns in the book, which enterprises can use as pointers for creating the action plan.

I am also passionate about sharing my knowledge, and this, along with my conviction about and belief in the power of agility are the key drivers for me to write this book. Being in ThoughtWorks, which has groomed and nurtured many well-known thought leaders, I harbored self-doubts about being an author and thereby potentially being compared with these great thought leaders.

However, my ex-colleague and now a good friend Matthew Stratford put things in perspective. He said, "Not every guitarist can be Jimmy Hendrix, but they can still make music which at least some people will like." I have drawn inspiration from this statement throughout this tough but highly fulfilling journey.

Value and limitations of the book

In an era where information on literally any topic can be "Googled," I initially wondered whether it was worth writing this book. However, the realization that my perspectives on agility and the narrative around them are unique gave me the courage and strength to write this book. With humility, I am hopeful that readers of the book will find them of some value.

The book is obviously limited to my knowledge and experience, and I wish to explicitly call out the following disclaimers in this regard:

♦ This book is based on both my experiences in software delivery and consulting, and my study on this subject. This means that my views are limited to the context of my experience and readings only. Therefore, what I have shared with regard to what will or will not work may not be applicable in certain contexts. Moreover, I have shared perspectives of external experts where I have felt appropriate, with a view to providing holistic perspective to the readers.

♦ The book doesn't cover many other important aspects of the enterprise such as innovation, marketing, and support functions such as legal, knowledge management and others, as I don't have experience in enhancing agility in these areas.

♦ I don't claim to be a "subject matter expert" in any of the topics covered in the book, which includes specialist topics such as technology and culture. Hence, the coverage of each topic in the book is limited to my knowledge and experience related to that topic.

♦ I have myself not held any enterprise-level leadership position in the post-Agile era. However, I have observed, advised, and worked with senior leaders across a variety of organizations across the globe and have derived my learnings about leadership in the context of agility based on these experiences.

♦ The scope of the book doesn't include what Agile is, the various methodologies under its umbrella, and their processes and practices. The scope also excludes describing the benefits of Agile. My hypothesis is that the intended audience of this book already has an awareness about these.

♦ I have used the terms Agile as a broad term that also encompasses other value-oriented frameworks such as Lean, Kanban, and so on. There is absolutely no intention of being disrespectful to the uniqueness of these frameworks.

♦ I have used the word enterprise also as a synonym of organization and business. I believe the word enterprise best conveys the wholeness of the entity.

Intended audience

This book is intended for any person that has influence in an enterprise that is aiming to improve its agility. The more the influence, the greater the value that the person will be able to derive from this book.

Specifically, the following roles associated with such an enterprise will benefit the most:

- ◆ "C" level leadership and senior executives
- ◆ Function heads
- ◆ Delivery managers
- ◆ People function managers
- ◆ Project management offices
- ◆ Enterprise and leadership coaches
- ◆ Organization development and change consultants

Having said this, I also believe the book can be an enabler for conversations between people who have an interest in enterprise agility.

What this book covers

Part 1 – The need for enterprise agility

This part examines the challenge of fast-paced change both from an opportunity and threat perspectives, and how the capabilities underlying agility can help the enterprise to leverage change to its advantage.

Chapter 1, Fast-Paced Change – Threat or Opportunity, deals with the impact of fast-paced change and the need for enterprises to reorient themselves to not only deal with change but also leverage the opportunities arising from it.

Chapter 2, From Agile to Agility, is about understanding the need for agility, how agility is different from Agile, and the underlying capabilities of agility.

Part 2 – The foundations of enterprise agility

This part examines the three foundational blocks of enterprise agility, namely, modeling the enterprise as a living system, mindset and culture, and leadership.

Chapter 3, The Enterprise as a Living System, explores shifting the enterprise from being a close-ended system to becoming a living system.

Chapter 4, Mindset and Culture, explores the significance of mindset and culture and how to influence them to become enablers for enhancing agility.

Chapter 5, Leadership, focuses on understanding the significance of leadership, and the key personal traits and behaviors of leaders which are critical for enterprise agility.

Part 3 – The components of enterprise agility

This part examines the six critical component of an enterprise, namely, organization structure, process, people, technology, governance, and customer, and suggests measures to unlock and enhance agility of these components, which will lead to enhancing agility of the enterprise.

Chapter 6, Organization Structure, covers the significance of organization structure and how to leverage this for enhancing enterprise agility.

Chapter 7, Process, covers the significance of process and how to leverage process for enhancing enterprise agility.

Chapter 8, People, covers the significance of people and how to leverage their capabilities for enhancing enterprise agility.

Chapter 9, Technology, covers the significance of technology and how to leverage technology for enhancing enterprise agility.

Chapter 10, Governance, covers the significance of governance and how to leverage governance mechanisms for enhancing enterprise agility.

Chapter 11, Customer, covers the significance of customer and how best to serve the customer for enhancing effectiveness of enterprise agility.

Part 4 – The blind spots

This part examines two blind spots of the enterprise, namely, distributed teams and technology partners, and suggests measures to unlock and enhance agility of these areas, which will lead to enhancing agility of the enterprise.

Chapter 12, Distributed Teams, examines the significance of distributed teams and how to leverage them for enhancing enterprise agility.

Chapter 13, Technology Partners, examines the significance of technology partners and how to enable them for enhancing enterprise agility.

Part 5 – The journey for enhancing agility

This part examines how to create an enterprise specific action plan for enhancing agility, and the enablers for facilitating change within the enterprise.

Chapter 14, Framework for Action, provides a framework for creating an action plan to enhance agility based on the specific circumstances of the enterprise.

Chapter 15, Facilitating Change, is about learnings that can help in facilitating change across the enterprise.

Learning outcomes

Readers will be able to learn about these topics:

- ◆ The meaning and significance of enterprise agility, and the importance of distinguishing it from Agile.
- ◆ Principles of complex adaptive systems (CAS), and how the enterprise can use these principles to enhance its agility.
- ◆ What an Agile mindset is, its attributes for leaders and teams, and the measures that can be taken to help leaders and teams make the transition from a traditional to Agile mindset.

- The significance of each of the following areas for a 21st century enterprise and specific measures in each of these areas to unlock and enable agility:
    - People
    - Processes
    - Structure
    - Governance
    - Technology
    - Customer

- The advantages and challenges of having distributed teams, and the measures to enhance agility and overcome the challenges of being distributed.
- Key considerations in building relationships with technology partners, and measures to help these partners align to Agile ways of working.
- A framework to create an enterprise specific action plan for enhancing agility.
- Insights for facilitating change.

The final word

The book is written with an intent to provoke thinking and not with an intent of providing prescriptive solutions. I have shared patterns that I have observed and experienced, which are inhibitors to and are enhancers of agility. If I can get the readers to just think about the relevance of the patterns in the context of their enterprise, I think my book would have served its purpose.

Conventions used

There are a number of text conventions used throughout this book.

Bold: Indicates a new term, an important word, or words that you see on the screen, for example, in menus or dialog boxes, also appear in the text like this.

References: In-text references include a bracketed number (for example, [i]) that correlates with the numbering in the *References* section at the end of the chapter.

Get in touch

Feedback from our readers is always welcome.

General feedback: Email feedback@packtpub.com, and mention the book's title in the subject of your message. If you have questions about any aspect of this book, please email us at questions@packtpub.com.

Errata: Although we have taken every care to ensure the accuracy of our content, mistakes do happen. If you have found a mistake in this book we would be grateful if you would report this to us. Please visit, http://www.packtpub.com/submit-errata, selecting your book, clicking on the Errata Submission Form link, and entering the details.

Piracy: If you come across any illegal copies of our works in any form on the Internet, we would be grateful if you would provide us with the location address or website name. Please contact us at copyright@packtpub.com with a link to the material.

If you are interested in becoming an author: If there is a topic that you have expertise in and you are interested in either writing or contributing to a book, please visit http://authors.packtpub.com.

Reviews

Please leave a review. Once you have read and used this book, why not leave a review on the site that you purchased it from? Potential readers can then see and use your unbiased opinion to make purchase decisions, we at Packt can understand what you think about our products, and our authors can see your feedback on their book. Thank you!

For more information about Packt, please visit packtpub.com.

—PART ONE—

THE NEED FOR ENTERPRISE AGILITY

This part of the book examines the challenge of fast-paced change both from the opportunity and threat perspectives, and how the capabilities underlying agility can help the enterprise to leverage change to its advantage.

1

FAST-PACED CHANGE – THREAT OR OPPORTUNITY?

This chapter deals with the impact of fast-paced change and the need for enterprises to reorient themselves to not only deal with change, but leverage the opportunities arising from it.

The chapter will explore the following topics:

♦ The significance of the fourth industrial revolution

♦ The impact of fast-paced change

♦ Change as an opportunity

The significance of the fourth industrial revolution

The world has been through multiple industrial revolutions. The first one was about mechanizing manufacturing, the second about scaling manufacturing, and the third about automating manufacturing and harnessing the power of information technology. Each of these revolutions has taken the world to the next level of prosperity. The impact of these revolutions on enterprises has also been significant. However, for the most part, enterprises have evolved quite well to become attuned to changes in the business environment.

According to the *World Economic Forum*, we are now entering the fourth industrial revolution:

> *"We stand on the brink of a technological revolution that will fundamentally alter the way we live, work, and relate to one another. In its scale, scope, and complexity, the transformation will be unlike anything humankind has experienced before."* [i]

Klaus Schwab, the founder and chairman of the *World Economic Forum* says:

> *"The new age is differentiated by the speed of technological breakthroughs, the pervasiveness of scope and the tremendous impact of new systems."* [ii]

The fourth industrial revolution is distinctly different from the earlier three in that the pace of change in the business environment, primarily led by technology, is exponential.

The impact of fast-paced change

Until not too long ago, enterprises were built to remain stable, consistent, and predictable. Tectonic shifts in the external environment happened only once every few decades, which meant that enterprises could take stability in customer expectations and competitive forces largely for granted. This scenario has seen a drastic change in recent years, starting with the onset of the information age, and continuing with the onset of the fourth industrial revolution. [iii]

David Burstein, author of *Fast Future: How the Millennial Generation is Shaping Our World*, argues:

"The future is coming at us faster and faster; the rate of change is increasing and the amount of change that takes place in a given year is skyrocketing as well. So much change has taken place so fast that our governments, businesses, and other large institutions haven't always had enough time to fully catch up." [iv]

The biggest challenge which enterprises are facing today is how to evolve at the speed at which change, largely originating from technological innovations, is taking place. Enterprises that have been modelled for incremental evolution are struggling to evolve at an exponential rate. This fast rate of change is resulting in the following far-reaching impacts:

Disruptive innovations

Disruptive innovation is a term in the field of business administration which refers to an innovation that creates a new market and value network and eventually disrupts an existing market and value network, displacing established market leading firms, products, and alliances [v]. The disruptions that have taken place, due to technological innovations, have been unprecedented and have had a huge impact on almost every enterprise.

Digital cameras have led to the demise of film-based cameras and related businesses. Smartphones have impacted all B2C businesses (including traditional businesses like banking), and self-driving and electric cars are starting to completely change the nature of automobile businesses. We have seen how platforms that facilitate exchange between consumers and producers/providers have led to the emergence of companies such as Uber and Airbnb, which have caused turmoil in their respective domains. Online stores are providing a holistic buying experience and are posing a serious threat to retail enterprises that are still relying primarily on physical stores.

By definition, these disruptions and their impacts are unpredictable and hence it is impossible to have a plan to deal with them. The key lies in the ability to spot newer technology trends and predict the resulting disruptions. As seen from the aforementioned examples, a disruption can appear suddenly and can be powerful enough to threaten the survival of an industry itself.

The key implication of this for enterprises is that they need to be integrated more closely with the environment and customers, have short feedback loops, and encourage experimentation and innovation. In short, enterprises need to have greater agility. The concept of agility is examined in detail in the next chapter.

Breakdown of traditional entry barriers

Until not too long ago, most businesses were "brick and mortar" businesses. By definition of being "brick and mortar," these businesses had significant entry barriers, especially related to capital, for example, investment in fiber optic networks in the telecommunications industry. However, innovations in technology are changing this rapidly. Entry barriers are collapsing in many industries. Here are a few examples of new age enterprises that broke entry barriers in their respective industries:

♦ **Netflix**: The company has very quickly gained immense popularity globally for online video and television streaming. It has nearly eliminated the DVD renting industry. Blockbuster, a DVD renting company that had outlets all across the USA, and whose revenue was $6 billion in 2004 and $4 billion in 2009, filed for bankruptcy in 2010. Netflix does not have any "brick and mortar" as part of its business, and by delivering its services online, it has eliminated the physical entry barriers in its industry. It has now created a different type of barrier for competitors by building strong relationships with movie and television studios.

- **WhatsApp**: With a team of just 55 engineers, and no "brick and mortar" infrastructure, WhatsApp has revolutionized the telecommunications industry. With WhatsApp providing free messaging, as well as voice and video calling, the traditional telecom companies are revisiting their customer engagement models. These companies are now beginning to focus on creating direct lines of communication with customers and offering services based on individual customer needs.

- **N26**: The bank, which is based in Germany, offers mobile-only banking, thereby having no need for physical branches. The bank arranges for video-based verification of its customers. It has purportedly developed its own core banking platform for a fraction of the cost of a platform for a "brick and mortar" bank.

- **Platform-based businesses**: Uber, Airbnb, and Alibaba are all platform-based businesses. They are very large-scale businesses but don't own traditional assets like cars, property, and retail inventory respectively. These platform-based businesses have clearly demonstrated that businesses in these industries can be started with minimal entry barriers.

The implication of the breakdown of entry barriers is that enterprises cannot take their survival for granted and need to have a strong sensing mechanism to spot opportunities, and threats, as early as possible. A start-up can come up with a product that can pose a sudden and unexpected threat to supposedly well-established enterprises (for example, Paytm [vi], a digital payments platform (acronym of payment through mobile) is fast gaining widespread acceptance across India, to the extent that it has posed a serious threat to debit and credit cards products).

According to the CEO of NITI Aayog, the premier policy think tank of the Government of India, credit and debit cards, and ATMs, will become redundant in three to four years due to the usage of mobile phones for conducting financial transactions. [vii]

Intersection of domains

Technology is enabling enterprises to break the shackles and extend their business into seemingly unrelated domains, for example, retailers are offering credit on purchases, telecom companies are offering basic payment services through mobile e-wallets and, travel portals are offering insurance.

Consumers have now begun to appreciate the availability of a wide range of connected products and services under a single roof, which is a huge tailwind for such convergences. These convergences can become a "win-win" opportunity for enterprises, depending on how well the bundled offering is received by customers.

For example, Netflix provides an option to buy broadband services along with a subscription to its service. Assuming that this offering is well received by Netflix's customers, Netflix and the broadband service provider will both benefit. Another example of a partnership across domains, and one that is enabled by technology, is between Nike and Apple. They created an offering that tracks fitness activity, while connecting people to their tunes.

The implication for enterprises is that they need to relentlessly and continuously pursue better-value propositions, through innovative ideas and create a better experience for their customers. They also need to be open to outside-of-the-box partnerships. An example of an unconventional partnership, which is based on an innovative idea, is between Uber and Spotify, which have very different products but a common goal: to add more users. The offering allows users to become the "DJ of their trip." [viii]

No place to hide

Due to the widespread prevalence of social media and hashtag-driven searches, the news of any slip up, or mistake, made at any level of an enterprise, can become globally viral within no time at all. A passenger dragged off a United Airlines flight [ix] or something more serious like Samsung batteries catching fire and exploding [x], are examples of events which the entire world came to know about very fast.

The challenge for enterprises is that they need to have the ability to recognize the occurrence of such failures early enough, and, more importantly, be able to recover from a failure quickly through engaging directly and swiftly with aggrieved customers.

Demanding customers

Today's customers are, among other things, tech savvy and demanding. They are ready to switch loyalties if they believe that there is an alternative product or service that offers better value, for example, a customer may choose to use Uber for travel, not necessarily because it is a cheaper option, but because it offers a superior end-to-end user experience that includes self-booking, vehicle tracking, automatic direct payment, and getting the receipt via email.

According to Senion, an indoor positioning systems and services company, the following factors are the ways in which 21st century customers are different:

"Experiential instead of transactional

Social instead of individual

Customization instead of conformity

Speed instead of price

Omnichannel instead of single channel." [xi]

The impact of this for enterprises is far-reaching. Specifically, businesses must do the following:

♦   Put the customer first

♦   Offer an experience, not just a product or service

♦   Shorten feedback loops

♦   Increase responsiveness to changing customer needs

♦   Innovate, with the goal of satisfying customers

Demanding employees

Today's employees are very different from their predecessors in that they are knowledge workers, rather than machine workers. What drives and motivates knowledge workers is very different from what previously drove and motivated workers who believed they were, and who were treated as, "faceless bodies." Moreover, the proportion of millennials in the workforce is rising very fast and they are expected to form 75% of the workforce by 2030. This generation is visibly different from their ancestors, as they do not want to work *for* enterprises, but work *with* enterprises.

According to Jeff Fromm, the president of FutureCast, a millennial marketing consultancy:

> *"Millennials embrace a strong entrepreneurial mindset and they are often on the lookout for opportunities that can continue to move them up the ladder, even if that means up and out of their current position. As digital natives, millennials have grown up in an era where the number of resources they have is almost infinite, making them more efficient problem solvers and critical thinkers." [xii]*

What this means for enterprises is that they will need a culture that enables learning, fosters collaboration, builds meaningful engagement drivers, and empowers its people. In short, a culture that values and nurtures knowledge workers.

Plentiful and cheap information

With the advent of the internet, the widespread adoption of smartphones and a drastic drop in the cost of data storage, there has been an "information explosion" across the globe. It is estimated that 90% of the data in the world has been created in the past two years, and that currently 2.5 quintillion (1 followed by 18 zeros) bytes of data is produced every day. A lot of that information is available freely or at very little cost.

Enterprises are grappling with the problem of "information overload." Due to the amount of information available, customers are getting distracted, becoming confused, and falling prey to the "analysis paralysis" syndrome, leading to delayed decisions. The problem is made worse as fake news and information is pervasive, thereby causing a need to validate the genuineness of information, especially if it is critical for decision-making.

This is in contrast to times when information was limited and leaders had to focus a lot of time and energy on acquiring information. Moreover, as the business environment was largely stable, information remained valid for longer periods and could be used as a source of power.

Taking all of this into account, decision-making needs to be decentralized, as the people who are closest to the customers are in the best position to filter out the clutter and focus on the most relevant information. Moreover, in a fast-changing environment, where information obsolescence is very high, enterprises no longer have the luxury of "pushing" ground level information up the layers of the hierarchy, losing valuable time and quality of information in the process.

Intuitive decision-making, based on "just enough" information, will become important, rather than waiting for "perfect information" [xiii] and a detailed analysis. Making decisions based on imperfect, but valid, information, and taking timely actions based on these decisions will provide early feedback.

What has worked in the past is unlikely
to work now

For many decades, the focus of enterprises was more inward, such as maximizing efficiencies and, return on capital and shareholder wealth. Maintaining stability and predictability were considered hallmarks of successful leadership. The fundamental approach to running enterprises was to treat them as mechanistic, or closed-ended, systems. This would control the extent to which the enterprise could be kept isolated from changes in the environment, which were mostly linear and largely predictable.

According to Richard Schutte, director at the National Australia Bank:

> *"The interplay between rapidly emerging technologies such as ubiquitous internet, artificial intelligence, genetics, automation, changing social and community expectations and shifts in our economy are disrupting and redefining every industry, organization and our society at large." [xiv]*

According to the *World Economic Forum*:

> *"The inexorable shift from simple digitization (the third industrial revolution) to innovation based on combinations of technologies (the fourth industrial revolution) is forcing companies to re-examine the way they do business. The bottom line, however, is the same: business leaders and senior executives need to understand their changing environment, challenge the assumptions of their operating teams, and relentlessly and continuously innovate." [xv]*

Enterprises that do not accept the reality of change, and are continuing with traditional methods, are struggling for survival. Kodak and Nokia are examples of enterprises that did not respond fast enough to a changing environment and therefore become irrelevant. Stephen Elop, Nokia CEO, said, "We didn't do anything wrong, but somehow, we lost" in his speech during the handover of Nokia to Microsoft in July 2013 [xvi]. While there may not have been anything "wrong" about not responding to change in the past, it can be extremely perilous in today's era, as the Nokia case study so starkly demonstrates.

Elop's words have a lot hidden under the surface. According to management trainer Ziyad Jawabra:

> *"They (Nokia) missed out on learning, they missed out on changing, and thus they lost the opportunity at hand to make it big. Not only did they miss the opportunity to earn big money, they lost their chance of survival." [xvii]*

There are many enterprises that are meeting a similar fate as Nokia. According to a study by Professor Richard Foster, from the Yale School of Management, the average lifespan of a company in the S&P 500 index decreased from 61 years in 1958 to just 15 years in 2012. His estimation is that at this churn rate, by 2027 more than three-quarters of the S&P 500 will be companies that we have not yet heard of. [xviii]

Given this tectonic shift in not only the way that change is happening but also the impact of change not being controllable, it is evident that what has worked for enterprises in the past, with respect to survivability and meeting the expectations of both internal and external stakeholders, is unlikely to work going forward.

Change as an opportunity

While most enterprises are struggling to deal with change, there are many enterprises that are succeeding in effectively dealing with it. Digitally driven enterprises, such as Apple, Amazon, and Google, are leveraging change for growth. Even traditional enterprises such as Ericsson, a 140-year-old firm, and Barclays, a 300-year-old bank, are doing things very differently in order to deal with change. Ericsson has over 100 small teams responding to its customers' needs in three-week cycles. At Barclays, over 800 teams are part of an organization-wide Agile transformation initiative aiming to deliver instant, frictionless, and intimate value at scale. [xix]

Enterprises that are dealing effectively with a rapidly changing environment appear to have drastically different characteristics compared to enterprises that continue to be rooted in the past. The following table brings out some of the key differences:

Characteristic	Enterprises struggling with change	Enterprises thriving on change
Primary motive	Profit	Purpose
Structure	Hierarchy	Flexible networks
Ways of working	Process driven	People driven
Leadership style	Directive	Empowering
Team organization	By roles/skills	By outcomes
Primary outcome	Efficiency	Value
Governance	Compliance driven	Value driven
Role of technology	Tactical	Strategic

Enterprises that are succeeding today realize that they operate in a complex environment where technology is disrupting business models, competitive advantage is transient, and outcomes are not linear. The critical differentiator between struggling and succeeding enterprises is the level of agility, which separates the winners from the losers.

According to Prosci, an organization offering change management-related solutions, "To be successful in this environment of rapid, concurrent and never-ending change, organizations must grow their change agility not just to thrive, but to survive." In fact, senior leaders are starting to acknowledge how important agility is to their success. In a PwC survey of 1150 CEOs [xx], 76% said that their ability to adapt to change will be a key source of competitive advantage in the future. [xxi]

The rest of this book is devoted to getting an enterprise ready to embrace change, with a view to treating disruptive change as an opportunity, rather than as a threat. Enhancing enterprise agility is imperative to achieving this.

Summary

In this chapter, we learned that enterprises today are challenged to keep evolving with the fast pace of change in the environment. Moreover, the world is at the cusp of the fourth industrial revolution, which means that the pace of change may accelerate even more. The impact created by this change will be unprecedented, and therefore enterprises will have to reinvent themselves to continue to survive. Enterprises need greater agility to not only minimize the threat to survival, but also to be able to leverage the opportunities arising from change for creating and sustaining competitive advantage. Enterprises have a choice to treat fast-paced change as a threat or an opportunity.

The next chapter is about understanding the need for agility, how agility is different from Agile and the underlying capabilities of agility.

References

[i] https://www.weforum.org/agenda/2016/01/the-fourth-industrial-revolution-what-it-means-and-how-to-respond/

[ii] http://whatis.techtarget.com/definition/fourth-industrial-revolution

[iii] https://www.weforum.org/agenda/2016/01/the-fourth-industrial-revolution-what-it-means-and-how-to-respond/

[iv] http://davidburstein.com/fast-future

[v] https://en.wikipedia.org/wiki/Disruptive_innovation

[vi] https://paytm.com/

[vii] https://timesofindia.indiatimes.com/business/india-business/debit-credit-cards-atms-will-be-redundant-in-4-years-niti-aayog-ceo/articleshow/61608511.cms

[viii] https://blog.hubspot.com/marketing/best-cobranding-partnerships

[ix] https://www.forbes.com/sites/forbesagencycouncil/2017/05/23/the-biggest-pr-crises-of-2017/#7c319c8950a8

[x] http://www.techradar.com/news/samsung-galaxy-note-7-battery-fires-heres-why-they-exploded

[xi] https://senion.com/insights/understanding-21st-century-consumer/

[xii] https://www.forbes.com/sites/jefffromm/2015/11/06/millennials-in-the-workplace-they-dont-need-trophies-but-they-want-reinforcement/#10943b1e53f6

[xiii] http://www.businessdictionary.com/definition/perfect-information.html

[xiv] https://www.linkedin.com/pulse/some-thoughts-fourth-industrial-revolution-leadership-richard-schutte/?trackingId=zfZ8 nYDk76FO6kvvzFbJLQ%3D%3D

[xv] https://www.weforum.org/agenda/2016/01/the-fourth-industrial-revolution-what-it-means-and-how-to-respond/

[xvi] https://www.youtube.com/watch?v=uGPBwUdYV3M

[xvii] https://www.linkedin.com/pulse/nokia-ceo-ended-his-speech-saying-we-didnt-do-wrong-incorporation/

[xviii] https://www.theatlantic.com/business/archive/2015/04/where-do-firms-go-when-they-die/390249/

[xix] https://www.forbes.com/sites/stevedenning/2016/11/26/can-big-organizations-be-agile/#42543c2038e7

[xx] https://www.prosci.com/change-management/thought-leadership-library/organizational-agility-as-a-strategic-imperative

[xxi] https://www.pwc.com/gx/en/ceo-survey/pdf/pwc_11th_annual_global_ceo_survey_e.pdf

2

FROM AGILE TO AGILITY

This chapter highlights the need for greater agility at enterprise level and calls out the fact that merely adopting Agile methodologies is not enough to enhance agility. With the onset of the Information Age in the mid-1990s, many enterprises began using **information technology (IT)** as a means to gain competitive advantage. They started expecting IT divisions/vendors to support changing priorities, increase the speed of delivery, iterate the solution based on regular feedback, and lower the costs arising from the changing requirements. However, for decades, software delivery was based on the waterfall methodology [i], which is a rigid and heavyweight approach. Agile methodologies such as Scrum, XP, FDD, and DSDM emerged as a reaction to the challenges arising from the waterfall methodology.

However, agility as a capability is far bigger than Agile. This chapter will bring out the distinction between Agile and agility, and also examine the various facets of agility including the properties, capabilities, and characteristics of enterprises with high agility.

The values and principles of Agile

While this book is about agility, it is important to briefly define what Agile is. Agile was formally born in 2001, as an abstracted set of values and principles. 17 people, who were practicing their individual methodologies came together to define the manifesto and principles, which they believed to be common to all the underlying methodologies.

The Agile Manifesto

> *"We are uncovering better ways of developing software by doing it and helping others do it. Through this work we have come to value:*
>
> *Individuals and interactions over processes and tools*
>
> *Working software over comprehensive documentation*
>
> *Customer collaboration over contract negotiation*
>
> *Responding to change over following a plan*
>
> *That is, while there is value in the items on the right, we value the items on the left more." [ii]*

The creators of the Agile Manifesto also specified 12 principles that address areas such as incrementally delivering the highest value, welcoming change, self-organizing teams, and seeking continuous improvement. [iii]

Agile is a resounding success in IT

Given that the origins of Agile are rooted in ways to address the challenges arising out of the waterfall methodology for software development, which was failing to enable businesses to deal with a fast-changing environment, it was obvious that Agile would be adopted almost exclusively by IT delivery teams. There is now consensus that Agile's success in IT has been resounding. There is plenty of empirical evidence available which suggests that the success rates are three times higher for Agile-driven projects when compared with waterfall projects and are even higher for large and medium-scale projects. [iv]

According to a global survey, 98% of the respondents said that their organizations have realized success from Agile projects [v]. The survey stated the following top five benefits which the respondent enterprises had realized from adopting Agile:

"Ability to manage changing priorities

Project visibility

Increased team productivity

Delivery speed/time to market

Team morale"

Agile has also made a difference to the business world

One of the biggest impacts of Agile, and something which is its primary differentiator, is that it has helped to bring the business and IT departments closer to each other, if not bringing them on "same side of the table," through specific working practices. On account of this, businesses have seen meaningful benefits such as increased speed to market, resulting in higher ROI, lower cost of change, and lower risk due to fast feedback loops.

Issues with Agile adoption and scaling

Impressed by Agile's success at the team level, several enterprises saw the potential for Agile to be adopted in a broader way, that is, at program, portfolio and even enterprise levels. Companies that took an interest in Agile include IBM, GE Suncorp, ING Bank, Barclays Bank, and others like Salesforce.com, PayPal, John Deere, the BBC, Universal Credit, and so on. A common term, which has been used for Agile adoption at enterprise level, is Agile transformation. However, studies indicate that very few enterprises have derived, or are on the path to deriving, meaningful and sustainable enterprise-wide benefits from Agile. This is due to a variety of reasons, some of the prominent ones being as follows.

Focus on "doing" Agile

As stated earlier, Agile has its roots in IT. The Agile Manifesto, the 12 principles, and the practices within the methodologies are all oriented toward optimizing the delivery of software. It is therefore not surprising that many enterprises have not only kept Agile adoption limited to IT delivery but have also limited the adoption of Agile by merely applying the list of practices. This is because Agile is seen as something to "do," rather than something to "be." The difference between "doing" and "being" Agile has major implications at the enterprise level, as will emerge throughout this book. For the average enterprise, the benefits of Agile relate largely to the benefits derived from Agile practices only.

Moreover, differences in ways of working, and the approach to "managing" people in parts of the enterprise which have adopted Agile versus those which have not, create unhealthy friction. The tensions arising from such friction are usually addressed by diluting Agile to render it a mere "checkbox" exercise.

Adoption without addressing systemic issues

Enterprises that limit the adoption of Agile to only a part of their business have often seen the changes made quickly regress to their original state, thereby losing all, or most, of the benefits derived from Agile adoption. This happens due to *Organizational Inertia* [vi]. The unaddressed systemic issues appear to overpower the "green shoots" in the Agile-adopted part of the enterprise. This behavior is akin to antibodies overpowering a newly entered virus in a human body.

Examples of systemic dysfunctions include the business and IT sectors having different measures of success, KPIs which encourage and reward individualistic behaviors, and a culture of pleasing the boss, because the boss is the sole decider of the salary and career progression of subordinates.

According to Steve Denning, author of multiple books including *The Leader's Guide to Radical Management*:

> *"Single-fix changes at the team level may appear to make progress for a while, but eventually the interlocking elements of the organizational culture take over and the change is inexorably drawn back into the existing organizational culture. This isn't like fixing a car where if you fix a tire, the tire stays fixed. Instead the organization acts more like an ingeniously morphing virus that steadily adapts itself to, and ultimately defeats, intended fixes and returns to its original state, sometimes more virulent than before."* [vii]

Adoption for wrong/unclear reasons

The benefits accruing from Agile adoption are now well recognized [viii]. Many enterprises, not wanting to be left behind, jumped on the Agile adoption bandwagon without truly understanding how to derive value from Agile.

Agile has become a "buzzword" for many, and therefore no enterprise wants to be seen as not having adopted Agile. Some businesses adopted Agile for merely optimizing their software development process, without much regard for business-driven outcomes such as an increase in customer satisfaction. Worse still, some others adopted Agile simply because "others are doing it."

Adopting Agile without linking it to a broader purpose, and without taking a systemic view, often results in unintended anti-patterns. An example of this is that in the quest to speed up delivery, teams have created technical debt, which, over a period of time, has been quite damaging. Another problem with merely "doing" Agile, that is, adopting Agile without the right mindset and culture change, is the wrong use of Agile practices. For example, story points are being used to measure and compare the productivity of teams. This, again, can create serious anti-patterns, as teams learn ways to "game the system" and thereby create a false sense of achievement, which can last only temporarily.

The "Cookie cutter" approach

The While Agile methodologies may be prescriptive to a certain extent, for example, Scrum prescribing the five "ceremonies," a one-size-fits-all approach does not work even for Agile practices, as the practices have multiple maturity levels. Adoption of Agile practices, without customizing for context, is a guaranteed recipe for failure.

The need for customization to context has tremendous significance for Agile adoption. It implies that both experience and expertise are needed to decide upon and facilitate the adoption of the appropriate practices. Moreover, Agile works on the principle of "inspect and adapt" and hence the adoption needs to be monitored closely and adjustments made swiftly as necessary.

Some enterprises have tried to save money by not engaging experienced coaches. Many have hired coaches who only appeared qualified. It is therefore not surprising that the benefits of Agile have been minimal or have not accrued at all for many companies. In many instances, half-hearted/incorrect adoption has caused serious damage to Agile's credibility and has also left teams in worse states than before they attempted adoption. The natural consequence is that leaders of such enterprises lost faith in Agile.

Early visibility of issues seen as a problem with Agile

One of the critical benefits of Agile practices is faster feedback. This implies that if something is failing, or not working well, it will become visible early. This is very valuable, as it provides an opportunity for early course correction. However, a lack of understanding of Agile has led to earlier visibility of issues, and even early failures, being seen as an impediment that slows down delivery. Ironically, a significant benefit of Agile has at times been erroneously seen as a problem with Agile, leading to Agile adoption being suspended or even abandoned.

Leaders feeling threatened

The problems that Agile helps to surface are not only related to what's broken in the delivery process, but also about systemic dysfunctions such as command and control culture, and silo-oriented optimization. These dysfunctions are almost always closely linked to leadership roles and behaviors.

When the dysfunctions related to their roles and behaviors start becoming visible, most leaders feel threatened and insecure. Such leaders, to protect themselves, have sabotaged and even stopped Agile adoptions, claiming that it is not meant for, or relevant to, their enterprise.

Wrong expectations

Agile, if implemented in the spirit of "being," brings positive outcomes early. Simple practices such as visualizing work in the pipeline, and daily stand ups, are highly impactful if used in the right way, even if they are implemented in the simplest form. The downside to this is that many enterprises have treated Agile like a "silver bullet" and expected it to act as a magic wand that can resolve all problems instantly. The reality is that Agile is not a problem solution framework, but a problem identification framework. Agile helps to surface problems early, through shorter feedback loops, as discussed in the previous point. Agile does not fix the dysfunctions in the system but helps to bring them out in the open early. Knowing the problems within the overall system is the fundamental step toward effectively enhancing agility in the enterprise.

Underestimating the extent and impact of change

A cardinal mistake, which most leaders and those helping enterprises to adopt Agile have made, is to underestimate and even ignore the breadth and depth of change and the ensuing impact of that change arising from Agile adoption. Agile, if adopted right, needs a significantly different mindset compared to traditional approaches. Change in mindset and behaviors is painful, for both leaders and teams. Change needs to be facilitated and steered, and that is a lot of hard work. Moreover, this type of intrinsic change almost always takes a very long time.

It took eight years for the insurance division of a large financial conglomerate in Australia, employing over 10,000 people, to achieve the mindset and culture change that began making a significant positive impact on its business.

In many cases, leaders have expected delivery teams to change their mindset while not doing much to enable that change. Even worse, many of them expect everyone to change but themselves. Consequently, many enterprises have ended up merely "doing" Agile and have either not attempted or have given up on a mindset and behavior change, that is, "being" Agile. Even merely "doing" Agile brings in benefits related to better visibility of the work pipeline, improved collaboration between delivery teams and business stakeholders, and so on, which puts teams in a much better position. Enterprises often miss out on bigger benefits by stopping at "doing" Agile, since they, albeit wrongly, believe that they have achieved the optimal benefits from Agile.

Even though agility is quite different from Agile, as explained in the following sections, the challenges encountered by enterprises in adopting Agile are very likely to be similar to those encountered when enhancing agility. Hence, it is important that enterprises draw lessons from these mistakes and avoid making them in the pursuit of enhancing agility.

The need for enhancing agility

The Meriam-Webster dictionary defines agility as:

> *"the quality or state of being agile." [ix]*

The views of two well-known experts bring out the essence of agility. According to David S. Alberts, author of the book, *The Agility Advantage*:

> *"Agility is the ability to successfully effect, cope with and/or exploit changes in circumstances".*

According to Jim Highsmith, one of the signatories of the Agile Manifesto:

"Agility is the ability to both create and respond to change in order to profit in a turbulent business environment. Agility is the ability to balance flexibility and stability." [x]

Every enterprise has some level of agility, and hence the concept of agility is not new in the business world. What is relatively new is the realization of the need for enterprises to have greater agility. It is now considered as one of the core qualities which an enterprise must have in order to survive and thrive in today's rapidly changing environment.

According to Wouter Agthina of McKinsey, with today's levels of uncertainty, ambiguity and volatility in markets, and globalization, agility is important for all companies. He further states:

"The opposite of fragile is something that gets stronger when I exert force or stress on it. In today's environment— with enormous changes coming from both inside and outside of the organization—that's what we think the aspiration should be. That's what I call agility: when you thrive on change and get stronger and it becomes a source of real competitive advantage." [xi]

Enterprises today must have greater agility than ever before, in order to deal with the implications of fast paced-change, as discussed in *Chapter 1, Fast-Paced Change – Threat or Opportunity?*. It is agility which will enable enterprises to not only deal with disruptions arising from change but also to create disruptions and gain/improve competitive advantage. Agility is necessary for the enterprise to evolve and renew itself, in order to be able to align itself to changes, which are happening at a very fast pace.

No amount of past glory and success is of any use when dealing with disruptions arising from change. No enterprise, even one with high agility, is in a position to predict when and how a disruption will create impact in the future, including posing a threat to survival. However, agility will enable the enterprise to be as prepared as possible to deal with disruptions, so that when those disruptions happen (it is not a question of if), they are in the best position to deal with them.

Enhancing agility, and maintaining it, requires constant commitment, dedication, and hard work. This is akin to an athlete making all efforts to get and stay in good shape, even when a competition for their sport is not on the horizon. Someone wanting to become an athlete while they are currently having a sedentary lifestyle will need more time and a lot more effort to even get close to being as fit as an athlete. For enterprises, it is a race for survival today. If they have any chance of staying in the race, they need to enhance agility to a level that is optimal for them, and then maintain it as well.

Adopting Agile is not enough

Enterprises that have adopted Agile are facing two hard realities: a) it is difficult to scale the benefits accrued from Agile and many times even to sustain them, and b) despite adopting Agile, it has made minimal or no difference to the enterprise's ability to deal with the disruptions arising from fast-paced change.

What these enterprises are lacking is a greater level of agility. Adopting Agile practices and methodologies, and even scaling them, does not increase agility. At the enterprise level, it is agility that matters most, not Agile. This is because agility encompasses a set of enterprise-level capabilities while Agile, though based on values and principles, is oriented toward software delivery. Enhancing agility at enterprise level usually requires profound changes across the enterprise. The rest of this book is devoted to the "why," "what," and "how" of achieving enhanced agility.

Enhancing agility is not the same as Agile transformation

Many enterprises are initiating Agile transformation initiatives, with the intent to enhance agility at enterprise level. However, Agile transformations usually mean scaling Agile practices across teams using a prescribed framework, implementing DevOps, changing the rigid structure to another rigid structure, and similar types of changes which not only aim for a fixed end state, but are also blindly copied from what purportedly is working for other enterprises.

The word transformation indicates moving from the current state to a new state, which is predicted in advance. This goes against the core philosophy of agility, which is to assume that a) the end state can be predicted in advance, and b) it is OK to remain in a fixed state.

Jurgen Appelo, author of the book, *Management 3.0*, has summarized an enterprise with high agility as follows:

> *"In the 21st century, successful organizations are hard and soft. Fast and slow. Solid and liquid. Organized and self-organized."* [xii]

Adopting Agile, assuming that it is done correctly, is a good start on the journey towards agility. However, it is incorrect to believe that adopting Agile practices, methods, and frameworks is enough to create agility. As we will see in the later part of this chapter, and the subsequent chapters, the breadth and depth of the initiatives and changes required to enhance agility are very different from those needed to optimize delivery using Agile methodologies.

Capabilities underlying agility

David S. Alberts breaks down agility into what he labels as six components [xiii]. They may be viewed as capabilities that enterprises need to develop in order to enhance agility. These can be treated as basic capabilities and enterprises can choose to modify this list based on their context.

Responsiveness

This capability means to recognize that some action is needed as a response to an event or a circumstance, to determine what action is to be taken and then to take that action at the appropriate time. The level of responsiveness depends on the speed at which the need and nature of the action is determined and implemented. The effectiveness of the responsiveness will depend on the outcome of the action taken and the timing of the action. It is about sensing and responding to both potential and actual change in circumstances that can be unfavorable, that is, there is risk.

Versatility

This capability helps to achieve the desired outcomes under new and varying conditions and circumstances. The true test of this capability is when the enterprise is undergoing stress, especially when the survival of the enterprise is threatened. A term that is used as a synonym for this capability is robustness.

Flexibility

This capability helps the enterprise to come up with alternate approaches to achieve the intended outcome. This may be needed when the original approach does not appear to be effective, either due to changes in circumstances or the fact that it was based on imperfect assumptions. The alternative approach may not be as optimal as the original one, but the enterprise has at least another option to respond with.

Resilience

This capability enables the enterprise to recover from a setback, by repairing, reconstructing or creating something new out of something that has been damaged, destroyed, or rendered obsolete.

Innovativeness

This capability enables the enterprise to come up with new approaches, that is, approaches hitherto never used, in order to best respond to current circumstances or those not encountered earlier. Innovations can be either discoveries or inventions.

Adaptability

This capability enables the enterprise to change, eliminate, or newly create its own components, for example, structure and processes. This capability is needed when the current components are an impediment to achieving the desired outcomes.

A fundamental capability, which is an enabler for the aforementioned capabilities, is the ability to probe and sense the environment. The quicker the enterprise is able to sense the changes happening, or that are about to happen, in the environment, the more effective the capabilities underlying agility will be.

It is important to note that these capabilities are needed not just at the enterprise level but at lower levels, for example, teams and programs.

Properties of agility

Enterprise agility has five key properties:

- ◆ It is a set of capabilities, as discussed earlier. It is not something which is monolithic and abstract.

- ◆ The capabilities reinforce each other and hence agility is greater than the sum of its capabilities. On the flip side, a capability is unlikely to work in isolation of the other capabilities, for example, it is difficult to build versatility unless it is supported by flexibility.

- ◆ Enterprise agility is holistic in nature, that is, it encompasses both tangible elements of the enterprise, for example, people, structure, process, governance and technology, and intangible elements as well, for example, mindset and culture. Each of these elements are discussed in detail in the upcoming chapters.

- ◆ It does not have an end state, that is, it is a journey and not a destination. This is unlike Agile transformation, which works backwards from a fixed end state.

- ◆ Its meaning and relevance is unique to each enterprise. Like health, agility too has general "good practices," but it must be customized for the context of each enterprise.

Characteristics of enterprises with high agility

Relatively well-established enterprises such as Google, Facebook, Amazon, and ThoughtWorks, and the newer "disruptor" enterprises such as N26 Bank, Tesla, and Netflix are some of the well-known enterprises that have a high level of agility. These enterprises are seen as success stories with respect to not only anticipating and dealing with a rapidly-changing environment but also for leveraging it for their competitive advantage.

While agility is unique to each enterprise, businesses with high agility share some characteristics in terms of the outcomes they are able to achieve consistently. These include the ability to do the following:

♦ Anticipate and recognize change in different circumstances, that is, to spot both opportunities and threats emanating from change early. Zara, the Spain-based world's largest clothing retailer, is known to spot fashion trends early.

According to Donald Sull, a senior lecturer at MIT Sloan School of Management:

> *"Zara consistently spots these opportunities because it has built-in systems to collect real-time market data, to supplement statistical reports with periodic exposure to raw market data, and to share information widely throughout the organization. Zara's cross-functional design teams pore over daily sales and inventory reports to see what is selling and what is not, and they continually update their view of the market." [xiv]*

♦ Leverage opportunities arising from change for gaining/improving competitive advantage.

According to Bart Schlatmann, ex-COO of ING Netherlands:

> *"Customer behavior, however, was rapidly changing in response to new digital distribution channels, and customer expectations were being shaped by digital leaders in other industries, not just banking. We needed to stop thinking traditionally about product marketing and start understanding customer journeys in this new omnichannel environment."* [xv]

Bart goes on to mention that customer satisfaction scores increased meaningfully after ING embarked on the initiative to enhance agility.

♦ Make quick decisions, involving the relevant stakeholders, thereby being able to respond to the changed circumstances and opportunities in the most effective manner.

Santander Bank acquired two UK banks (Alliance & Leicester and Bradford & Bingley) where it had no presence earlier. This is a good example of a company's ability to make a quick decision to seize an opportunity. The acquired banks were struggling in the aftermath of the Lehman Brothers collapse, and Santander moved quickly to acquire them.

♦ Consistently deliver value, in alignment with the purpose/mission/vision and strategy of the enterprise.

Apple is a fine example of an enterprise which is known for delivering value in line with its vision and mission statements. The vision statement explicitly spells out values such as innovation and making great products, which are core to Apple's value propositions for its customers.

♦ Embrace digital technologies.

JetBlue, Domino's, and Walmart are examples of companies that are considered to be success stories of digital transformations [xvi]. These companies were able to quickly launch digital initiatives to improve the customer experience, thereby blurring the lines between technology and business.

Optimal agility

As stated earlier, the desired, or optimal, level of agility will be specific to the circumstances of an enterprise. Attaining and maintaining agility will involve the investment of time, money, and effort, which are finite resources.

Hence, the goal should be to have as much agility needed to influence potential events, such that the chances of adverse events and/or the impact of adverse events on the enterprise are minimized, and the chances of favorable events are maximized and/or the impact of such events creates opportunities to make positive outcomes. Just like living healthily cannot guarantee good health, agility does not guarantee positive outcomes or that the enterprise will be insulated from negative outcomes. However, the optimal level of agility will definitely increase the probability that an enterprise can cope with adverse circumstances and exploit the favorable circumstances arising as a result of change.

Summary

In this chapter, we learned that adopting Agile methodologies has been a significant enabler for the technology function to improve the effectiveness of software delivery, thereby positively impacting business outcomes as well. However, scaling the adoption of Agile methodologies across a business is not adequate to enhance the agility of the enterprise.

Agility at the enterprise level has six basic underlying capabilities: responsiveness, versatility, flexibility, resilience, innovativeness, and adaptability, with an underlying capability to sense the environment also needed. It is these capabilities underlying agility which will enable companies to not only survive but also thrive on change.

The next chapter is the first of the three chapters in the foundation section. The chapter explores shifting the enterprise from being a close-ended system to becoming a living system.

References

[i] https://en.wikipedia.org/wiki/Waterfall_model

[ii] http://agilemanifesto.org/

[iii] http://agilemanifesto.org/principles.html

[iv] https://www.scrumalliance.org/community/articles/2016/october/what-we-really-know-about-successful-projects

[v] http://stateofagile.versionone.com/?utm_campaign=soa&utm_source=pressrelease&utm_medium=social

[vi] https://managingresearchlibrary.org/glossary/organizational-inertia

[vii] https://www.forbes.com/sites/stevedenning/2015/07/22/how-to-make-the-whole-organization-agile/#4f713e845841

[viii] https://www.forbes.com/sites/forbestechcouncil/2016/05/09/the-benefits-of-using-agile-software-development/#7b2f2dc0b0f8

[ix] https://www.merriam-webster.com/dictionary/agility

[x] http://jimhighsmith.com/what-is-agility/

[xi] http://www.mckinsey.com/business-functions/ organization/our-insights/the-keys-to-organizational- agility

[xii] https://medium.com/agility-scales/stop-your- agile-transformation-right-now-6cf2ef2fa1a

[xiii] http://www.dodccrp.org/files/agility_advantage/ Agility_Advantage_Book.pdf (p. 203)

[xiv] https://www.mckinsey.com/business-functions/ organization/our-insights/competing-through- organizational-agility

[xv] https://www.mckinsey.com/industries/financial- services/our-insights/ings-agile-transformation

[xvi] https://www.cio.com/article/3149977/digital- transformation/8-top-digital-transformation-stories- of-2016.html?page=2

—PART TWO—

THE FOUNDATIONS OF ENTERPRISE AGILITY

This part of the book examines the three foundational blocks of enterprise agility, namely, modeling the enterprise as a living system, mindset and culture, and leadership.

3

THE ENTERPRISE AS A LIVING SYSTEM

This chapter is about the need to liberate the enterprise from the grip of the mechanistic model and the criticality of treating a business as a living system. The chapter also covers the key characteristics of living systems and their implications for a company.

For decades, enterprises have been modeled as closed-ended systems, the rationale for which is discussed in this chapter. Closed-ended systems, for example, machines, are largely insulated from the external environment and incapable of learning on their own. Hence, although they are highly predictable and stable, systems are not capable of sensing, responding, and adapting to changes in the environment. Open-ended systems, also known as living systems, on the other hand, interact with the environment through the exchange of information, learn from interactions with the environment and, therefore, are able to evolve by adapting and responding to change, for example, humans have evolved from apes.

It can be concluded that organizations modeled as close-ended systems find it extremely difficult to evolve with a changing environment. For an enterprise to sense, respond, and adapt to change, it needs to be transformed to become an open-ended or living system.

The chapter will explore the following topics:

♦ The mechanistic approach, which is outdated for enterprise modeling

♦ The widening sustainability gap for businesses

♦ Need to reinfuse "life" into enterprises

♦ Complex adaptive systems (CAS) – a proven model of high agility

♦ Reasons for high agility in CAS

♦ Implications of CAS for organizations

The mechanistic approach that is outdated for enterprise modeling

Looking back in history, the period from 1945-71, also known as the Golden Age of Capitalism [i], saw an unprecedented boom in business activity. The only major problem that businesses appeared to have in this period was how to produce more, to satisfy the ever-increasing demand for their products and services. Most enterprises had limited product and service offerings and custom-made offerings were an exception. Companies during this period were production- or inward-focused. Competition was not very intense and the business environment was largely stable and predictable, compared to today.

The focus of companies was largely on standardization and maximizing efficiency. Processes and tools were, by far, more important than people. People were mandated to adhere to processes and comply with "orders" from "bosses." Innovation and creativity were limited to research and development departments, if considered at all.

In this period, enterprises were modeled on mechanistic systems that were appropriate for manufacturing activity. According to *The Law Dictionary*:

> *"This type of organization is hierarchical and bureaucratic.*
> *It is characterized by its (1) highly centralized authority,*
> *(2) formalized procedures and practices, and (3) specialized*
> *functions. Mechanistic organizations are relatively easier and*
> *simpler to organize, but rapid change is very challenging." [ii]*

This model works on the premise of control, that is, it implies that companies, like machines, can be designed to behave exactly as expected and every part of the enterprise will execute its functions in a repetitive and predictable way, without any variability. The business is expected to change its behavior only when there is deliberate intervention. The model follows the idea that the natural evolution of a mechanistic system only means wear and tear or obsolescence. Like machines, mechanistic organizations have no life and, therefore, little or no agility.

However, the most critical element of any enterprise is its people and unlike machines, people have feelings and aspirations, are curious and, being naturally social in nature, like to engage with other people. Employees get bored doing repetitive work. Machines do not. Machines, by definition, cannot be creative. People, by definition, are creative. People-centricity is the essence of agility and the mechanistic model hinders enterprises from becoming people-centric.

Taylor's scientific management theory – the roots of mechanistic modeling

It is important to understand the roots of mechanistic modeling so that its limitations can be addressed in the most effective manner. The roots of mechanistic modeling for businesses lie in Frederick Taylor's *Theory of Scientific Management* [iii].

Taylor's theory revolutionized the way that enterprises were run. It helped businesses to maximize efficiencies and to scale operations quickly. The theory helped companies to master the craft of manufacturing, which is about designing an object upfront and producing that object repetitively to exact specifications. Prior to this theory being adopted, there was no known systematic way of running a business, especially related to manufacturing. Taylor's theory points toward the following three key beliefs.

Managers should "think" and workers should "do"

This implies that the "doers" should "put blinkers on" and do exactly as they are told. Whatever information they gather from the environment, they are expected to pass it on to their managers, who are deemed more capable of making decisions.

Efficiency is the most important outcome to aim for

This implies that the work being done is repetitive in nature, thereby making it possible to apply scientific methods to improve productivity. The statement also implies that the doer should optimize their part of the work, without worrying about the overall outcome.

Processes and methods should drive ways of working

This implies that standardization is important, and not creativity, that most work-related circumstances and instances can be predicted in advance, and will have minimum variations or exceptions, and that people should not apply their own mind. Most importantly, the statement suggests that people are easily replicable like cogs in a wheel, and processes and methods are robust enough to smooth out the disruptions arising from people churn.

These beliefs, especially the "thinker versus doer" separation, are the primary reason for an organization to become mechanistic in nature, and thereby the people within the firm become mechanistic "resources" as well. While Taylor's theory was revolutionary in helping businesses to scale their activities, it is a huge impediment to enterprise agility in the following ways:

- ♦ The "thinkers," that is, the leaders and middle managers are removed from the customers, as they are largely kept busy preparing reports and plans and attending endless internal meetings.

- ♦ The "doers" have very little or no autonomy to make any decision that might please the customer. They are expected to follow the standard operating procedure and have to seek approval for deviations. Sometimes, the deviation has to traverse multiple levels up in the hierarchy for the decision to be made.

- ♦ It forces people to organize activities around specializations, rather than around outcomes and the delivery of value, which is almost always not optimal from the perspective of the customer and therefore for the enterprise as well.

- ♦ By the time the information has traversed the hierarchy and has reached the manager, it usually has become diluted and also outdated. Decisions made on information which may not reflect the context at that moment are likely to be suboptimal, especially considering that the manager may have very little information about the ground-level realities.

♦ The "doers" do not get a voice in defining and shaping strategy, which leads to them not feeling engaged with their work. There is no incentive for people to be passionate about their work, which severely limits excellence. Customers will likely feel the indifference of the "doers."

♦ If the number of managers becomes large, then more managers are needed to manage these managers, thereby adding more unproductive layers to the hierarchy of managers. The value these additional layers in hierarchy bring to the enterprise is highly questionable, as the managers in these middle layers are mere channels to pass information between the hierarchy layers.

♦ The extreme importance given to compliance and adherence to processes leaves no incentive to innovate.

Does this imply that we should simply abandon the scientific management theory? Of course not. It would be akin to "throwing the baby out with the bath water." Even living systems have some parts which work mechanically and which need to be treated as such, for example, in a human body, the heart works like a machine. Moreover, focus on optimizing efficiency will always remain a critical element of profitability for a company, for example, a global online retailer's fulfilment centers across the globe are run on principles of Taylorism, due to the repetitive nature of the work, so the teams in the offices are set up for enabling knowledge work and creativity.

What is needed is recognition that enterprises need to "live and breathe" in order to evolve with and adapt to change, and that continuing with the mechanistic model in its purest form, just because it has been widely successful in the past, is likely to severely impair agility.

Companies need to examine which aspects of this model have become outdated and therefore the impediments to agility in their specific context and address those impediments in order to infuse life into the business. Peter Drucker, considered to be the father of modern management, predicted the rise of knowledge work, which takes place in people's brains, as opposed to mechanistic work, which is primarily performed by machines. This has major implications as the primary resource used by businesses shifts from tangible assets such as land and labor to an intangible asset: knowledge.

In an article in the Harvard Business Review, Rick Wartzman, author of the book, *Drucker: A Life in Pictures*, states:

> *"Drucker had been anticipating this monumental leap — to an age when people would generate value with their minds more than with their muscle — since at least 1959, when in Landmarks of Tomorrow he first described the rise of knowledge work. Three decades later, Drucker had become convinced that knowledge was a more crucial economic resource than land, labor, or financial assets."* [iv]

Businesses have always evolved and will continue to evolve in order to adapt to the changing environment. Some enterprises, such as Toyota, despite being a purely manufacturing-oriented business, began recognizing the importance of people much earlier than many organizations of that scale and size. This importance is reflected in *The Toyota Way* [v], which has several principles that are people-centric.

However, the issue is that the mechanistic model is so deeply embedded in many enterprises that they are finding it difficult to evolve at the speed at which the external environment is changing. This is creating a sustainability gap for companies, which is getting wider with the onset of the digital age. Businesses looking at a wide sustainability gap face a threat to their survivability.

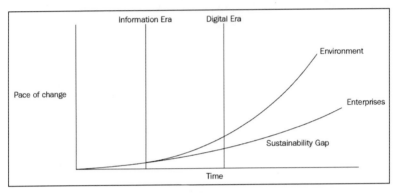

Figure 3.1: The sustainability gap facing enterprises

The preceding diagram depicts the widening off the sustainability gap due to enterprises being unable to keep up with the pace of change of the environment. The gap has been widening at a faster rate, especially after the start of the digital era.

Empirical evidence suggests that companies are finding it difficult to bridge the sustainability gap. According to Wouter Aghina, a partner at McKinsey & Co.:

> *"When machine organizations have tried to engage with the new environment, it has not worked out well for many. A very small number of companies have thrived over time; fewer than 10 percent of the non-financial S&P 500 companies in 1983 remained in the S&P 500 in 2013. From what we have observed, machine organizations also experience constant internal churn.*

According to our research with 1,900 executives, they are
adapting their strategy (and their organizational structure)
with greater frequency than in the past. Eighty-two percent
of them went through a redesign in the last three years.
However, most of these redesign efforts fail — only
23 percent were implemented successfully."

The only possible way that enterprises can bridge this gap is through enhanced agility, which will enable them to keep up with or even exceed the pace of change of the environment.

Need to reinfuse "life" into enterprises

A fast-changing environment necessitates that businesses have agility, that is, they should be organic like living systems and not lifeless like machines.

According to Michelle Holiday, president of Cambium Consulting:

"This new story is emerging all around us, though few have
connected the dots. Why does a flat, networked organization now
seem the better choice, when we've relied on rigid hierarchy for
so long? Why do we need to engage the passion of people within,
when for so long we've considered them simply 'labor'? Why do
we need to engage customers in meaningful conversation, when for
so long it was enough to deliver a quality product? The answer
is that each of these is a move in the direction of resilience,
adaptability and creativity. In other words, it's a move in the
direction of life." [vi]

A timeless fact about businesses is that they have always had people. Of course, while machines may be more significant in some companies than others, depending on the nature of the industry they are in, the indisputable fact is that people have been and still are an enterprise's most valuable asset. This can be easily corroborated by examining the extent of people-centric agility that a business has at the startup stage. Most businesses lose agility as they grow in scale, as the mechanistic model gets applied after the enterprise grows beyond a certain size. Exceptions to this are companies such as Google and Apple, which appear to maintain their agility despite continuing to grow in size. Given that the mechanistic modeling of companies is stifling agility, it is necessary to free the enterprise from the clutches of this largely obsolete model and bring the business back to life.

Complex adaptive systems (CAS) – a proven model of high agility

The challenges of environments becoming highly dynamic, interconnected, and unpredictable might be new in the context of business, but they are widely prevalent in life and social sciences and have existed since eternity. Prominent examples are humans, ecology, the global macroeconomic network within a country, or group of countries, the stock market and complex webs of cross-border holding companies, social insect (for example, ant) colonies, and any human social group-based endeavor. These systems are better known as **complex adaptive systems** (**CAS**). These systems have demonstrated a pattern of evolving, that is, adapting and responding to change.

According to Martin Reeves, co-author of *Your Strategy Needs a Strategy*, and others in an article in the *Harvard Business Review*:

> *"We stress that companies are identical to biological species in an important respect: both are what's known as complex adaptive systems. Therefore, the principles that confer robustness in these systems, whether natural or manmade, are directly applicable to business."* *[vii]*

Given how consistently and effectively these systems have demonstrated agility, it is worth exploring whether there are any learnings from CAS for enterprises, with respect to dealing with change.

What are CAS?

According to BusinessDictionary.com, CAS is defined as:

> *"Entity consisting of many diverse and autonomous components or parts (called agents) which are interrelated, interdependent, linked through many (dense) interconnections, and behave as a unified whole in learning from experience and in adjusting (not just reacting) to changes in the environment."* *[viii]*

One of the most popular definitions of CAS was offered by John H. Holland, a pioneer in the study of CAS:

> *"A Complex Adaptive System (CAS) is a dynamic network of many agents (which may represent cells, species, individuals, firms, nations) acting in parallel, constantly acting and reacting to what the other agents are doing. The control of a CAS tends to be highly dispersed and decentralized.*

If there is to be any coherent behavior in the system, it has to arise from competition and cooperation among the agents themselves. The overall behavior of the system is the result of a huge number of decisions made every moment by many individual agents." [ix]

According to Wikipedia:

Complex adaptive systems are complex in that they are dynamic networks of interactions, and their relationships are not aggregations of the individual static entities, that is, the behavior of the ensemble is not predicted by the behavior of the components. They are adaptive in that the individual and collective behavior mutate and self-organize corresponding to the change-initiating micro-event or collection of events.[x]

The following diagram is a pictorial model of a CAS [xi]:

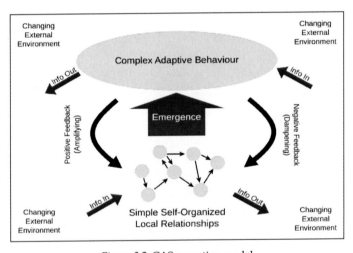

Figure 3.2: CAS operating model

The preceding diagram depicts the operating model of CAS, at a high level. Self-organizing agents interact with each other, which creates complex adaptive behavior through emergence. The agents receive both positive and negative feedback on their behaviors, which helps them to adjust their behaviors. Moreover, the agents and their behaviors influence and also get influenced by the external environment.

Characteristics of a CAS

We will now look at the key characteristics of a CAS and their implications for enterprises with respect to moving the companies away from the mechanistic model and bringing "life" back into them.

Continuous evolution

The most important characteristic of a CAS is that it evolves continuously. Let's take human beings as an example. We, as a CAS, have evolved over millions of years from apes to our current form. We have shed the tail, as it was of no use to us. We branched into multiple races. We are still evolving and will continue to do so. Another example is economies, which were long ago based on a barter system and then went on to paper and credit money and now seem to be moving toward cryptocurrencies. The evolution of a CAS keeps pace with the changes in the environment. This is the primary reason for the resilience in a CAS, which significantly improves its chances of survivability.

Autonomous and self-organizing agents

A CAS comprises of agents that interact with the environment and with each other and adapt and respond based on feedback. In an economy, the agents might be individuals or households. In an ecosystem, the agents are species. In a brain, the agents are nerve cells. Agents can be non-living entities like banks in financial markets, political parties in a democracy, and so on.

As depicted in the pictorial model of a CAS, there is constant action and reaction to what is happening in the environment and to what other agents are doing, thus making the system constantly dynamic. Agents may be able to relate to each other through a structure, but the structure changes and evolves based on the need to adapt to context.

There is no single centralized control mechanism that governs the behavior of the agents or the system itself. Agents have the autonomy to behave as they deem fit, subject to boundaries and some restrictions, for example, humans have the freedom to decide when to marry, but will be punished if they threaten someone into marriage.

Although the interrelationships between agents in the system produce coherence, the agents are constantly reorganizing to find the best fit with the environment, for example, a new honey bee queen is created when the number of bees in a hive becomes too many.

Agents' interactions influence system behavior

CAS behavior is driven by the inter-relationships, inter-action, and inter-connectivity of the agents within a system and between a system and its environment. The relationships and interactions between the agents are generally more important than the agents themselves, for example, in a human body, the brain operates quite independently and so does the digestive system. However, the interaction between these subsystems, which are agents themselves, is critical for the optimal functioning of the larger system. The digestive and respiratory system may seem disconnected, but digestion cannot happen unless the respiratory system provides it with oxygen, and the respiratory system cannot function unless the digestive system converts food into energy. Some systems are based entirely on interactions between agents, for example, an economy cannot function unless there are both buyers and sellers for goods and services.

Agents' behavior is driven by purpose

The driver behind agents interacting with the environment and with other agents is always some purpose. For example, the primary purpose behind all living species interacting with the environment is survival. While this interaction is necessary and unavoidable, it may not be so for other purposes, for example, people trade in the stock market to create wealth and people join a social organization like the Rotary Club for multiple purposes, like social service and fellowship. Even people getting together to celebrate a birthday or a wedding is a purpose-driven behavior.

Loosely-coupled agents

The agents in a CAS are loosely coupled. This implies that when some agents are removed or when a part of the system fails, the rest of the system is either not impacted or recovers quickly, for example, if some investors leave the stock market, the market continues to function normally. When a large financial institution like the Lehman Brothers collapses, it might bring down a few other institutions with it and make the economy wobble a bit. However, the economy will eventually recover.

The key to being loosely coupled is flexibility in the structure of the system and the diversity of behavior of the agents. If the agents behave in a coordinated or unidirectional manner, the system's behavior will change to being tightly coupled. A stock market crash leading to panic selling and a run on a bank are examples of tightly coupled behaviors.

Variety is a source of strength

The more variety there is in a CAS, the stronger it is. The diversity in a CAS leads to ambiguity and paradox. However, a CAS uses contradictions and uncertainty to create new possibilities to evolve with and adapt to the environment. This reinforces the idea of bounded instability or the edge of chaos that is characterized by a state of paradox: stability and instability, competition and cooperation, order and disorder.

Democracy and financial markets are examples of a CAS where a variety of agents leads to the strength of these systems. In living systems, the importance of genetic diversity has also been widely recognized.

According to The National Gardening Association:

"Genetic diversity strengthens a population by increasing the likelihood that at least some individuals will be able to survive major disturbances, and by making the group less susceptible to inherited disorders." [xii]

Emergent behavior

Complexity in a CAS refers to the potential for emergent behavior in complex and unpredictable phenomena. There is constant action and reaction to what other agents are doing. From the interaction of the individual agents arises some kind of global property or pattern, which is something that could not have been predicted from understanding each particular agent, for example, the overall behavior observed in the economy is a result of the countless decisions made by millions of individual people. Any coherent behavior in a system arises from competition and cooperation among the agents themselves.

A poignant example is that if we were to take all the food shops in a town and divide all the food by the number of people living there, we would find a pattern that there is always one-to-two weeks' worth of food supply in the town. However, this is achieved without a food plan for the town or a formal controlling process.

Another example is of a termite hill that has an amazing architecture, with a maze of interconnecting passages, large caverns, ventilation tunnels, and much more. Yet there is no grand plan, the hill just emerges as a result of the termites following a few simple rules.

The nonlinear relationship between cause and effect

In a CAS, the relationship between cause and effect is not necessarily linear, and sometimes not even correlated. Small changes can have a surprisingly profound impact on overall behavior, or vice versa, a huge upset to the system may not affect it. An example of a nonlinear relationship is how Bearings Bank was brought to closure by the actions of just one person, Nick Leeson. The fluttering of butterflies in Brazil causing tornadoes in the state of Texas in the USA [xiii] is an example of a lack of direct correlation between cause and effect. Hence, the causes of many effects may be found only in hindsight, which then may lead to interpreting them over a period of time as patterns.

There is a fine line between order and chaos. A system in equilibrium does not have the internal dynamics to enable it to respond to its environment and it will slowly (or quickly) die. Too much order implies too many constraints and that stifles innovation and creativity. An automobile is an example of an orderly system, which (usually) behaves in a very predictable manner. A system in chaos ceases to function as a system, until order is restored, for example, a severe traffic jam due to a failed traffic signal at a busy intersection. Hence, the most productive state to be in is at the edge between order and chaos, where there is maximum variety and creativity, leading to new possibilities. CASs function best when they combine order and chaos in an appropriate measure, for example, there are some unwritten rules about traffic in Johannesburg, South Africa [xiv], which have emerged from the city being on the edge of order and chaos.

The key to understanding the word chaos in this context is to understand it not as anarchy, but as a lack of structure. A CAS is ruled by the second law of thermodynamics: it is in a constant state of equilibrium, entropy, or disorder, which will keep increasing such that the system will wind down and eventually die, unless it renews itself.

In a CAS, the rules governing the functioning of the system are quite simple. A classic example is that all the water systems in the world (all the streams, rivers, lakes, oceans, waterfalls, and many more, with their infinite beauty, power, and variety) are governed by the simple principle that water finds its own level. The simplicity in rules enables self-organization, which is the key to the system being on the edge of order and chaos, and effectiveness over efficiency.

A CAS, once it has reached the state of "being good enough," that is, the energy wasted is less than the energy spent on improving itself, will trade off increased efficiency every time in favor of greater effectiveness. A simple example is the human body, which will start burning stored fat in the absence of food.

Patterns of behavior

The collective behavior of the agents leads to the formation of broad patterns, which are far more predictable than the behaviors of an individual or a group of agents. The economy has patterns of recession-recovery-boom-slowdown. The weather has a pattern of seasons. While the patterns are largely predictable, the timing of the onset of a pattern is much less predictable. When the economy is in recession, when the recession will end and when recovery will start cannot be predicted.

Reasons for high agility in a CAS

The analysis of CAS characteristics helps in understanding the key reasons why a CAS has high agility. These are as follows:

♦ Agents, that is, employees in the context of an enterprise, are empowered to deal with the environment and interact with other agents, in a manner which they deem as best for the situation at hand

♦ Agents learn based on feedback and change themselves and adjust their behaviors accordingly

♦ Agents are actively and purposefully engaged with the system

♦ Agents and the system discard what is not working, and constantly evolve to find the best fit with the environment

♦ CAS purpose, structure, and processes are dynamic and evolve based on emergent information

Implications for enterprises

The characteristics of a CAS provide meaningful pointers for reinfusing life into companies. The following table is a summary of the implications for businesses, which are derived from the characteristics of a CAS:

CAS characteristic	Implication for enterprises
Continuous evolution	Enhanced agility
Autonomous and self-organizing agents	Responsive structure
Agents' interactions influence system behavior	Build social density
	Amplify success stories
	Encourage healthy friction
Agents' behavior is driven by purpose	Link purpose to work
Loosely-coupled agents	Balance proximity and modularity
Variety is a source of strength	Cultivate diversity
Emergent behavior	Build on emergence
Nonlinear relationship between cause and effect	Shorter feedback loops
	Experiment with lever points

The fine line between order and chaos	Balance order and chaos
	Selective destruction
	Simple rules
	Safe to fail experiments
Effectiveness over efficiency	Prioritize effectiveness over efficiency
Patterns of behavior	Monitor and leverage patterns

The explanations of the implications are as follows:

Enhanced agility

The overarching implication is that enterprises will need to be attuned to the changes in the environment, and reform and reinvent themselves accordingly. The critical point is the pace of adaptation, as that needs to keep up with the blistering pace of change, that is, change as fast as change itself. To do this, businesses will need high maturity in all the capabilities that are underlying agility: responsiveness, versatility, flexibility, resilience, innovativeness and, of course, adaptability.

Responsive structure

The enterprise needs to have a structure that supports autonomous, decentralized, and outcome-oriented teams, which will facilitate interoperability and information sharing among people. This structure should have a wider periphery, which facilitates closer interaction with the environment and therefore enables the company to be more responsive.

According to Niels Pflaeging, author of *Organize for Complexity*:

> *"It is the periphery that learns from the market easiest. That can best adapt to and respond to markets — quickly and intelligently. In complexity, the center loses its information monopoly, its competence advantage:*

it can hardly issue any meaningful commands anymore. The coupling between periphery and center must consequently be designed in a way that enables the organization to absorb and process market dynamics. For that, the periphery must steer the center through market-like mechanisms and own the monetary resources". [xv]

This aspect is discussed at length in *Chapter 6, Organization Structure.*

Build social density

Social density is the number of interactions that are likely to happen between agents within a given space. Enterprises should put enablers in place to encourage social density between people, giving special attention to social density between the people whose interactions are more critical for the business.

Attention given to ensuring adequate social density is particularly important when change is recently introduced and agents are still getting used to being in a common space, which they did not share before the change, for example, DevOps bringing together the development and operations teams, which prior to the change had a "wall" between them. A concrete measure to increase social density for these agents can be to include operations in project inception and release meetings, thereby engaging them right from the beginning of the delivery cycle.

In case the social density appears to be low, the underlying cause needs to be fixed, for example, if team members are always overloaded with work, and are frequently multitasking, the conditions are not right for them to have meaningful interactions. **Communities of Practices (CoPs)** are a highly effective way of enabling social density. The Spotify model [xvi] (Squads, Tribes, and so on) is a popular model for establishing CoPs.

Amplify success stories

Stories too are agents, albeit logical and in an enterprise, and hence success stories should be identified and socialized across the company. The more the desire for other agents to connect to the success story, or to create another one, the higher the chances of coherence around the desired outcomes.

Encourage healthy friction

Healthy friction among agents is one of the key reasons for higher resilience in a CAS. While at the agent level the objectives might appear contrary, at the system level it is important to align the agent-level objectives to the broader objective of the enterprise. Marketing may want to increase spend on advertising, but finance may be keen to control costs. Both are valid objectives at the respective agent levels and may appear contrary, but a balance needs to be achieved between them to meet the business' objective of increasing sales. It may be possible that the agents will work out a better way to increase sales with minimal additional spend on advertising. The key is that the agents have autonomy to resolve the conflict in a manner that best meets the broader objectives and they are enabled to do this with integrative thinking skills.

According to Roger Martin, a former dean at Rotman School of Management at the University of Toronto in Canada:

> *"Integrative thinkers aren't satisfied with simply making an unpleasant trade-off. Instead, they master the ability to constructively face the tensions of opposing models, and instead of choosing one at the expense of the other, they generate a creative solution of the tensions in the form of a new model that contains elements of the individual models but is superior to each." [xvii]*

Healthy friction and an integrative thinking approach will enable employees to come up with out-of-the-box solutions to deal effectively with the unique challenges presented by the dynamic environment. The creative solutions that emerge, through employee interaction, can provide a significant boost to agility.

Link purpose to work

The purpose of the enterprise, broken down into vision, mission, strategy, and initiatives, must be socialized across the business such that the agents, namely, people in the enterprise, are able to establish a connection between the work they are doing and the purpose of the company. Staff being aligned with an organization's purpose is a necessary condition to be able to effectively deliver value-driven outcomes. Besides autonomy and mastery, purpose is a key factor in intrinsically motivating people who are knowledge workers. This topic will be discussed in more detail in *Chapter 6, Organization Structure* and *Chapter 8, Process*.

Balance proximity and modularity

Given the criticality of the interaction between the agents in shaping the outcomes and evolution of the system, it is important to ensure that no agent remains disconnected or connected weakly with the agents they are supposed to interact with. The connectedness should help in improving the flow of information and knowledge between agents. It is critical to remember that agents include external entities like vendors and, of course, the customers.

While connectivity is important, the right level of modularity should also not be overlooked. Modularity helps in achieving coherence, as well as in increasing the ability of the system to absorb shocks better. Modularity may involve reorganization of the agents, which might cause short-term pain but could result in significant long-term benefits, for example, if teams are structured as component teams, then increasing connectivity within the component teams, which are specialized to work on a layer of a feature (for example, the user interface), will surely yield some benefits. However, far greater and more sustainable benefits can be achieved if the teams are restructured as feature teams, that is, teams which work on the entire feature. This topic is discussed in detail in *Chapter 6, Organization Structure.*

Cultivate diversity

For decades, businesses had the tendency to resist change. Heavyweight approval processes, change control boards, and so on, were put in place to ensure that only a selected few had the right to decide what changes should be made, if at all. The higher the predictability, the more reassured the leaders were that "everything is under control." There was a defined process for everything, compliance to processes was expected and rewarded, and those committing "deviations" were punished. Standardization, therefore, not only became the means to achieve predictability, but in many cases became the goal itself.

Standardization consequently leads to homogeneity, which is the opposite of diversity. However, biological species are known to become more vulnerable as they become more genetically homogenous. Nature has therefore put in a mechanism of sexual reproduction, which leads to the random matching of chromosome pairings. This results in more permutations and more variety in offspring.

According to William Hamilton, an evolutionary theorist from the University of Oxford, "enemies," that is, harmful germs, find it much harder to adapt to a population born through sexual reproduction, as opposed to one born via parthenogenesis.

In the context of an enterprise, people are chromosomes, the genetic material that creates variety and diversity. Therefore, a business must strive for diversity in its people (gender, ethnicity, education, and experience), and, more importantly, encourage diversity of thought. A company must also leverage the fresh perspectives that newly hired talent can provide.

Without internal variety and diversity, a business will find it very difficult to deal with the variety and diversity of today's external environment. Diversity also means having the right balance between process standardization and autonomy for the people closest to the environment to override processes, as needed, if that helps to deliver greater value.

Build on emergence

In a dynamically changing environment, it is futile to try to predict the long-term future state accurately. Hence, rather than working backwards from an imaginary and inaccurate future state, it makes much more sense to work forwards based on the current state, which is known. Complexity implies that the end solution to a problem cannot be predicted at the outset. Moreover, the nature of the problem itself may undergo change, with a change in circumstances and the emergence of new information.

Not defining a future state should not mean lack of clarity about the goals and intended outcomes. However, the means to achieve the goals and outcomes must remain flexible. Hence, instead of having a detailed plan, which is supposed to show the exact way to get to the future state, a rolling plan should be prepared to ensure and maintain alignment with the broader intended goals and outcomes.

The plan should be detailed closer to current time, with progressive lower levels of details into the future. It is important to keep this as an organic element and to keep evolving this continuously, based on "today's reality." The plan should emphasize higher predictability in the near term and higher flexibility in the medium and long term.

The following diagram is a visual depiction of a rolling wave plan:

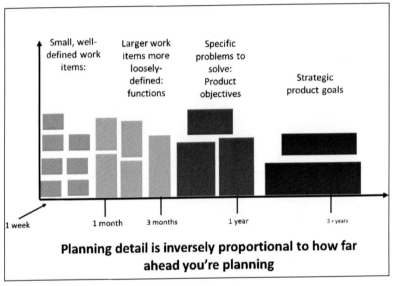

Figure 3.3: Rolling wave plan

In the preceding diagram, strategic product goals are defined for a longer period and the product objectives, functions, and work items are defined at progressive lower granularity, with the lowest granularity defined for work to be done closest to the current time.

The parts of a CAS cohere around common goals and hence the plan should clearly reflect the goals of the enterprise. Agents will self-organize in conducive conditions and do what it takes to achieve the goals. Building on emergence implies that the goals and outcomes may also need to undergo change, based on changes in the external environment. In such a case, the plan needs to change to reflect the revised goals and outcomes, and also the means to achieve the outcomes.

Another critical aspect of emergence is to work with "just enough" information. What is just enough is totally context-specific. However, it should be adequate to conform to an existing pattern or to form a new pattern. Seeing information as patterns is especially important as it is quite easy to get lost in data, which is available in abundance.

Information being valid for investigation and exploration should be the driver to guide the next steps. A practical example is the amount of time to travel from destination X to Y, by taxi. In terms of planning, it is good enough to know that it takes roughly 20-25 minutes for the journey. Knowing that it took 21 minutes and 33 seconds and 24 minutes and 10 seconds the past two times is valuable, but estimating to the last second for the next journey adds very little value.

Emergence also means that the enterprises have to be ready to deal with unforeseen circumstances, for example, customers venting their anger about a poor product or service on social media and its immediate and widespread negative impact is something which may not have been initially anticipated by companies. However, now that this behavior has become a pattern, businesses have no option but to put in a mechanism to spot such complaints and mitigate them as early as possible.

Shorter feedback loops

As outcomes can be nonlinear and, more importantly, can often result in unintended and unwanted consequences, feedback loops across the enterprise need to be as short as possible. Feedback is much more valuable when it is timely. A simple example is of a software defect. The direct and indirect costs of the defect are much lower if the defect is detected closer to when the code is written, versus if the defect is found when the code is in production.

Feedback loops should be made shorter and stronger at all levels including between team members, between teams, between teams and customers, teams and leadership, team and code, and so on. It is not only important to act appropriately based on feedback but also to learn from it by drawing out patterns based on the received information.

Feedback should be sought actively rather than waiting for the concerned entity to provide the feedback. It is often wrongly assumed that when no feedback is received, everything is fine. This is a truly wrong assumption to make. If we examine our own experiences as customers, how often have we taken the time and effort to provide feedback, whether positive or negative, when it has not been solicited?

It is worth calling out that a CAS is able to deal with change effectively not only due to short feedback loops but also because it is structured in a way which enables the agents to collect and respond to feedback effectively.

Experiment with lever points

Most management theories and practices are based on a deterministic cause and effect principles, for example, incentivize employees with more money and they will deliver more/work harder. However, one of the core properties of a CAS is nonlinear or disproportionate causation, that is, a small action resulting in a disproportionate effect and vice versa. Actions that are inexpensive but lead to significant positive outcomes are called **lever points**. These points can be identified through experimentation or learned based on patterns of empirical evidence.

Agile practices have many such lever points, which enhance agility, for example, putting up a visual board to depict the pipeline of work in a process usually has a highly positive impact in terms of identifying blockers, managing dependencies, and focusing on higher priority items. Another example is a daily stand-up meeting.

Lever points can also be used quite effectively in influencing culture change. A senior leader could participate in a retrospective exercise to learn about why something failed and then encourage the team to learn from that mistake, sending positive signals across the enterprise, especially if the employees of that business are generally afraid of failure. Socializing success stories is another lever point that has usually resulted in broad-based positive outcomes across companies.

Balance order and chaos

In order to deal with change, enterprises, like a CAS, need to undergo change themselves. This change can be in the form of reorganization, selective destruction and renewal, reshaping or something else. As mentioned earlier, a firm cannot be at equilibrium for any meaningful period, as the forces acting upon it are changing constantly. The very basic definition of equilibrium is that "it is a state of an object in which all forces acting upon it are balanced."

Essentially, a CAS will do "whatever it takes" to survive under changing conditions. All CAS appear to follow this pattern. It is only by being in this "sweet spot" that CASs are able to deal most effectively with change.

The implications for enterprises are as follows.

Selective destruction

An example of selective destruction in a CAS is how forest fires have been found to be a crucial factor in regenerating healthy forests. The key takeaway for companies is that destruction is part of evolution. In practical terms, it means getting rid of anything that has become obsolete and is no longer delivering value. In the prism of a fast-changing environment, obsolescence is defined by relevance and not age. Examples include obsolete IT solutions, non performing business units, and at more granular level, a practice or a process followed by a team, which is no longer adding value.

A key point to remember is that intervening to prevent something that needs destruction can prove disastrous. The major fire in Yellowstone Park in the USA, in 1992, is a good example of this. As stated earlier, forest fires are considered healthy for the regeneration of forests. However, forest fires were prevented from happening for decades in Yellowstone Park, through human intervention. Gradually, the forest floor accumulated a very thick layer of debris. Eventually, a lightning strike caused a fire that could not be contained. Decades of accumulated debris burned hotter and longer than normal. This incinerated large trees and destroyed living components of the soil, which would have otherwise survived a normal fire. The fire wiped out 25% of the park.

Enterprises must build a culture where people can challenge anything that may not be adding value now. It is fairly common to see people doing things because "we have always done it that way." Going further, teams also need to be empowered to stop or modify what no longer adds value, be it a process, practice, role, communication pattern, and so on.

Selective destruction also needs to be viewed from the point of view of "destroying" something where a better alternative has emerged, for example, the possibility of hosting IT infrastructure in the "cloud" can lead to getting rid of a physical IT infrastructure, as the former may be both more effective and efficient. Selective destruction, when appropriate, will not only enable a business to remain lean, but it is also a huge enabler for a company to keep evolving in line with the changes in the environment.

Simple rules

As stated earlier, all CASs operate on simple and minimal rules. For an enterprise, this means setting appropriate boundaries and keeping the rules simple and minimal. It also means letting the people, and networks of people, interact among themselves and with the environment to organize through an iterative process of creative exploration and selective destruction. Agility is most effective when the people who are closest to the environment have the space and freedom to interact with the environment as they deem appropriate and make the necessary modifications in the system. For example, an organization that is recognized for successfully transforming to Agile has only two rules for the teams: iteration length should be two weeks and the shared electronic tool should be updated with all relevant data on a real-time basis.

Safe to fail experiments

The disruptions caused by change, particularly change that is technology related, mean that a business will repeatedly encounter unprecedented situations, for example, blockchain, which was perhaps unimaginable a decade ago. It can be a threat or an opportunity, depending on how a bank deals with it.

An enterprise must have the culture of innovation, if it is to spot and also create opportunities that a changing environment presents. Innovation can come only from experimentation. To foster a culture of innovation, the business should encourage people to stay away from the "we have always done it this way" mindset and more toward a culture of trying something new.

However, risk and experimentation go together, and if risk is not understood and contained, it can be disastrous for the company. The Ford Edsel car is a classic case study in this regard. Ford wanted to develop a premium car for middle class Americans. Ford was so confident about the car that it planned to introduce 18 variants of the car at launch. At launch, the car was too expensive, was a "gas guzzler," and was mocked in the press. Ford had to write off $350 million for this failure, which in today's terms is close to $3 billion.

Some ideas can be just ahead of their time (for example, the Newton MessagePad introduced in the early 1990s) while the customers may simply not like some ideas (for example, Crystal Pepsi). From an enterprise perspective, there are two takeaways: 1) it's important to get feedback as early as possible to know whether something should move forward or should be stopped, and 2) risks should be taken only to the extent where it is possible to recover quickly from failure and ensure that the risk does not prove fatal for the company. In summary, an enterprise must strive to strike that fine balance between order and chaos, as too much order impedes agility and chaos destroys agility.

Prioritize effectiveness over efficiency

Under perfect conditions of stability, trade-offs may not be necessary between effectiveness and efficiency. However, in reality, this trade-off is always there. Most businesses, as a rule of thumb, appear to favor efficiency over effectiveness. Some of the key reasons for this include the following:

- Manufacturing orientation, where identical things are produced in large quantities

- Short-term profit maximization orientation, due to pressure to show increasing profits every quarter

This becomes starkly clear when examining the KPIs chosen to define success and also those based on which C-level executives are incentivized and rewarded. A CAS, however, prioritizes effectiveness over efficiency, when the trade-off has to be made. This is perhaps the best way to deal with a changing environment when survival is at stake.

Enterprises need to change their orientation to prioritize effectiveness over efficiency, when there is a necessity to make the trade-off. A business may be highly efficient by producing its products at the lowest possible cost, but, to save costs, it may not spend on learning about the customers' changing preferences. As a result, the company can achieve higher profitability in the short run, but will lose customers in the long run, thereby losing both revenue and profits. The swift downfall of Blockbuster [xviii], which was the leader in the video rental industry, is a case in point. A critical part of its revenue model was charging late fees to customers. When Netflix came up with a model which made late fees redundant, Blockbuster went bankrupt in no time.

An organization must spend, as needed, time, effort, and money on enabling a learning and knowledge-driven culture, which helps its people to effectively adapt and respond to the fast-changing environment. Knowledge workers should primarily be accountable for effectiveness, that is, getting the desired outcomes, and secondarily for efficiency, that is, doing things at the least cost.

Monitor and leverage patterns

The emergent nature of CAS implies that patterns will surface at all levels of the enterprise, which will be based on the behavior of the agents, as well as the behavior of the system itself, for example, people becoming tense during performance appraisal periods could be a pattern. These patterns can lead to outcomes that are both desirable and not desirable.

An example of an undesirable pattern is that decisions are being made by the **HIPPO** (short for, **highest paid person's opinion**). Hence, patterns need to be monitored on a continuous basis, to encourage behaviors that lead to desired outcomes and conversely discourage behaviors that lead to undesirable outcomes.

It is also important to examine patterns that have become mental models, and challenge them, as some may be impediments to change. These patterns, therefore, should be dealt with first before introducing additional changes. Unless the feedback is a one-off, feedback should be consolidated into patterns. Patterns help in understanding the core issue quickly, without getting lost in the details. While details are important, not everyone should see the details or see them at all times. Patterns help in making information more consumable, thereby aiding the speed of communication, as well as knowledge transfer. There are significant implications of CAS modeling for leadership, which will be covered in *Chapter 5, Leadership*.

Summary

In this chapter, we learned that today enterprises are facing challenges which CASs have dealt with since time immemorial very effectively. They have been able to do so as they have all the capabilities of agility, only because they are living systems.

Understanding CAS modeling and embracing it, in order to infuse life into the business, is the first and fundamental step that companies should take as they embark/continue their journey toward agility. It will create a strong foundation that will support all other measures to boost agility.

The next chapter is the second of the three chapters in the foundation section. The chapter explores the significance of mindset and culture and how to influence them to become enablers for enhancing agility.

References

[i] http://atheistnexus.org/forum/topics/golden-age-of-capitalism-1945-1971

[ii] https://thelawdictionary.org/mechanistic-organization/

[iii] http://www.economist.com/node/13092819

[iv] https://hbr.org/2014/10/what-peter-drucker-knew-about-2020

[v] https://en.wikipedia.org/wiki/The_Toyota_Way

[vi] http://www.managementexchange.com/hack/organizations-living-systems-crafting-new-story-life-center-its-plot

[vii] https://hbr.org/2016/01/the-biology-of-corporate-survival

[viii] http://www.businessdictionary.com/definition/complex-adaptive-system-CAS.html

[ix] https://en.wikiquote.org/wiki/Complex_adaptive_systems

[x] https://en.wikipedia.org/wiki/Complex_adaptive_system

[xi] https://commons.wikimedia.org/wiki/File:Complex_adaptive_system.svg

[xii] https://garden.org/courseweb/course2/week2/page18.htm

[xiii] https://en.wikipedia.org/wiki/Butterfly_effect

[xiv] https://www.news24.com/mynews24/yourstory/rules-for-driving-in-johannesburg-20110727

[xv] https://www.linkedin.com/pulse/flat-hierarchies-just-another-step-wrong-direction-niels-pflaeging

[xvi] http://www.full-stackagile.com/2016/02/14/team-organisation-squads-chapters-tribes-and-guilds/

[xvii] http://rogerlmartin.com/thought-pillars/integrative-thinking

[xviii] https://www.forbes.com/sites/gregsatell/2014/09/05/a-look-back-at-why-blockbuster-really-failed-and-why-it-didnt-have-to/#80977c51d64a

4

MINDSET
AND CULTURE

This chapter is about what mindset and culture are, their importance in enhancing agility, which variables influence them, and how to influence those variables.

As discussed in the previous chapter, for an enterprise to have greater agility, it must treat knowledge workers, that is, its people, as its most valuable asset. It is people who will build and enhance the capabilities underlying agility. People need to come together to work as teams that are committed to a common purpose and which need to figure out the best way to achieve that purpose through interactions and feedback-based learning. Hence, people who have the right mindset, and are supported by a people-centric culture, are at the foundation of enterprise agility.

The chapter will explore the following topics:

♦ What is mindset?

♦ What is culture?

♦ The culture and mindset ecosystem

♦ Changing mindset and culture

♦ Values aligned to agility

♦ Behaviors aligned to agility

♦ Enabling behavior changes

♦ Aligning the workplace to an agility-enabling culture

Significance

Our minds, for several centuries, have been used to a much slower pace of change. Our brains have been wired to favor predictability, certainty, and risk aversion. However, the basic properties of complexity are unpredictability and uncertainty. We have a hindsight bias which makes us believe that things are predictable, even when they are not.

According to Peter Green, who led a grassroots Agile transformation at Adobe from 2005 to 2015:

> *"Hindsight bias leads us to treat complex work as predictable. Instead of using empirical processes based on transparency and frequent inspection and adaptation loops, we do extensive up-front planning and implement stricter controls to meet the original plan. Years of "lessons learned" sessions caused us to move further and further from the right approach." [i]*

Until very recently, and perhaps even today, our formal education was largely oriented towards a linear way of thinking, tight cause-effect relationships, frowning on ambiguity, rewarding conformity, discouraging challenging with a different perspective, and, most importantly, believing that there is one right way or one best way of doing things.

However, many things around us as individuals, and in the business environment, have changed, and changed quite fast, with the advent of the internet era. They are expected to change at a faster rate still in the fourth industrial revolution.

What is needed in this highly-dynamic era, and a complex environment, are the abilities to deal with uncertainty, to adapt to change, to unlearn what does not work, and to learn what works and how best to respond to change. A mindset that has these key qualities is the agility-oriented mindset. Having this mindset is an absolute must for achieving agility, as without it, all overt measures to enhance agility are extremely likely to fail or at best have very little impact.

According to Steve Denning, author of multiple books, including *The Leader's Guide to Radical Management*:

> *"Having an Agile mindset is central. If you had the right mindset, it hardly mattered what tools and processes you were using, the Agile mindset made things come out right. Conversely, if you didn't have an Agile mindset, it didn't matter if you were implementing every tool and process and system exactly according to the book, no benefits flowed." [ii]*

The point made by Denning is critical, as it highlights the irrefutable fact that Agile is about "being" and not "doing." The abilities of adapting and learning are intrinsic in nature and can be acquired, developed, and exhibited only if one has the Agile mindset.

The case of enterprise culture is similar to that of mindset, in that a culture that is agility-oriented is very different from the culture of a business not set up for agility. As seen in the previous chapter, companies need to become "living" systems if they aspire for greater agility. The basic trait of a living enterprise is that it is based on people-centric values such as trust and transparency, rather than machine-centric values such as compliance and control.

What is DNA to humans, is culture to organizations. It is embedded in every single element of the enterprise, right from leadership and strategy, to people, processes and structure. Hence, as difficult as it might be to change the culture of a business, it is absolutely imperative to have a culture that not only helps to enhance agility but to sustain it as well.

Mike Dargan, the group head of technology at UBS, believes that:

> *"culture is the most important platform a bank can build."*

He adds:

> *"A strong culture ensures that everyone is focused on delivering for our clients, not ourselves. A strong culture allows us to challenge the status quo, learn from our mistakes and act with integrity. A strong culture insulates a bank from over-reliance on any single leader. It diversifies leadership risk over time. A strong culture of collaboration and trust allows for the most complex problems of an organization to be solved. Without it, they can fester for years, if not decades." [iii]*

Before delving into how mindset and culture can be aligned for agility, it is important to understand what they are and what influences them.

What is mindset?

There is no mention of the word *mindset* in the Agile Manifesto or the principles. Nonetheless, it is now widely recognized and accepted that agility needs a specific type of mindset, as indicated in aforementioned Denning's quote.

There is a formal definition available of the word mindset, but not in the context of Agile or agility. The word mindset is defined as "a set of assumptions, methods, or notations held by one or more people or groups of people." [iv] The closest anyone has come to defining the Agile mindset is Linda Rising, the author and lecturer, who made a clear distinction between the fixed and Agile mindsets, by contrasting their characteristics. According to Rising, an Agile mindset has the ability to grow like a muscle and has learning as the primary goal. The outlook towards challenge is to embrace it and be resilient and to view failure as something which provides information, alongside a belief that effort leads to mastery. [v]

In simple terms, mindset reflects an individual's mental inclination or way of thinking. What underlies an individual's mindset is their attitudes, beliefs, perceptions, and values:

- ◆ **Attitude**: A firm way of thinking about something, which can be positive or negative, for example, I will not hesitate to ask for help when I am having difficulty in solving a problem because I am inspired by others' success

- ◆ **Belief**: A state of mind which treats something as true, regardless of whether it is provable or not, for example, diversity of thought leads to better decisions or constructive feedback is helpful

- ◆ **Perception**: An interpretation of reality, as seen through a "lens," for example, I am paid a fair salary

- ◆ **Value**: The worth/importance attached to something, which is sometimes used as a synonym for principle, for example, respect or courage

What is culture?

Organization culture as a topic has been widely taught and researched by academics and specialist practitioners for decades. Yet, like mindset, there is no universally accepted definition of culture. Some popular definitions are as follow.

Edgar Schien, a former professor at MIT Sloan School of Management says:

> *"A pattern of shared basic assumptions that a group
> has learned as it solved its problems of external adaptation
> and internal integration that has worked well enough to be
> considered valid and therefore, to be taught to new members
> as the correct way to perceive, think, and feel in relation
> to those problems". [vi]*

Geert Hofstede, a professor and expert in organizational anthropology and international management at Maastricht University states:

> *"Organizational culture is defined as the way in which members
> of an organization relate to each other, their work and the
> outside world in comparison to other organizations. It can
> enable or hinder an organization's strategy." [vii]*

Henry Mintzberg, author of multiple books, including *Designing Effective Organizations* says:

> *"Culture is the soul of the organization — the beliefs
> and values, and how they are manifested." [viii]*

Terrence Deal and Allan Kennedy, authors of *Corporate Cultures: The Rites and Rituals of Corporate Life* define culture as:

> *"the way things get done around here." [ix]*

Essentially, culture is to a team, program, or company, what mindset is to an individual. The preceding definitions provide a sense of the multidimensional nature of business culture. As seen in the ecosystem of mindset and culture, enterprise culture influences and is influenced by the values of the organization. The values underlying the company's culture are reflected in people's behavior.

The culture and mindset ecosystem

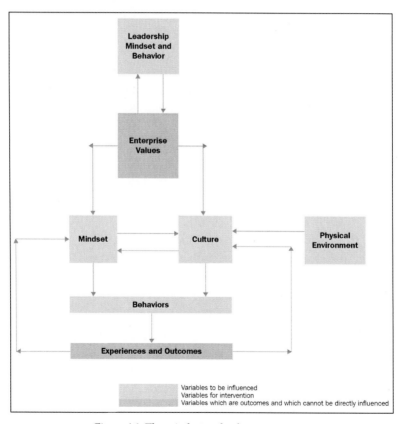

Figure 4.1: The mindset and culture ecosystem

The ecosystem of mindset and culture is extremely complex, as depicted in the preceding diagram, because of these factors:

♦ Mindset and culture influence each other

♦ Mindset and culture are directly influenced by multiple other variables

♦ Mindset and culture influence other variables, which indirectly influence mindset and culture

Let's examine the key influencing relationships in brief:

Mindset influences culture: As stated earlier, culture is at the level of a group or groups of people. Hence, if most people in that group have a similar mindset, it is very likely to influence the culture of that group.

Culture influences mindset: The culture of the group to which an individual belongs is highly likely to influence their mindset if an individual has a belief that feedback is helpful for continuous improvement, but if they join a team which does not have a culture of feedback, then it is possible that the individual may suspend their belief while they are in the team. The contrary is also possible: the individual can influence the team and bring in a feedback culture in the team, as called out in the earlier point.

Culture and mindset influence behavior: The only outward reflection of both mindset and culture is through the behavior of people, individually or collectively. The behavior can be in the form of doing something or avoiding to do something.

Behavior is the only honest indicator of the prevailing mindset and culture: Many enterprises have explicit cultural statements (for example, we strive to satisfy our customers) prominently displayed and also formally agreed upon. However, if the behavior of the people in the company is otherwise, then it indicates that the real culture is something different.

Behavior influences outcomes: This relationship is relatively more linear than others, for example, if a team strives to satisfy the customer, then it is quite likely that the outcome will be a happy customer and the team therefore experiences a sense of fulfillment.

Outcome influences both mindset and culture: Outcomes, both positive and negative, will either reinforce the existing mindset and culture or influence the modification of the mindset and culture, for example, the outcome of a happy customer, and the team feeling good about it, is highly likely to reinforce the culture of customer satisfaction.

It is critical that people do not get mixed signals due to additional intervention, otherwise the impact on the culture can be nothing or even negative, for example, if the team has gone a little over budget to please the customer, with the consent of their immediate manager, but someone from the finance department sends a nasty email to the team about the overspend, the positive outcome will have lost all relevance in terms of making a positive impact on mindset and culture.

Business values influence both mindset and culture: Again, this is a relatively more linear relationship. Values may be stated explicitly or reflected through purpose, vision, and mission statements, for example, Apple Inc, has values of innovation and product excellence, which purportedly influence the mindset and culture.

The most important thing about values, as in the case of culture, is that they mean nothing unless they are seen in practice, for example, if the enterprise states that it values gender diversity, but its workforce comprises of 90% males, then that value is questionable and is unlikely to be reflected in the mindset and culture. It is possible that mindset and culture can influence enterprise values. However, this relationship is not material from the perspective of influencing mindset and culture and hence not discussed.

Leaders influence enterprise values: This relationship is well established and well understood. Leaders such as Jeff Bezos of Amazon, Steve Jobs of Apple, Lee Iacocca of Chrysler, and Jack Welch of General Electric are well known for significantly influencing values in their respective organizations.

Company values influence leaders: If the values are strongly embedded within the business, then a leader joining the company will be influenced by the values core to it. There are examples aplenty of "C-level" executives joining enterprises with well-established values, who left within a short period of time, primarily because they were unable to align themselves with the values, and consequently the culture, of the enterprise. Vishal Sikka quitting as CEO of one of the largest IT companies, Infosys, and the firm bringing back Nandan Nilekani, one of the co-founders who had stepped away from the company for quite some time "to bring the continuity of culture and values" is an example of a value and culture misfit leading to a leadership-level exit. [x]

Other influencing relationships, such as the influence of experiences, outcomes, and the physical environment, on leaders do exist and are also important. However, we will not discuss them in this chapter. The model is by no means comprehensive, as there could be many other variables which can impact mindset and culture, and those which mindset and culture influence. This is just a broad framework to bring some structure to the variables that impact and are impacted by mindset and culture. Enterprises may wish to modify this model or create another one, which better reflects their context.

Changing mindset and culture

As seen in the preceding model, the ecosystem of mindset and culture is highly complex. In terms of changing mindset and culture, the key takeaway is that it is extremely difficult to establish a direct cause-and-effect relationship between the variables that influence them and also to what extent they influence them. Given how deeply culture is entrenched in every element of an enterprise, changing a company's culture is difficult and also takes a lot of time. Among all the changes which a business needs to make to enhance agility, culture change, by far, is the most difficult one. According to the 11th State of Agile survey [xi] "company philosophy or culture at odds with core Agile values" is the biggest challenge faced by companies attempting to adopt and scale Agile.

Given this, the best that companies can do is to introduce interventions to the variables that are likely to cause an impact on mindset and culture. Like any complex system, the system of mindset and culture will respond to the "disturbances" caused by the interventions and this will lead to a new state of mindset and culture, based on emergence. The interventions may need to be changed, if the system is not responding as per expectations. To summarize, the approach to changing mindset and culture is a "trial and error" approach, as is always the case when attempting to change a complex system. The change can be put into effect only through influence, and not through direct impact. According to the model, there are three areas of intervention that can lead to impacting mindset and culture: employee behaviors, working environment, and leadership and mindset behaviors.

It is important to clarify that leadership in this context means any person or group of people which has an influence at the enterprise level. This is especially true if the leader is the founder of the business. The reasons for treating leadership mindset and behaviors as a separate variable are that leaders perform the following:

- Play a significant role in defining and shaping the vision of the organization. This is especially true if the leader is the founder of the enterprise.

- Are seen as role models, which implies that people tend to emulate them.

- Have the authority to incentivize and discourage specific behaviors.

- Define what a crisis is and may exhibit and expect a different set of behaviors during the crisis. This can send positive or negative signals, depending on how leaders react to a crisis.

In this chapter, behavior and working environment interventions will be discussed. The leadership-level mindset and behaviors will be discussed in *Chapter 5, Leadership*.

Values aligned to agility

Companies that have a high level of agility have a common pattern of enterprise values. These values are not only a sign of high agility but are also enablers to enhancing agility. Values can be broadly categorized into internal-oriented values, that is, how people inside the company treat each other, and external-oriented values, namely, how the enterprise treats its external entities and how it expects to be seen by the external world. These values may overlap with each other.

Internal-oriented values

Some of the methodologies under Agile have explicitly specified the values that enhance agility. Scrum has specified the following values, along with their meanings: focus, courage, openness, commitment, and respect [xii]. **Extreme Programming (XP)** has specified the following values, along with their meanings: simplicity, communication, feedback, respect, and courage. [xiii]

There is also a view that the Agile Manifesto reflects four key values of agility. Some other values that are aligned with agility are: cooperation, craftsmanship, creativity, enthusiasm, excellence, flexibility, initiative, integrity, reliability, self-discipline, transparency, and trust.

Many enterprises encourage teams to pick and decide upon five to six values for the team from a set of values. Amazon has spelled out its values in the form of leadership principles [xiv], while Netflix has gone to great lengths to describe its culture [xv], and has expressed as here what makes Netflix different from other companies:

♦ Encourage independent decision-making by employees

♦ Share information openly, broadly, and deliberately

♦ Be extraordinarily candid with each other

♦ Keep only our highly-effective people

♦ Avoid rules

External-oriented values

An enterprise's external-oriented values are usually reflected in its purpose, mission and vision statements, for example, Apple's mission and vision statements are based on values of product excellence and innovation, among others. Companies with high agility not only have their external-oriented values aligned to agility but also complement their internal-oriented values.

Behaviors aligned to agility

Before delving into interventions for changing behaviors, it is important to examine patterns of behavior which align with agility and therefore help in enhancing it.

Treat failure as a learning opportunity

Despite best intentions and efforts, delivered outcomes may fail to meet expectations or even turn out to be adverse. There can be varied reasons for this, including making incorrect assumptions, a change in circumstances leading to assumptions being invalidated, human errors, and unanticipated circumstances.

Knowledge work, that is, work which is creative and not mechanical or repetitive, particularly work done with the objective of being innovative, is experimental in nature, and by definition is liable for failure. People and teams are consciously cognizant of this fact, and hence treat failure as an experience to be learned from rather than treating it as an event that is to be forgotten after blaming someone as the cause of it. The individual will retrospect to identify the actual underlying problem which caused the failure, crystalize the learnings and actively factor those learnings into decisions when similar situations arise in the future, thereby doing their best to avoid a repeat of the failure.

Corollary to learning from failure is also the willingness to try new things and therefore have the appetite to fail and recover from it. Continuous improvement and innovation can happen only if there is a willingness to challenge the status quo and also experiment to try something different. People and teams are not only courageous enough to own their failures, but also willing to share them with the wider organization so that others also can learn from them.

Focus on continuous improvement

In line with a willingness to experiment, a person with an agility-oriented mindset is always thinking about continuous improvement. The person believes that small improvements made over a period of time do lead to major improvements. The person is capable of observing anti-patterns in processes and practices and is willing to call those out in the early stages (the "smell" stage). While retrospectives and visual indicators provide excellent clues to anti-patterns, the person has the ability to take a step back and look at the situation objectively.

A by-product of this mindset is that the person is always seeking opportunities to get feedback and as early as possible. Continuous learning is also an essential element of continuous improvement. The person has the intrinsic desire to get better at their respective craft and gain mastery in their field. This would reflect in people investing time in reading about new trends and advancements in their respective fields, attending conferences, publishing blogs and books, and, most importantly, sharing the learnings within their respective communities, both internally and externally.

Value team spirit over individual heroics

There is a realization that when everyone works toward making the team successful, the whole is greater than the sum of parts. Hence, team members avoid the temptation to become individual heroes, which most often leads to adverse effects like the breaking of trust and a dent to the spirit of collaboration. Some of the visible traits of this behavior include people helping someone who is struggling with a piece of work or reorganizing themselves to focus on completing the highest value work, should the team be falling behind in its commitments.

People strive to align themselves to the purpose they are working towards. This includes alignment at all levels, right from the organization level objectives to the goals of the current iteration. One of the most visible clues of this behavior is how often the word *we* comes in conversations, as opposed to *I*. The team spirit of a team with an agility-oriented mindset can be compared with that of a sports team. What matters more than goals scored by an individual player is the win by the team.

Willingness to share knowledge

People with an agility-oriented mindset willingly share knowledge with others and do not treat knowledge as a source of power. People associate their self-worth not only with their individual mastery but also in contributing toward mentoring other team members and helping them to learn and grow. The knowledge-sharing culture within a team helps to significantly speed up the on-boarding process of any new person, particularly anyone with little or no experience, joining the team. The existing team members recognize this, and leverage pairing, even across roles, to make this happen. Having an appetite for learning and a desire to share knowledge go hand in hand. Team members, including those with experience, are always seeking to learn and improve, and hence participate actively in knowledge-sharing sessions. In a team with an Agile mindset, such sessions are organized by the team itself.

Diversity of thought valued

People with an agility-oriented mindset recognize the power of collective thought and therefore welcome diversity of thought. This brings creativity into problem-solving, enhances learning, and significantly reduces risks in decision-making.

Lack of diversity often leads to "groupthink," which can lead to suboptimal decision-making. According to *Psychology Today*, "Groupthink occurs when a group with a particular agenda makes irrational or problematic decisions because its members value harmony and coherence over accurate analysis and critical evaluation. Individual members of the group are strongly discouraged from any disagreement with the consensus and set aside their own thoughts and feelings to unquestioningly follow the word of the leader and other group members. In a groupthink situation, group members refrain from expressing doubts, judgments or disagreement with the consensus and ignore any ethical or moral consequences of any group decision that furthers their cause."

Having a culture where people feel "safe" about expressing their views, that is, without the fear of being judged, and where everyone believes that they have an equal voice on the table are the key enablers to minimizing "groupthink." While expertise in a given area, as well as past experience, is certainly important, in an era where having to frequently deal with unprecedented situations is a stark reality, a fresh perspective can provide a point of view which an expert is likely to miss.

The ability to embrace diversity of thought reflects that the people in a company are open to their existing knowledge and beliefs being challenged, and more importantly, are open-minded enough to keep their biases and mental models aside when they come across a totally different perspective. It also implies that they will respect the decision of the majority, even if their point of view is not accepted as the way forward. The team may ask for a person outside of the team to facilitate a discussion, if they believe that the discussion topic is sensitive and a neutral person can help in objective evaluation of diverse opinions and alternatives.

Practice "brutal" transparency

While Agile practices like daily stand-up meetings, retrospectives, and so on are huge enablers for the team to be transparent, they are not effective unless people in the team have embraced transparency as a value. A team with an Agile mindset is transparent in "words, deeds, and spirit" not only among themselves, but also with stakeholders outside the team, namely, other teams in the business and leadership.

The word "brutal" is used to emphasize that transparency should not be selective, that is, it must exist under all circumstances, both good and bad, and also with all people, regardless of their stature or seniority. Given that trust is the primary enabler as well as an outcome of transparency, leaders and managers need to be extra cautious about punishing the "messenger" who brings bad news.

People being transparent with each other is not just about being open about what they are working on, but, more importantly, it is about a willingness to admit and accept mistakes and being able to recognize that they need help to solve a problem. People realize that being transparent, particularly about one's vulnerabilities, is the foundation on which trust is built, and that trust among the team members is perhaps the most critical element of agility in the team. Transparency indicates the courage to face reality as is, including limitations, shortfalls, failures and mistakes, learn from them and then work together with the concerned stakeholders to find the best way forward.

Effective feedback

People view feedback as a means to strengthen confidence and to improve themselves. The spirit of giving negative feedback is not about finding fault or fixing blame, but to give pointers and perspectives on how the receivers of the feedback can improve themselves.

The person giving feedback is honest, yet courteous and respectful and the tone of the feedback is about how the receiver of the feedback could have/can do better.

The goal is to point out specific areas of improvement and, if possible, suggest actions that can help the person to make that improvement. Equally important is that the receiver of the feedback is willing to listen with an open mind and not become defensive when they hear something negative about themselves. People seek to get feedback from each other on a regular basis, both after a specific event and/or at regular periodic intervals. Similar to transparency, trust is the primary enabler for open and effective feedback.

Recognize the last responsible moment

People recognize and appreciate that the business environment is changing at an exponential rate and the implication of this is to not only embrace change but also to keep things lean. Hence, people are very conscious about not overengineering anything (in line with the Agile principle of "maximize the work not done") and delaying decisions until the last responsible moment. They apply the principle of simplicity to not only design and code but also to artefacts such as user stories, metrics, and workflow. Team members, especially developers, stay away from the temptation of "gold plating" [xvi]. The following this principle with a view to keep waste to a minimum also means that teams try to automate repetitive manual steps, so that precious brain power is not wasted on doing mundane activities.

Driven by value

People recognize the importance of value-based outcomes and hence are constantly focused not only on delivering value but also on delivering highest value first. They actively collaborate with PO/business to ensure that they align delivery to business priorities, based on regular feedback.

They actively suggest solution options to ensure that the highest value is delivered most efficiently and effectively. They strive to always view the "big picture" of the business and understand the business drivers and are therefore able to better visualize the impact of delivery on these drivers. They measure their success on the outcome and impact of their work, and not on task completion or effort spent.

People not only strive to deliver value, but to do it on a continuous basis. Hence, they are always aiming to optimize on the batch size and flow of work. These employees actively watch out for risks that might erode value and raise awareness about these risks with the concerned stakeholders, so that appropriate mitigations can be put in place in time.

Enabling behavior changes

The following measures can be helpful in enabling change of behaviors towards achieving the intended outcomes.

Align the metrics

> *"Tell me how you measure me and I will tell you how I will behave".*
>
> — *Eliyahu Goldratt* [xvii]

This quote highlights the significance of metrics on influencing behavior. Expecting different behavior is futile if the way people are measured continues to reward nonaligned behaviors, for example, if the expected behavior is that people should collaborate but rewards are given to people for individual level outputs, it is futile to expect people to collaborate.

Similarly, if the expected behaviors are punished or discouraged, it is obvious that people will not exhibit those expected behaviors, for example, if the expectation is that people should innovate through experimentation but any failure is punished, it is again pointless to expect people to experiment.

While fair monetary compensation is important for everyone, providing direct monetary incentives as a primary means for a behavior change should be avoided, as incentivizing on a continuous basis over a long period is not sustainable, and, more importantly, the change is driven by an extrinsic factor rather than it being intrinsic. It is only when the behavior change happens intrinsically, that the behavior becomes an integral part of the culture, for example, on examination of the key performance drivers, a company found that collaboration and a sense of purpose were more important than monetary incentives for its employees. They moved from giving individual bonuses for performance to celebrating how teams improved customer satisfaction.

Levelling environment

A levelling environment is one where everyone, regardless of role, seniority, and so on is treated equally. It is one of the critical factors for an enterprise to become people-centric. Specifically, it translates into the following:

- ◆ Every person in the business has equal opportunity to "have a voice on the table" and be heard. This applies to matters at all levels, right from the team to the entire enterprise. This results in a healthy friction of ideas, thereby leading to an increase in the antifragility of the organization.

- ◆ Every person in the enterprise is treated fairly, and the definition of fairness is uniform for everyone. This means:

- ○ No favoritism and cronyism in hiring, pay raises, promotions, and so on.

- ○ Reasonable parity in compensation, considering parameters such as role and years of experience. Fairness of compensation is mostly relative, that is, if a person comes to know, or even believes, that their peers are getting a disproportionately higher compensation than them, they are very likely to believe that they are being treated unfairly.

- ○ The same perks and facilities for everyone, for example, if lunch is served in the office, everyone in the office, regardless of seniority, should have access to the same food and also eat in the same area, without any differentiation whatsoever.

- ○ With respect to compensation, the only differentiator should be the monetary components of the salary. As far as possible, all allowances should be equal to all people.

- ○ The consequences of unacceptable behaviors should be same for everyone, for example, if an organization has a zero-tolerance policy on anyone raising their voice over another person, the zero tolerance should be applied even to the senior leader of the organization.

- ◆ Every person in the enterprise is treated with the same level of respect and courtesy, be it the janitor or the CEO.

Leadership involvement

Senior leaders, including leaders from the business side, need to be continuously involved in a mindset and culture change. While the HR function can play a large role in facilitating this change, for the culture change initiative to be seen as credible and to become sustainable, the entire senior leadership of the organization, without exception, must have their "skin in the game." Without the involvement of senior leaders on a continuous basis, there is a risk that the change initiative can become a "tick box" exercise.

Identify what needs to change about the current mindset and culture

Every enterprise will have pockets of mindset and culture that are enabling the business to do well, or else the company will not be in existence. The starting point to change, therefore, should be the identification of what the positives of the current mindset and current culture are and what's not working or is holding back the organization from having greater agility. According to Schien, "When that (what isn't working) is clearly defined as a business problem then we can ask the question: well given the culture, is that going to help you solve the problem or hinder you, and it always ends up being both. There are always parts of the culture that help solve the problem and other parts of the culture that get in the way. Then you're finally at the point of saying — well maybe I need a culture change program — but you got there by thinking about the business problem you are trying to solve." [xviii]

While diagnosing problems with the current mindset and culture, care should be taken to not mistake the symptom for the problem, for example, if the culture is about lack of accountability, the underlying problem could be a culture of zero tolerance for mistakes.

Link a behavior change to business outcomes

A mindset and culture change should not be approached in a "big bang" way, but rather to impact one or two critical business outcomes. This will increase the likelihood of seeing a difference to those outcomes in a much shorter timeframe. When people see the positive impact of behaviors on the outcomes, these behaviors will spread, not because people are told about a behavior change, but because they actually see it making a positive impact. Consciously publicizing success stories across the organization, and the behavior that led to those successes, goes a long way in creating an appetite for a behavior change.

Call out gaps between expected and actual behaviors

Behavior changes can sometimes take time to become a habit. However, it is important for people to realize that their behaviors are not aligned with expected behaviors. Quite often, such realization can come only from feedback from another person. Moreover, the fact that people's behavioral changes are being observed should help employees to become self-aware of the behavioral gaps. There are two potential reasons for the discrepancy between expected and actual behavior:

♦ Wrong behaviors are being rewarded and/or right behaviors are being discouraged or punished. An often-seen example of this is where on the one hand leadership is passing the message that they would like to foster a culture of experimentation and innovation, but, on the other hand, employees are blamed and also punished for failed experiments.

♦ The vision of the new culture is interpreted incorrectly, for example, in an enterprise, the new culture was defined as "becoming a more customer-focused organization." The organization expected new behaviors in terms of becoming more responsive to customer demands and wanted to remove inefficiencies within the production processes so that those benefits could be passed to the customers. However, the workers on the shop floor interpreted the expectations of new behaviors as exploitation. Hence, it is important to verify if the vision and expectations of new behaviors have been interpreted correctly.

Have clarity and consensus around trade-offs

Building and nurturing a culture based on specific desirable behaviors will invariably lead to some tough trade-off choices, for example, if collaboration is a desired behavior, as talented and skilled as a potential employee may be, if they prefer to work in isolation, then they are not a good fit and hence should not be selected. Another example is if everyone getting an opportunity to voice their opinion on a critical decision is the desired outcome, then the trade-off might be the time and energy that leaders would have to spend to hear and discuss the issue across the entire organization.

Deal with individual negative behaviors on a case-to-case basis

There will always be a group of people who will respond to a mindset change in negative ways. This is particularly because in this process, most people will have to come out of their "comfort zone." Usually, people respond with negativity due to one of the following reasons:

- They need appreciation and encouragement to make the change and seek recognition but believe that they are not getting it. However, questions from "wise fools" [xix], who have spotted failings in the approach and who are not afraid to ask unpopular and politically risky questions may actually be helping the cause.

- They fear that they might lose their relevance and importance in the new mindset and culture, and therefore ultimately become redundant for the organization.

- They have a "fixed" mindset, that is, they believe that they are good enough as they are and do not see the need to change.

The way to deal with the negativity will depend on what is causing it, and more importantly, whether the concerned individual is showing willingness to truly give their best to making the mindset change happen. The important thing is to spot the negativity as early as possible and provide the necessary support and encouragement to overcome it.

Look out for broader anti-patterns

Just as some individuals may display negativity toward a mindset and culture change, at an organization level, there could be lingering anti-patterns or even fresh ones cropping up such as the following:

- The passionate and nontraditional thinkers have become silent and have stopped voicing their views.

- People do not openly challenge impossible deadlines and unrealistic plans, but prefer to complain offline to people they trust.

- People rely on the informal grapevine for finding out what's going on within the organization. Unwarranted rumors are being created.

♦ Managers and subordinates are seldom seen together.

♦ There is always palpable tension in the air.

These anti-patterns are mere symptoms that the mindset changes are not happening. Rather than focus on treating the symptom, the root causes of such toxic symptoms need to be investigated and adjustments to the culture change initiative need to be made accordingly.

It is possible that some people may have a deep-rooted traditional mindset, so they either are unable to, or just do not want to change themselves to suit the new mindset and culture. Under such circumstances, it might be in the best interest of such people and the enterprise to consider parting ways.

Go beyond logic

A natural consequence of people being engaged at work is that they will invest their emotions in their work and in the business. This has implications for influencing behavior changes, as they are a function of the need for change as perceived by each individual. This, therefore, means that mere objective/logical conviction may not be adequate to influence different behaviors. People will try to, either consciously or subconsciously, answer the question "what's in it for me?" with respect to changed behavior expectations, and if the answer to this question is not convincing, the behavior change is not likely to be meaningful and sustainable.

Hence, engaging with employees informally, to gauge their mood and to understand their concerns with respect to the behavior change, will provide meaningful insights to modify the communication around the behavior change.

Aligning the workplace to an agility-enabling culture

As discussed earlier, the physical workplace is one of the few variables which directly impacts the culture of an enterprise and is also a reflection of the culture of the company. People sitting behind closed doors and in cubicles, formally dressed and speaking in hushed voices, indicates a very different culture compared to groups of workers sitting in close proximity around large tables and where there is a constant din of voices.

Assuming that the firm is embracing values aligned with agility, it is critical that the workplace be aligned to support those values. Otherwise, the workplace can become a huge impediment in the values becoming a part of the culture, for example, managers and leaders sitting behind closed doors, with the cabin size directly correlated to seniority in the hierarchy is not a conducive work environment when the enterprise is trying to imbibe transparency, openness, and equality as values.

The following are some of the primary considerations in creating a workplace for agility:

- The people (HR), infrastructure, and technology departments must come together to create the Agile workplace. Each of these departments can have their concerns, challenges, and a limited view of Agile, for example, the infrastructure team may have concerns about exiting during an emergency, if the tables are being placed too close to each other. The HR team might believe that Agile means flexible working hours. An acceptable solution can be found only when this cross-departmental team works together to fulfill a common objective.

- The workplace needs to have the right balance of open and flexible workplaces: private areas, conference rooms, and areas for teams to gather and collaborate.

♦ The infrastructure provided to people and teams should enable mobility and collaboration. Teams should have access to large monitors and also table space, and laptops which enable flexibility in seating and working remotely, and so on.

♦ The money spent on this should not be treated as a cost, but as a necessary investment.

♦ Ensure that the needs of people with different abilities are taken care of. An Agile workplace respects the diversity of people, and employees with physical limitations should be as comfortable as others in the workplace, for example, the workplace should be able to accommodate workers on wheelchairs or with limited vision, and so on.

♦ People should be able to have a say on how the new workplace should be created. This will not only help to bring out common concerns early on but there will also be a greater sense of ownership among staff.

♦ Implement ways of working that are based on the core values of communication, collaboration, and transparency, which implies that teams will actively use information radiators and whiteboards. There should be enough space and infrastructure around the team area for these tools.

An Agile workplace should be inclusive, comfortable, open, fun and, most importantly, promote collaboration. It should be a place which makes people want to come to work every day. While it is fine to draw inspiration from Agile-friendly workplaces (for example, the Google office is designed for people to bring their pets to work), this may not be what every enterprise would like to do. The key is to involve those who are going to use the workplace in designing the space.

Dealing with losing their individual desk, and not having a fixed place, can be very challenging for people, especially those who have been used to working in that kind of set up for a long time. Employees get used to pinning their family photographs up and keeping personal items on their desk, and to not have these around when sharing a large table can be an emotionally disturbing experience. It is not reasonable to expect that all people will adapt immediately to the new workplace design. The concerns and feelings of people finding this transition difficult must be dealt with using patience, empathy, and encouragement. Co-locating a few teams and giving workers time to try out the new set up, rather than mandating it en masse, can be one of the ways to ease the transition.

Summary

In this chapter, we learned that the mindset of employees and a company's culture are foundational for enhancing agility. They are difficult to change, as they not only reinforce each other but they also influence and get influenced by multiple variables. The three primary variables, where intervention for changing mindset and culture will be most effective, are employee behaviors, working environment, and leadership mindset and behaviors.

This chapter has covered specific behaviors that align with agility and measures to change these behaviors. We have also considered how to align the workplace for greater agility.

The next chapter is the last of the three chapters in the foundation section. It focuses on understanding the significance of leadership, and the key personal traits and behaviors of leaders which are critical for enterprise agility.

References

[i] http://agileforall.com/this-cognitive-bias-kills-our-ability-to-address-complexity/

[ii] https://www.forbes.com/sites/stevedenning/2016/06/07/the-key-missing-ingredient-in-the-agile-manifesto-mindset/#7dc1529267ff

[iii] https://www.linkedin.com/pulse/tech-most-important-platform-we-can-build-strong-culture-mike-dargan/?trackingId=begadRSouMxrijqFV2c%2F2w%3D%3D

[iv] https://en.wikipedia.org/wiki/Mindset

[v] https://www.slideshare.net/AgileSparks/mindset-better-60-min

[vi] http://pateglinton.weebly.com/organizational-culture.html

[vii] https://www.hofstede-insights.com/models/organisational-culture/

[viii] http://www.trentglobal.edu.sg/wp-content/uploads/2016/09/Unit-5-Organisational-Culture-and-Change.pdf?x80301

[ix] https://en.wikipedia.org/wiki/Organizational_culture

[x] http://www.spjimr.org/blog/infosys-story-cultural-differences

[xi] https://www.versionone.com/about/press-releases/versionone-releases-11th-annual-state-of-agile-report/

[xii] https://www.scrumalliance.org/why-scrum/core-scrum-values-roles

[xiii] http://www.extremeprogramming.org/values.html

[xiv] https://www.amazon.com/p/feature/p34qgjcv93n37yd

[xv] https://jobs.netflix.com/culture

[xvi] https://en.wikipedia.org/wiki/Gold_plating_(software_engineering)

[xvii] https://en.wikiquote.org/wiki/Eliyahu_M._Goldratt

[xviii] http://www.cultureuniversity.com/culture-fundamentals-9-important-insights-from-edgar-schein/

[xix] http://trailridgeconsulting.com/blog/the-wise-fool/

5

LEADERSHIP

This chapter focuses on the leadership aspect of a business and probes the leadership capabilities that are fundamental for enhancing enterprise agility.

The leadership of a firm has a very high bearing on the extent of agility which the company can achieve. Leaders are in a position to influence just about every aspect of a business, including vision, mission, strategy, structure, governance, processes and, more importantly, the culture of the enterprise and the mindset of the employees. As discussed previously, leaders are influencers not only because they make decisions about resource allocation priorities but also because they are looked up to as role models and therefore they are in a position to influence the behavior of people across the organization.

The chapter will explore the following topics:

♦ The significance of leadership in enterprise agility

♦ Dimensions of leadership

♦ Personal traits of leaders, which are critical for enterprise agility

♦ The behaviors of leaders, which are crucial for enterprise agility

Significance

Empirical evidence corroborates the criticality of leadership in enhancing agility. Company philosophy or culture being at odds with core Agile values, lack of managerial support, and general resistance to change in an organization are three of the top four challenges faced by enterprises in adopting and scaling Agile, according to a global survey released in 2017. [i]

Leaders are recognizing the growing complexity in the business environment and also admitting that they are struggling to deal with it. This goes back as far as 2010, when IBM interviewed 1500 CEOs and published the findings in a detailed report. [ii]

The report states:

> *"Our interviews revealed that CEOs are now confronted with a "complexity gap" that poses a bigger challenge than any factor we've measured in eight years of CEO research. Eight in ten CEOs expect their environment to grow significantly more complex, and fewer than half believe they know how to deal with it successfully."*

This recognition and realization is very significant, as higher complexity and a need for greater agility are highly correlated. Leaders are recognizing that the challenges of today are unprecedented and hence, what has worked in the past is unlikely to work in today's era. Leadership in the past emphasized stability and maintaining the status quo, while leadership today needs to embrace change, enable innovation, and motivate knowledge workers.

According to Jayesh Ghatge, the market partner for India at ThoughtWorks:

"Principles passed down from the industrial economy are inapplicable today, because businesses are functioning in a Knowledge Economy. We are living in an age of creativity that calls for a new paradigm of leadership. The kind of leadership that creates long-term value and invests in employee and stakeholder engagement, one that builds a learning organization, which is lean and innovates quickly. And, most importantly, a leadership that creates a successive management pipeline that will ably respond to current and future business challenges." [iii]

What the leaders of today need is "leadership agility." Bill Joiner, CEO of ChangeWise Inc., and Stephen Josephs, principal at Stephen Josephs LLC, define leadership agility as "the ability to lead effectively under conditions of rapid change and mounting complexity." [iv] Leadership agility is based on underlying capabilities and not on the authority which the leadership position carries.

Dimensions of leadership

Kevin Cashman, the author, speaker, and pioneer in executive development, says that there are five dimensions which are crucial for leadership in the context of agility. These are as follows:

- ◆ **Mental agility:** Thinking critically to penetrate complex problems and expanding possibilities by making fresh connections

- ◆ **People agility:** Understanding and relating to other people, as well as tough situations, to harness and multiply collective performance

- ◆ **Change agility**: Enjoying experimentation, being curious, and effectively dealing with the discomfort of change
- ◆ **Results agility**: Delivering results in first-time situations by inspiring teams and exhibiting a presence that builds confidence in themselves and others
- ◆ **Self-awareness**: Being reflective, knowing themselves well, understanding their capabilities, and being aware of their impact on others

From the description of the dimensions, it is apparent that each of them is critical in enabling leaders to enhance enterprise agility. Each of these dimensions need to be supported by specific underlying capabilities. These capabilities exist at two levels:

- ◆ Personal traits
- ◆ Behaviors

These capabilities, mapped to the dimensions, are as follows:

Dimensions	Personal traits	Behaviors
Mental agility	Willingness to expand mental models	Systems thinking
People agility	Emotional intelligence	◆ Tolerance toward failure ◆ Connection with peers ◆ Connection through engagement ◆ Servant leadership ◆ Inclusivity and diversity ◆ "Humble inquiry"

Change agility	♦ Creativity ♦ Courage ♦ Resilience	♦ Comfortable with VUCA ♦ Leverage risk
Results agility	Responsiveness	♦ Guide and facilitate teams ♦ Technology awareness
Self-awareness	♦ Self-awareness ♦ Passion for learning ♦ Aware of cognitive biases	Not applicable, as it does not directly get reflected in behaviors

Obviously, these capabilities are in addition to basic capabilities such as communication, focus, commitment, honesty, ability to inspire, and integrity.

Personal traits

Personal traits are by definition intrinsic in nature. They enable the personal development of an individual and are also enablers for certain behaviors.

Willingness to expand mental models

According to Wikipedia:

> "A mental model is an explanation of someone's thought process about how something works in the real world. It is a representation of the surrounding world, the relationships between its various parts and a person's intuitive perception about his or her own acts and their consequences." [v]

Essentially, a mental model is an individual's perception of reality and how something works in that reality. A mental model represents one way of approaching a situation and is a form of deeply-held belief. The critical point is that a mental model represents an individual's view, which may not be necessarily true.

While it is natural for every individual to have mental models, the limitations of the models are something which leaders need to be consciously aware of. This is because mental models drive the way an individual applies reasoning, makes decisions, and behaves. When mental models are deeply rooted, the individual will see a problem only from one perspective, for example, a leader believed that money and people's productivity are very highly directly correlated. So, when the trend of the throughput of his team showed a decline for a couple of months, he announced a bonus for the team if their productivity improved by x%. Due to his deeply held mental model, he could not think of an alternative way of addressing this problem.

The reality was that the team's productivity was hit due to a change in process, which created dependency on another team and was slowing this team down. Hence, despite the team's best efforts, there was no increase in productivity. Due to his deep-rooted mental model, the leader thought that the bonus would make a difference. Needless to say, this did not affect productivity, as giving more money was an inappropriate solution to solving this problem. Subsequently, the leader added another mental model to his repertoire, believing that process change could lead to a drop in productivity. He was then able to see a drop in productivity from two perspectives, as compared to just one perspective.

Leaders must also consciously let go of mental models that are no longer relevant today. This is especially important for those leaders who have spent a significant part of their career leading enterprises based on mechanistic modeling, as these models will create impediments for agility in "living" businesses.

For example, using monetary rewards as a primary motivator may work for physical work, which is repetitive in nature. However, it does not work as a primary motivator for knowledge workers, for whom intrinsic motivators, namely, autonomy, mastery, and purpose, are generally more important than money. Examining the values and assumptions underlying a mental model can help in ascertaining the relevance of that model.

As leaders deal with unprecedented circumstances, viewing a problem purely from the perspective of what has worked in the past has very little chance of being effective. In order to expand their set of mental models, leaders must temporarily suspend their existing mental models, which will enable them to look at additional models with an open mind. A passion for learning and encouraging new ideas, and a willingness to put the new ideas to the test, are critical to expanding mental models.

Self-awareness

Self-awareness helps leaders to become cognizant of their strengths and weaknesses. This will enable the leaders to consciously focus on utilizing their strengths and leveraging the strengths of their peers, and teams, in areas where they are not strong. Leaders should validate their view of their strengths and weaknesses by seeking feedback regularly from people that they work with. An objective view of their own strengths and weaknesses can help in creating effective personal development and skills improvement plans.

According to a survey of senior executives, by Cornell's School of Industrial and Labor Relations:

> *"Leadership searches give short shrift to 'self-awareness,' which should actually be a top criterion. Interestingly, a high self-awareness score was the strongest predictor of overall success.*

> *This is not altogether surprising as executives who are aware*
> *of their weaknesses are often better able to hire subordinates*
> *who perform well in categories in which the leader lacks*
> *acumen. These leaders are also more able to entertain the*
> *idea that someone on their team may have an idea that*
> *is even better than their own." [vi]*

Self-awareness, a mostly underrated trait, is a huge enabler for enhancing other personal traits.

Creativity

Since emergence is a primary property of complexity, leaders will often be challenged to deal with unprecedented circumstances emerging from within the enterprise and also in the external environment. This implies that what may have worked in the past is less likely to work in the new circumstances, and new approaches will be needed to deal with them. Hence, the ability to think creatively, that is, "out of the box," for coming up with innovative approaches and solutions is critical.

Creativity of an individual will have its limitations, and hence leaders must harness the creativity of a broader group of people in the enterprise. A leader can be a huge enabler to this by ideating jointly with a group of people and also by facilitating discussions by challenging status quo and spurring the teams to suggest improvements. Leaders can also encourage innovation through experimentation.

With the fast pace of change in the external environment, and consequently the continuous evolution of businesses, leaders will often find themselves out of their comfort zone. Leaders will therefore have to get comfortable with being uncomfortable. It will be easier for leaders to think more creatively once they accept this new reality.

Emotional intelligence

Emotional intelligence (EI), also known as **emotional quotient (EQ)**, is defined by Wikipedia as "the capability of individuals to recognize their own emotions and those of others, discern between different feelings and label them appropriately, use emotional information to guide thinking and behavior, and manage and/or adjust emotions to adapt to environments or achieve one's goal/s." [vii]

EI is made up of four core skills [viii]:

◆ Self-awareness

◆ Social awareness

◆ Self-management

◆ Relationship management

The importance of EI in people-centric enterprises, especially for leaders, cannot be overstated. While people in a company may be bound by purpose, and by being a part of a team, people are inherently different from each other in terms of personality types and emotions. This can have a significant bearing on how people in a business deal with and react to circumstances, especially adverse ones. Having high EI enables leaders to understand people "from the inside." This helps leaders to build better rapport with people, thereby enabling them to bring out the best in employees and support them as needed. EI enables the leader to boost staff morale when needed, thereby being able to create and sustain positive energy in the workplace.

Lack of EI, or low EI, in leaders can lead to negative behaviors such as insensitivity, arrogance, and selfishness. A leader displaying these negative behaviors is unlikely to have meaningful relationships with peers, as well as with others in the enterprise. Such behaviors will result in the leader getting disconnected from people and becoming isolated, and thereby becoming ineffective.

EI is also important at a personal level. Like everyone else, leaders too can have negative emotions such as anxiety, insecurity, and even anger. However, EI can help leaders to become aware of their emotions and thereby have the ability to manage them, especially in crisis situations. Leaders' reactions during crisis situations can have a severely negative impact on the mindset and culture of a company, and hence leaders have a greater responsibility to manage their negative emotions. Unlike **intelligence quotient (IQ)**, EI is not static. EI can be evolved and increased by training the brain with specific techniques. EI can also be enabled by mindfulness and a strong desire to change oneself.

Courage

An innovative approach to dealing with an unprecedented circumstance will, by definition, carry some risk. The hypothesis about the appropriateness of that approach can only be validated by putting it to the test against reality. Leaders will therefore need to be courageous as they take the calculated risky bets, strike hard, and own the outcome of those bets.

According to Guo Xiao, the president and CEO of ThoughtWorks:

> *"There are many threats—and opportunities—facing businesses in this age of digital transformation: industry disruption from nimble startups, economic pressure from massive digital platforms, evolving security threats, and emerging technologies. Today's era, in which all things are possible, demands a distinct style of leadership. It calls for bold individuals who set their company's vision and charge ahead in a time of uncertainty, ambiguity, and boundless opportunity. It demands courage." [ix]*

In a survey carried out by ThoughtWorks, in 2017, of C-level executives across the globe, 87% of the executives agreed that taking risks is necessary to achieving goals and maintaining competitive advantage. Another 62% said their willingness to take risks that their competitors wouldn't is what sets them apart from other C-suite executives. [x]

Taking risks does not mean being reckless. Rather, leaders need to take calculated risks, after giving due consideration to intuition, facts, and opinions. Despite best efforts and intentions, some decisions will inevitably go wrong. Leaders must have the courage and humility to admit that the decision went wrong and own the outcomes of that decision, and not let these failures deter them from taking risks in the future.

The essence of being courageous is to overcome the fear of failure. Traditionally, a failure almost always led to a sense of shame and also blaming oneself or others. However, taking no risk in the bid to avoid failing is simply not an option today. It can lead to enterprises missing unprecedented opportunities emerging from technological disruption and change.

Richard Branson is an example of a courageous leader. He founded Virgin Group, which comprises of over 400 companies. His path to success has been laden with multiple failed initiatives including Virgin Cola, Virgin Cars, and Virgin Digital. [xi] However, he is known to have learned from his failures, for example, the failure of Virgin Cola was attributed to the product not having any uniqueness about it. These failures have not deterred him from taking risks post the failures.

Taking risks on bets that have the potential for significant outcomes, in a highly dynamic environment, has become necessary, as making incremental changes will lead to insignificant outcomes.

A passion for learning

Learnability is the ability to upskill, reskill, and deskill. In today's highly-dynamic era, it is not what one knows, or what skills one has, that matters as much as the ability to quickly adapt to a different skill set. It is about understanding what is needed to optimize success and what skills and abilities are necessary, from a leadership perspective, to make the enterprise as a whole successful.

The fundamental step toward learnability is to understand and acknowledge, the gap between existing skills and abilities, and those which are needed. Inquisitiveness and curiosity are essential for learning to be effective and for learnability to become sustainable.

Leaders need to shed inhibitions about being seen as "novices" while they acquire and practice new skills. The fact that leaders are willing to acquire new skills can be hugely impactful in terms of encouraging others in the enterprise to do the same. This is especially important in terms of bringing in and encouraging the culture of learnability across the business. Learning can happen through various ways including reading, attending conferences, listening to expert-level talks, group discussions, training, and coaching. Of these, reading appears to be highly popular among executives. According to Jim Kwik, a brain fitness expert, the average CEO is reading four to five books per month. [xii] As busy as leaders might be at work, they will need to take dedicated time for learning. This time is essential not only for actual learning but also for reflection. Time spent on learnability and reflection must be given value and importance and should be treated as part of work. Sharing the learnings through discussions is also very effective.

Awareness of cognitive biases

Cognitive biases are flaws in thinking which can lead to suboptimal decisions. Leaders need to become aware of these biases so that they can objectively assess if their decisions are being influenced by any biases.

Cognitive biases lead to short cuts in decision-making. Essentially, these biases are an attempt by the brain to simplify information processing. These biases are the brain's way of dealing with human limitations of memory and attention span. Leaders today are challenged with an overload of information and also the need to make decisions quickly. These factors can contribute to decisions and judgements being influenced by cognitive biases.

Taking mental shortcuts in decision-making for routine or repetitive matters is obviously helpful and perhaps even warranted. However, a tendency to take a shortcut while making decisions which can have a far-reaching impact can be highly detrimental for the enterprise. Cognitive biases should not be confused with logical fallacy, as the latter is an error in logical argument, while the former is a mental mistake arising from limitations of memory and attention. Over decades, psychologists have discovered a huge number of biases. [xiii] However, the following biases are more important from the decision-making perspective.

Confirmation bias

This is the tendency of selectively seeking and holding onto information to reaffirm what you already believe to be true. This bias affects the logical reasoning ability and therefore can lead to suboptimal decisions. Confirmation bias leads to ignoring or bypassing information that does not support existing beliefs, for example, a leader believes that a recently-launched product is doing well, based on the initial positive response.

He has developed a bias that this product is successful. However, although the product is succeeding in attracting new customers, it is also losing existing customers. The confirmation bias is making the leader focus only on data pertaining to new customers, so he is ignoring data related to the loss of existing customers.

Bandwagon effect bias

Also known as "herd mentality," this bias encourages doing something because others are doing it. The bias creates a feeling of not wanting to be left behind and hence can lead to irrational or badly-thought-through decisions. Enterprises launching the Agile transformation initiative, without understanding the implications of the long and difficult journey ahead, is an example of this bias.

"Guru" bias

This bias leads to blindly relying on an expert's advice. This can be detrimental, as the expert could be wrong in their assessment and therefore the advice could also be wrong. Also, the expert might give advice that is primarily furthering his or her interests over the interests of the enterprise.

Projection bias

This bias leads the person to believe that other people have understood and are aligned with their thinking, while in reality this may not be true. This bias is more prevalent in enterprises where employees are fearful of admitting that they have not understood what their "bosses" have said, asking questions to clarify or expressing disagreement. The bias leads to poor communication and can be a major impediment to reaching a consensus.

Stability bias

Also known as "status quo" bias, this bias leads to a belief that change will lead to unfavorable outcomes, that is, the risk of loss is greater than the possibility of benefit.

It makes a person believe that stability and predictability lead to safety. For decades, the mandate for leaders was to strive for stability and hence, many older leaders are susceptible to this bias.

The way to minimize the chances of decisions being influenced by biases is by taking a step back and seeing the potential impact of making or not making a decision from a systemic perspective. Sounding the decision to an "outsider," that is, someone who is not an interested party in the decision and getting candid feedback from that person can also help to uncover the biases. Leaders must encourage others in the enterprise to challenge biases, which can uncover "blind spots" arising from them. Once decisions are made, attention should be paid to information coming from feedback.

Humans have a natural tendency to develop biases and hence many of the biases are unavoidable. However, being aware of the biases can increase the chances of avoiding their unfavorable influence on decision-making.

Resilience

Resilience is the capacity to quickly recover from difficulties. Given the turbulent business environment, rapidly-changing priorities, and the need to take calculated risks, leaders are likely to encounter difficult and challenging situations quite often. Under such circumstances, having resilience will help the leader to "take knocks on the chin" and keep moving forward.

According to Dr. Linda Rising, co-author of the book, *Fearless Change*, in an Agile mindset, the reaction to challenge is resilience, as opposed to the reaction to challenge being helplessness in a fixed mindset. [xiv]

Resilience is also about maintaining composure when something fails, analyzing the failure with the team in an objective manner and learning from that failure. The actions of leaders are watched by the people in the enterprise even more closely in periods of crisis and difficulty, and hence leaders showing resilience goes a long way in increasing resilience across the company.

Mistakes, disappointments, and failures will leave scars. Resilient leadership is about embracing those scars and deriving strength from overcoming difficult times and situations. Periods of difficulties and crisis should be treated as an opportunity to strengthen leadership capabilities. Difficult periods will almost always result in higher levels of stress. However, managing the stress levels to minimize the negative impact of stress is critical for becoming resilient.

Resilience is also about having patience and persistence about a transformational type of change, especially related to mindset and culture. Change can be very difficult, especially in the early stages, and in an era driven by instant gratification, it can be hard to maintain conviction about having done the right thing. This is precisely where leaders need to be resilient.

Responsiveness

Responsiveness, from the perspective of leadership, is the ability to quickly grasp and respond to both challenges and opportunities. Leaders must listen to feedback coming from customers and the marketplace, learn from it, and adapt accordingly. Leaders must be ready to enable the morphing of the enterprise's offerings in order to stay relevant for customers and also to exploit opportunities. This implies that leaders must be willing to adjust the "pivot" of their offerings based on feedback, for example, the journey of Amazon Web Services, which was an internal system, but has now grown into a highly successful business [xv]. Other prominent examples are Twitter, which was an offshoot of Odeo, a website focused on sound and podcasting, and PayPal's move from transferring money via PalmPilots to becoming a highly robust online payment service. Feedback coming in after customers use the product, and competitors and even partners copying the offering and coming up with a better one, can necessitate the repivoting of the original offering. Leaders must be responsive by taking this feedback quickly and making changes to the product.

Behavioral capabilities

Behaviors are extrinsic in nature and hence have influence at a wider level across a business.

Tolerance toward failure

As stated earlier, emergence being a core property of a living system implies that leaders and teams will frequently come across unprecedented situations. For these situations, no best practice exists, but, more importantly, any approach to dealing with such a situation can be seen as an experiment. By definition, experiments are fraught with risk and therefore carry the possibility of failure. Leaders recognize this fact consciously and are usually tolerant of failures, particularly those arising from experiments that are consciously undertaken. Leaders facilitate their teams to derive appropriate learnings from failures and guide their teams to avoid similar failures in the future.

As previously mentioned having resilience is a huge enabler toward recovering from failure and treating it as learning opportunity. Leaders should create an environment where people feel "safe to fail," that is, an environment where people are not afraid of being judged and blamed for failure, and therefore are not afraid to experiment. Going beyond this, leaders must encourage their teams to come up with creative solutions to complex problems and also provide guidance and confidence to teams to choose and execute the most appropriate solutions.

From a personal perspective, leaders need to recognize and accept that they themselves cannot be right all the time and may not have answers to all problems. Great leaders are not afraid of exposing their vulnerability by saying, "I don't know the answer. Let's figure it out together."

Connection with peers

Functional leaders, for example, **chief marketing officer (CMO)**, **chief technology officer (CTO)**, and so on, are usually heavily focused on optimizing their respective functions. Given that the core characteristic of **complex adaptive systems (CAS)** is of the interaction between agents creating value, functional leaders can create tremendous incremental value for the enterprise by interacting and collaborating with their peers in a holistic manner.

According to a study of CMOs by Thomas Barta and Patrick Barwise, authors of *The 12 Powers of a Marketing Leader:*

> *"The ability to reach beyond the marketing silo to executives in areas such as IT and finance explained an additional 13 percent of the variation in both business impact and career success."* [xvi]

These interactions should extend beyond formal meetings and should be aimed at winning the hearts and minds of peers. Informal relationships, which are based on helping each other to maximize the functional impact at the enterprise level, can only result in a "win-win" for the functional leaders and also for the business. The interactions can be about bouncing ideas off each other and working together to address shared concerns.

Leadership, particularly at higher levels, can be a lonely place. This can lead to negative feelings such as insecurity and self-doubt. A meaningful support system of peers can go a long way in enabling leaders to effectively deal with the loneliness.

Comfort with "VUCA"

Leaders need to welcome and become comfortable with **VUCA** (stands for, **volatility, uncertainty, complexity,** and **ambiguity**) and in working with information that may be inadequate in both breadth and depth.

Relying heavily on traditional management techniques, such as detailed planning and forecasting, and statistical methods for monitoring and controlling variability, and so on, will not be helpful in dealing with VUCA.

Leaders should be able to abstract patterns based on whatever information is available to them and then use these patterns as feedback for decision-making. They must validate these patterns and update them as necessary based on emergent information, and also socialize them with other stakeholders. Leaders are therefore able to go to the source of complexity, and collaborate with subject matter experts, enabling the participation of teams that are working closer to the source of the complexity, in order to figure out the best way to handle it.

According to Bill George, a senior fellow at Harvard Business School:

> *"With external volatility the prevalent characteristic these days, business leaders who stay focused on their mission and values and have the courage to deploy bold strategies building on their strengths will be the winners. Those who abandon core values or lock themselves into fixed positions and fail to adapt will wind up the losers." [xvii]*

On the other hand, enforcing predictability and stability can contradict with VUCA. If predictability and stability are enforced on a living system, it will take life out of the system slowly but surely. For example, the stock market is a complex system, which not only survives, but thrives on VUCA. The market will stop functioning if predictability and stability are enforced on it.

There is no doubt that a certain level of predictability and stability is needed in any living system, including enterprises. Allowing for reasonable variation, and letting predictability and stability emerge from the system itself, rather than enforcing it, should be the approach.

Ability to guide and facilitate teams

The adage "you can lead a horse to water, but you cannot make it drink" aptly brings out the point about the behavior of living systems. Living beings and systems, unlike machines, have a mind of their own and, if left on their own, will do something only when they see value in doing it. Continuing the analogy of the horse, the being who best knows whether the horse is thirsty or not is the horse itself. All the owner/manager should do is to recognize that the horse might be thirsty and make the water available. Forcing the horse to drink water is simply not going to work.

Humans are the most intelligent living beings and therefore value their freedom the most. The basic nature of humans is that they resent being "told" what to do. If people are to remain engaged and take ownership, leaders should change their approach from managing and directing, that is, "telling" what and even how to do, to guiding and facilitating. The local context is best known to the people closest to it, but leaders will have a better view of the bigger picture. Providing guidance based on the bigger picture and then giving freedom to people to make localized decisions should result in optimal outcomes across the enterprise. While doing this, leaders must instinctively know when to stay away, when to step up, and when to serve.

Ability to leverage risk

In businesses that are being led and managed as closed-ended systems, the mandate for leaders is to keep things predictable and stable. Consequently, leaders in such enterprises strive to eliminate risk to the extent possible or at least put mitigations in place to minimize it. While risks that have only potentially negative outcomes are obviously to be avoided and/or mitigated, a general risk avoidance culture is detrimental to innovation, as well as continuous improvement.

Risk needs to be looked at not just as a threat, but from an opportunistic point of view as well, that is, something that can lead to positive outcomes. Trying new things in the pursuit of continuous improvement and innovation will inherently have the possibility of both positive and negative consequences. The key to mitigating the risk of negative consequences is to shape and monitor experiments which are small enough to not "rock the boat," in case they fail, and also to have robust feedback and governance mechanisms so that what is beginning to fail can be identified as early as possible, in order to enable the containment of the failure.

Continuous improvement and innovation will not happen unless people are encouraged to take risks and feel safe in doing so. Hence, the role of leadership has to change from blindly avoiding risks to leveraging risk.

Connection through engagement

Many companies are so obsessed with maximizing their top and bottom lines that their mindset, intentionally or otherwise, is toward exploiting their employees and customers. Some common ways of customer exploitation include substandard quality, warranty-related surprises in terms of what is not covered, false claims on what a product can do, and so on.

Employee exploitation happens through denying vacations or having staff cancel them at the last minute, forcing staff to work on weekends, bullying, coercion, and so on. Exploitation happens with suppliers/vendors in the form of intentionally delaying payments, creating dependence and then squeezing them for lower prices, and so on.

The roots of this noninclusive thinking lie in viewing everything, including people, as "resources." Resources, by definition, are meant to be exploited. The basic assumption is that it is alright to think about self-interest, even if it comes at the cost of someone else.

Given the importance of interaction between agents in a living system, it is imperative for leaders to move away from an exploitation mindset, to that of engagement. Leaders must view these stakeholders as an integral part of the ecosystem to which the enterprise also belongs and strive to maximize value for all entities, such that the value is maximized at the ecosystem level through a "win-win" for the business and its stakeholders. Maximizing value for the company at the cost of other stakeholders in the ecosystem may yield short-term benefits, but is unlikely to result in other stakeholders helping to unlock hidden value. Having been "exploited" by the firm, these stakeholders may not have any interest in helping the company to derive additional value.

Kevin Kruse, the bestselling co-author of *We: How to Increase Performance and Profits Through Full Engagement*, in his article, *Employee Engagement: The Wonder Drug for Customer Satisfaction*, states:

> *"I've tracked over 30 studies that show how engagement correlates to decreases in absenteeism, turnover, accidents, and defects, while it also correlates to increases in customer service, productivity, sales, and profits."*

In the same article, Kruse depicts the engagement-profit chain as follows:

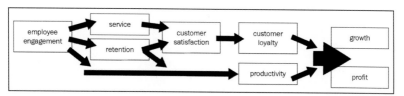

Figure 5.1: Showing how employee engagement positively triggers a chain of variables, which, through greater customer satisfaction, leads to higher growth and profit

In the digital era, where customers are directly connected to enterprises via mobiles and can easily leverage the power of social media, customer engagement is not just a necessity, but, if done well, can be a tremendous enabler for improving customer satisfaction, and thereby increasing loyalty.

According to the thought leadership research division of Forbes Media:

"In order to survive today's ever-changing landscape, businesses need to provide real-time, personalized experiences that reach customers just as they need them. Whether it be a mobile push notification promoting a sale or an email confirming an order, customer engagements now take many forms. By promoting relevant and consistent communication throughout the customer experience, businesses have an opportunity to engage with their audiences like never before." [xviii]

Ability to apply systems thinking

Traditionally, leaders have been mandated to optimize around their respective functional areas and the related spheres of influence, the boundaries of which are clearly earmarked. This has encouraged leaders to work in silos, due to which the systemic perspective is largely neglected by such leaders.

While silos may have their use in enabling leaders to focus on a function, they can become a huge barrier to enhancing agility if a leader's view is limited to the respective silo. Such a restricted view will usually result in local optimization, which can negatively impact the speed of delivery and creating value for the customer.

A living system is greater than the sum of its parts, as the parts have interdependence and the behavior of the system is driven by the interactions between its parts. The implication of this is that when a part of the system needs a fix, or needs to be optimized, the systemic impact must be considered. Otherwise, the overall outcome is likely to be suboptimal. This can be demonstrated by the following example. A commonly used metric in call centers to evaluate the performance of the representatives is **average handle time (AHT)**. It is calculated as follows:

$$AHT = \frac{(\text{Total Talk Time} + \text{Total Hold Time} + \text{Total Post-Call Work})}{\text{Number of Calls Handled}}$$

The metric is useful in that it provides insights into productive hours and aids capacity planning, and so on. However, it penalizes those reps who may be spending more time handling complex calls, in order to ensure that the customers are satisfied at the end of the call. The metric has no linkage with critical outcomes like customer retention, and so on.

If this metric is used as the primary performance metric, and the goal is set to lower it as much as possible, to get more throughput, the following can be the systemic impact:

- Reps will aim to end the call as quickly as possible. There is a very high probability that the customer will not be satisfied at the end of the call and may end up calling again, leading to not only time being wasted, but also an unhappy customer.

- While the customer is interested in getting the issue resolved regardless of how long it takes, the rep is interested in finishing the call as quickly as possible. This leads to no alignment between the interest of the rep and the interest of the customer.

- The pressure to end the calls quickly can result in poor engagement with the customer, thereby leaving the customer unhappy and the rep demoralized.

While it is a perfectly legitimate objective to reduce AHT, in order to avoid the aforementioned unfavorable outcomes, the focus has to be on impacting variables in the system which can impact AHT. The following systemic measures can help in reducing AHT:

- Investing in a robust and user-friendly support portal. Once the portal is in place, calls can be kept short by guiding customers to online references. Over time, customers get used to looking for help on the portal first, before calling the call center.

- Focusing on the entire customer journey and training reps to take the next issue avoidance approach, that is, proactively delving into the next steps in the process with the aim of preventing the next issue from occurring, can significantly reduce the calls. This requires the reps to be aligned to customer value as the key business goal to be achieved.

- The customer calling the call center is a mere symptom of problems that lie somewhere in the customer journey. The key is to go to the root of the problems and resolve those, so that the customer will not have the need to call. According to a blog published by Kayako, a company in the business of helping to improve customer experience, the following questions should be addressed:

  - Why are customers even calling?

  - What was their support journey before they called?

  - What are you doing to prevent the call in the first place? [xix]

The preceding example clearly highlights how systems thinking easily trumps the local optimization approach. Some of the leadership behaviors which reflect systems thinking are:

- Leaders make their silos as porous as possible to facilitate collaboration and the flow of information across the value stream.

- Leaders always aim to optimize at system level, rather than at local level, for example, if a manager in charge of release asks for a person from the development team to help to speed up a particular release, the development team manager will help the release manager. The impact of a person helping to take something live faster is greater than the impact that that person would make while being in the development team.

♦ Leaders consider the potential impact of their decisions at systemic level, for example, a bank deciding to levy a hitherto free service, which would increase revenue, but could have far more negative consequences if the customers feel aggrieved by this move and decide to terminate their relationship with the bank. In such a case, the leaders would carefully weigh the systemic impact of the decision to levy the fee, before actually making the decision.

♦ When slip ups and failures happen, and when people behave in a nonaligned manner, the focus is on finding and fixing the root cause of the problem, as opposed to "quick fixing" a symptom. Reacting to a symptom is like treating a fever with paracetamol, without ascertaining whether it is merely seasonal flu or something serious. A business-related example of a symptom is defects in software. The root cause could be missed requirements, poorly-written unit tests, missed test scenarios, differences in development and production environments, and so on. If a nonaligned behavior from a person has caused an issue, the leader will see if the system rewards bad behavior and if so, will fix the underlying problem to encourage the desired behavior.

Being technology aware

The fact that businesses are becoming technology-driven is a stark reality of today. Technology has become an integral part of strategy for enterprises across all industries. Yet, there are far too many companies that have no representation of people in their Board of Directors who understand technology.

Furthermore, the Board members of most firms do not have even basic awareness of technologies relevant to the business, even when their business is fully dependent on technology, for example, online retail. The lack of awareness of technology is accentuated at the lower levels of the hierarchy, in the leaders at the lower levels. The mindset of most leaders is, "It's too complicated. Talk to someone in IT about it." This "not my problem" mindset toward technology, particularly among senior executives, has the following consequences:

♦ It concentrates power in the CIO/CTO/VP-technology, who heads the technology function. This can result in this person's decisions being based on a limited perspective and not being challenged. Also, this person's view of what's possible and what is not with respect to technology, can result in a "learned helplessness" culture in the enterprise, for example, the business wants new features rolled out around Christmas time, but the CIO says that this is not possible due to a code freeze and he does not want to take the risk of destabilizing the system by introducing new features at the time of peak sales through the website. The business leaders are not in a position to challenge the decision of the CIO and feel totally helpless.

♦ The Board may not be able to appreciate the value of initiatives put forth by the head of IT, which can lead to the technology function not being able to keep up with change.

♦ There is a huge risk that the strategy of the enterprise may not be leveraging the power of technology and, even worse, may be disconnected from technology.

♦ Opportunities to enter into value-adding technology partnerships may be missed or existing technology partners could work in a way which compromises the interests of the enterprise.

While it is fine to have an expert in charge of the technology function, given that most of the disruptions that are impacting companies are technology-driven, the Board and senior leaders need to have basic understanding of how technology enables the business and cannot afford to be blind to emerging technology trends which can impact the enterprise.

According to Sarrazin and Willmott of McKinsey:

"To serve as effective thought partners, Boards must move beyond an arms-length relationship with digital issues (exhibit). Board members need better knowledge about the technology environment, its potential impact on different parts of the company and its value chain, and thus about how digital can undermine existing strategies and stimulate the need for new ones. They also need faster, more effective ways to engage the organization and operate as a governing body and, critically, new means of attracting digital talent." [xx]

The fundamental characteristic of a living system is that it spares no effort in making sense of the environment and the changes happening to it. Given that technology is such an integral part of the environment today, leaders have no option but to understand enough about technology to enable their businesses to leverage it for improving competitive advantage.

Following servant leadership

Even though this phrase was coined by Robert Greenleaf, the founder of the Greenleaf Center for Servant Leadership, in 1970, it became prominent with the advent of Agile and is now widely acknowledged as the primary trait of an Agile leader. Simply put, servant leadership is about putting the needs of people and teams who are producing value above everything else. It is about providing guidance and perspectives to people and teams, without directly influencing them or "telling" them what to do. On the contrary, leaders use their wider influence to remove any obstacles and provide all the resources required for people and teams to be able to work most effectively and efficiently.

Leaders recognize that the people and teams who are actually producing value are the closest to the business and customers, and that they are in the best position to understand the context and to respond to challenges related to that context. Hence, even if the team, after due deliberations, decide to take a different course of action than to what the leader had in mind, the leader wholeheartedly supports the team with the decision that they have collectively made. The leader should obviously challenge them to ensure that the decision is well thought out, but must respect the team's decision, as long as it does not violate something which has been agreed on upfront as being non-negotiable.

Servant leadership is also about empowering the people and teams at the lowest level of the hierarchy and trusting them to decide the best way forward, thereby making the lowest level of the hierarchy the most empowered layer in the hierarchy. People like to be led and not managed. Servant leadership is about the former.

Balancing the paradoxes

A complex system is abounding with paradoxes. Leaders need to balance paradoxes like nimbleness and discipline. These paradoxes may appear contradictory and hence can lead to the temptation of choosing one way, while giving up on the other. However, balancing the paradoxes is about being in the middle and being guided by the system itself on how to balance them. Paradoxes can be best dealt with by adapting to, and building on, emergent outcomes and by empowering teams and people producing value to balance the paradoxes in their contexts, guided by the "maps of intent."

According to Jim Highsmith, author of *Adaptive Leadership: Accelerating Enterprise Agility* and a signatory of the Agile Manifesto:

"Paradoxes do not have solutions, they have resolutions."

He adds:

"Agile proponents, and opponents, get hung up on the issue of architecture — to develop architecture up front or to evolve architecture over time. This isn't a problem, it's a paradox. There isn't a single solution to the question, but a series of balanced resolutions that depend on the specific organizational and project or product context. Ultimately, the architecture issue requires a balancing of early skeleton work combined with evolutionary updates. Balancing early versus evolution makes management more difficult than a black and white problem solution, but balancing resolutions over time will deliver far better performance." [xxi]

Leaders do not treat paradoxes as problems and do not try to resolve them one way or the other, as doing so leads to detrimental outcomes in a CAS-type organization and a VUCA-type environment. Leaders stay away from "there can be only one right way of doing this" type of thinking. More importantly, paradoxes can throw up interesting opportunities for the organization, which may emerge from the intersection of objectives and approaches.

As Highsmith says:

> *"It's easy to be an "or" leader. Pick a side and state your case loudly, over and over until the opposition gives up. It's much more difficult to be an "and" leader, balancing between seemingly opposite strategies. However, in our ever-changing and turbulent world, slavishly following the "one right answer" is a recipe for disaster." [xxii]*

As individuals, leaders too are complex and therefore will have paradoxical characteristics. According to Dr. Travis Bradberry, co-author of *Emotional Intelligence 2.0*:

> *"Most wildly successful people are complex—so complex that many of their defining qualities are paradoxical. Rather than an "either/or" set of static characteristics, they're more likely to demonstrate both. This is a key to their success." [xxiii]*

Bradberry gives many examples of paradoxical individual characteristics, one of which is convergent and divergent thinking. He states:

> *"Convergent thinking is what's measured by IQ tests: rational thinking that typically results in a single right answer. Divergent thinking, on the other hand, is less precise.*

It's about generating ideas and asking questions that have no solid right or wrong answers. Both are important. No matter how high your IQ is, you're not going to be successful if you can't think outside of the proverbial box. On the other hand, you need rational thinking skills to correctly judge whether your ideas have merit. That's why this particular paradox is so important."

Encouraging inclusivity and diversity

With the world feeling smaller each day, with interesting possibilities emerging through the intersection of domains, and with innovation in all spheres happening at breakneck speed, leaders must recognize that inclusivity and diversity are critical for the organization to foster learning and creativity.

Diversity and inclusivity should span both people and ideas. There is tremendous value when people across varying backgrounds and experiences bring in ideas and opinions from their very different perspectives. A healthy tension between these diverse ideas and opinions not only leads to lowering risks in making decisions but becomes a source to funnel innovation and creativity.

According to Boris Groysberg, a professor at Harvard Business School, and Katherine Connolly, a research associate at Harvard Business School, in an article in HBR:

"A diverse workforce also prevents an organization from becoming too insular and out of touch with its increasing heterogeneous customer base."

In a survey they found that:

"CEOs asserted that it is crucial for a company's employees to reflect the people they serve."

Valuing inclusivity and diversity will help leaders to recognize their biases and mental models, which will enable them to keep an open mind and examine various perspectives objectively. Leaders need to recognize that, at times, some decisions may get slightly delayed when multiple views and ideas need to be debated. However, decisions made taking an inclusive approach are highly likely to be better and, more importantly, the concerned stakeholders will willingly take ownership of the decision, due to their participation in the decision-making process. Leaders should respect people for who they are and for the unique experiences and perspectives they bring to the table. This makes employees be themselves at work, thereby enabling the company to maintain diversity.

"Humble inquiry"

Edgar Schein, the "guru" of organization development, who has written an entire book on this topic, defines humble inquiry as:

> *"the fine art of drawing someone out, of asking questions to which you do not know the answer, of building a relationship based on curiosity and interest in the other person."*

In a complex world, and particularly for knowledge work, humble inquiry means actively seeking the opinions of subordinates, and ensuring that they are feeling comfortable enough to share their views without the fear of being judged. Going a step further, the leaders who practice humble inquiry have such a trust-based relationship with the subordinates that if their team notice the leaders making a mistake, they will feel comfortable in pointing it out. The leaders benefit immensely from humble inquiry, as they are likely to get information from their subordinates, which they would not be able to get using formal influence and authority.

Studies have been carried out on the causes of disasters, like airplane crashes, oil spills, and so on, and in almost all instances it was found that the junior people might have had information about something not being right, but did not feel safe to tell the truth to their supervisors/managers. For example, the Deepwater Horizon Oil Spill, which happened in April 2010, was due to a series of simple oversights. [xxiv] It is quite unlikely that the people on the ground would not have been aware of these oversights.

Consistently practicing humble inquiry creates an environment where the subordinates feel safe to share the truth, even when not prompted to do so. On the flip side, the leader is not afraid to be vulnerable by saying that he/she genuinely does not know the answer and that he/she needs help.

Humility is an integral part of humble inquiry. From a leadership perspective, it is about giving credit to colleagues, especially those who are less powerful, for positive outcomes. Humility is about using power and authority to empower people and enable them to give their best. The opposite of this is having a sense of entitlement about indulging in what Prof. Robert Sutton, of Stanford University, calls "disrespectful, demeaning and downright mean-spirited behavior." [xxv] He believes that such oppressive behaviors are quite common. He goes on to add in his book, *The Asshole Survival Guide*, that even a single exposure to negative behavior, like the receipt of an insulting email, can turn a person into a "carrier," like a common cold. Therefore, it is quite easy for such behaviors to spread across the enterprise and cause irreparable damage to a people-centric mindset and culture. Leaders, therefore, need to be extremely vigilant and strict about applying the "no jerks" rule, without exception, to themselves and to everyone in the business as well.

Summary

In this chapter, we discovered that leaders are the primary catalysts for any enterprise aspiring to enhance agility. Leaders need specific capabilities, which are over and above the standard leadership capabilities, in order to take the business on the path of enhanced agility. These capabilities comprise of personal traits and behaviors that are intrinsic in nature and enable leadership agility, which is foundational for enhancing agility.

This chapter concludes the foundation section. The next chapter is about organization structure, which is the first component in the third section of the book (about the components of a company). The chapter will cover the significance of organization structure and how to leverage this for enhancing enterprise agility.

References

[i] https://www.versionone.com/about/press-releases/versionone-releases-11th-annual-state-of-agile-report/

[ii] https://www-01.ibm.com/common/ssi/cgi-bin/ssialias?htmlfid=GBE03297USEN

[iii] https://info.thoughtworks.com/rs/199-QDE-291/images/LeadershipInTheAgeofComplexity.pdf

[iv] http://www.changewise.biz/?page_id=474

[v] https://en.wikipedia.org/wiki/Mental_model

[vi] https://www.forbes.com/sites/victorlipman/2013/11/18/all-successful-leaders-need-this-quality-self-awareness/#1642c4eb1f06

[vii] https://en.wikipedia.org/wiki/Emotional_intelligence

[viii] https://www.forbes.com/sites/travisbradberry/2014/01/09/emotional-intelligence/#456686251ac0

[ix] https://www.thoughtworks.com/insights/blog/next-big-disruption-courageous-executives

[x] https://info.thoughtworks.com/courageous-executive-lp.html?utm_source=web&utm_medium=insights&utm_campaign=survey-report-launch

[xi] https://www.entrepreneur.com/article/295312

[xii] https://www.inc.com/brian-d-evans/most-ceos-read-a-book-a-week-this-is-how-you-can-too-according-to-this-renowned-.html

[xiii] https://en.wikipedia.org/wiki/List_of_cognitive_biases

[xiv] https://www.slideshare.net/AgileSparks/mindset-better-60-min, slide 12

[xv] https://techcrunch.com/2016/07/02/andy-jassys-brief-history-of-the-genesis-of-aws/

[xvi] https://www.mckinsey.com/featured-insights/leadership/why-effective-leaders-must-manage-up-down-and-sideways

[xvii] https://www.forbes.com/sites/hbsworkingknowledge/2017/02/17/vuca-2-0-a-strategy-for-steady-leadership-in-an-unsteady-world/#20ab9c1d13d8

[xviii] https://www.forbes.com/sites/forbesinsights/2015/01/29/6-strategies-to-drive-customer-engagement-in-2015/#3703297a325c

[xix] https://www.kayako.com/blog/why-average-handle-time-is-a-terrible-metric/

[xx] https://www.mckinsey.com/business-functions/digital-mckinsey/our-insights/adapting-your-board-to-the-digital-age

[xxi] http://jimhighsmith.com/embracing-paradox/

[xxii] https://assets.thoughtworks.com/articles/adaptive-leadership-accelerating-enterprise-agility-jim-highsmith-thoughtworks.pdf

[xxiii] https://www.linkedin.com/pulse/eight-paradoxical-habits-wildly-successful-people-bradberry/

[xxiv] https://listverse.com/2013/03/02/10-deadly-disasters-we-should-have-seen-coming/

[xxv] http://nymag.com/daily/intelligencer/2017/09/robert-sutton-asshole-survival-guide.html

—PART THREE—

THE COMPONENTS OF ENTERPRISE AGILITY

This part of the book examines the six critical components of an enterprise, namely, organization structure, process, people, technology, governance, and the customer, and suggests measures to unlock and enhance the agility of these components, which will lead to enhancing the agility of the business.

6

ORGANIZATION STRUCTURE

This chapter focuses on the structure of the enterprise and provides insights on optimizing it for enhancing agility at its structure and consequently at the enterprise level as well.

The structure of an organization is to a business what a skeleton is to a human body. The structure not only defines the shape and form of the enterprise, but it also determines how flexible a enterprise can be in responding to changing circumstances.

For enterprises to have greater agility, they need a structure that enables cross functional and self-organizing teams to deliver value. The structure must be an enabler for teams to develop and sustain all capabilities that underlie agility, namely, responsiveness, versatility, flexibility, resilience, innovativeness, and adaptability. This is radically opposed to a structure that separates the "thinkers" from the "doers," and which is aimed at optimizing efficiency, predictability, and stability.

The chapter will explore the following topics:

♦ The significance of the organization structure in agility

♦ Structural impediments to agility

♦ Structural enablers for agility

Significance

Structure influences agility in the following ways. It determines:

♦ The speed of decision-making and thereby the responsiveness to customer needs and changes in the environment

♦ How efficient and effective the feedback loops are, that is, the speed at which the enterprise is able to sense the changes in the environment, and how quickly this information reaches the relevant stakeholders

♦ The level of collaboration between people within and across teams

♦ The alignment of teams toward delivering valuable outcomes

♦ How effectively the strategy of the enterprise is executed

♦ How optimally synergies across the business are identified and leveraged

♦ The extent to which an enterprise can scale and descale quickly

♦ The distribution of power and authority across a firm

It should be noted that among all the tangible elements of an enterprise, its structure is perhaps the most difficult to change. However, on the flip side, the *right* structure can be the biggest enabler for enhancing enterprise agility.

Inhibitors to agility

The following factors related to organization structure are key barriers for enterprises to enhance and sustain agility.

A "tall" hierarchy

In any system of humans, the distribution of power is seldom equal, that is, some roles have more power than others. In the absence of defined roles, a leader or leaders will emerge who voluntarily, or by force, have more power than others in the system. An enterprise is also a system of humans, and hence the existence of power centers, both formal and informal, is a reality that must be accepted. The hierarchical structures in companies reflect this reality.

However, enterprises have used hierarchy as a means to provide "growth" to their employees. The belief that "climbing up" the hierarchy denotes growth and also more power is widely prevalent in organizations across the globe. Unfortunately, in most traditional enterprises, the lure of rising in the hierarchy is generally the only way that employees are motivated. This is because increase in salary is tightly linked to the levels in the hierarchy. Moreover, increase in growth, status, and power are directly associated with a rise in the hierarchy.

There is another reason why enterprises have a hierarchical structure, which needs to be examined. The roots of hierarchy can be uncovered in author Frederick Taylor's *Theory of Scientific Management*. The most important premise of this theory is that the "thinker" and the "doer" should be separate. The biggest consequence of the thinker-doer separation was the creation of the hierarchical organization structure, where the primary job of the managers was to "think" and direct and control those lower in the hierarchy. Command and control styles of management became the order of the day. As enterprises scaled, they hired senior managers to manage the relatively junior managers and the number of layers in the hierarchy become highly correlated with the size of the enterprise. A hierarchical structure is best for ensuring compliance and thus people were required to comply with the instructions given by their "bosses."

While some hierarchy may be necessary or even inevitable, a "tall" hierarchy, that is, a hierarchy that has multiple layers, is one of the major impediments to agility. A classic symptom of a tall hierarchy is the high ratio of managers to people who are directly involved in producing value. Sometimes, the total number of managers is greater than the number of "producers," which does not make any sense, especially when the enterprise is trying to enhance agility.

The problems with an unnecessarily tall hierarchy are many:

♦ The decision makers, being higher up in the hierarchy, are not connected to the realities on the ground. This can have a severe impact on the quality of decisions made by them.

♦ The flow of information, needed for making decisions, is vertical. This not only leads to delays in making and communicating decisions, but the information itself may get diluted before it reaches the appropriate level in the hierarchy.

To make things worse, taking advantage of the fact that the "big bosses" are removed from ground realities, their immediate juniors, who are usually also not connected to the ground realities are tempted to "dress up" the information provided to their superiors, in order to look good in the eyes of the "bosses."

♦ By definition, a hierarchy creates silos. This encourages the tendency to optimize locally, creates barriers to collaboration, and slows down delivery due to handoffs and dependencies. The silos also are a disincentive for sharing and learning. A silo encourages individualism over team spirit, as the focus is to keep the "boss" happy, because the "boss" has the biggest influence on how the performance of the subordinate is rated.

♦ A hierarchy embodies a command and control style of management, due to the premise of thinker-doer separation. People are expected to follow the orders and instructions of the bosses. Therefore, the accountability for success or failure does not lie with the "producers," but with the "bosses." A command and control style is diametrically opposed to the concept of autonomous, empowered, and self-organizing teams, which is the cornerstone of agility.

Organizing primarily for efficiency

For decades, when scarcity of resources was one of the biggest concerns for enterprises, and the levels of complexity and uncertainty in the business environment were much lower than today, companies organized people around specializations and activities. Driving for efficiency was seen as a key enabler to the cost leadership strategy adopted by many organizations during those times.

Today, fast-paced change leads to high uncertainty and complexity. Delivering value to satisfy customers is driving competitive advantage, and being organized for effectiveness is critical. However, a structure that optimizes activities, can do so at the cost of handoffs leading to delayed delivery, which narrows the focus of people to activity completion and output maximization, rather than being aligned to achieving the business outcome. This can be a huge impediment to enhancing agility. Moreover, a structure focused on maximizing efficiency is driven by vertical optimization, that is, optimization of functions (for example, sales, technology, and customer service and so on). However, agility needs something that is diametrically opposite, that is, horizontal optimization. Horizontal optimization aims for optimizing value driven outcomes for the entire value chain, which covers ideation, creation, delivery, and support.

Devaluing knowledge workers

According to MSG:

> *"A knowledge worker is one who uses knowledge as the capital for work and who uses brain power rather than brawn power to get the job done. In other words, knowledge workers "think for a living.""* [i]

This term was created by Peter Drucker as far back as in 1959, in his book *The Landmarks of Tomorrow* [ii]. Knowledge workers have become significantly prominent in recent times due to the rise of knowledge economy which is enabled by information technology. Moreover, there has been a significant rise in service economy across the globe, which also falls in the category of knowledge work.

Contrast this with the first industrial revolution, where work was heavily oriented toward manufacturing. In contrast to mechanistic types of work, knowledge work requires creativity, intuition, and decisiveness. There is tremendous value addition to outcomes when knowledge workers collaborate with each other. Knowledge workers aspire to understand the *why* behind everything they do. The critical implication, therefore, is that the "thinker and doer" separation, as advocated in Frederick Taylor and discussed in *Chapter 3, The Enterprise as a Living System,* is highly inappropriate for knowledge work.

Another important characteristic, which distinguishes knowledge workers, is that intrinsic variables such as autonomy, mastery, and purpose are critical for motivating them. The Agile Manifesto and principles are explicit about enabling knowledge workers. The Manifesto values "individuals and interactions over processes and tools," and the following two principles reflect this:

♦ The best architectures, requirements, and designs emerge from self-organizing teams.

♦ Build projects around motivated individuals. Give them the environment and support they need, and trust them to get the job done.

On the contrary, if teams are tied down by heavy-weight processes, mandated to follow instructions of the higher ups in the hierarchy without having a meaningful say in decision-making, measured on completion of tasks and activities rather than on delivering outcomes and such other things that devalue knowledge workers, the enablement of agility is seriously compromised.

Centralization of core capabilities

It is logical for enterprises to centralize certain functions such as marketing and sales, assuming that there are synergies to be leveraged across products, customer segments, and so on. However, confusing functions with capabilities, particularly those capabilities that are critical to agility and therefore need to be pervasive across the enterprise, can be an impediment to agility. Examples include customer insights and innovation. The respective functions for these are market research and development, which may be centralized, but it is not smart to centralize the capabilities associated with them.

Taking the example of customer insights forward, every person in the enterprise, especially those who interact directly with customers, should be striving to understand customer needs and expectations as deeply as possible. While people directly facing customers play a slightly more important role in satisfying them, this cannot happen at all unless the entire value stream from "concept to cash" is aligned to facilitating it. Centralizing this capability will send a wrong signal that having this capability is limited to only people in that team. Moreover, this centralized team will find it very difficult to get alignment from the rest of the business to act on the insights gained by them, as other teams' priorities may be different.

Some enterprises recognize the capabilities that are critical for agility and also the fact that it takes a mindset and culture change for people to have these capabilities. They try to create a separate "cell" to build and nurture these capabilities in a limited number of people, along with changing the mindset of these people and having a different culture in these teams. However, integrating these teams into the mainstream of the enterprise subsequently is extremely difficult, particularly due to the mindset and culture differences between these teams and the rest of the enterprise.

Leadership-level silos

Companies that are pursing agility often fall into an anti-pattern, where the teams that produce and deliver are restructured as cross-functional teams, that is, silos are broken down at the team level, while maintaining the silos at the management/leadership levels. This anti-pattern is particularly visible in business and IT functions, for example, the CIO and product head are in silos. Sometimes, the anti-pattern is also seen within these functions, for example, the chief architect and chief of infrastructure are in silos, while the rest of the department leaders have broken the silos between them.

Silos at the leadership level become a huge impediment, as the ill effects of silos include local optimization of a function or activity, lack of accountability for business outcomes, resistance to collaboration, and many more. These practices are highly likely to cascade to the teams. So while the teams may appear to be cross-functional, it may just be a façade, as the team members may align themselves to the silos of their respective leaders. Silos may be lead to unfruitful disagreements due to the tendency of "guarding the turf," and these disagreements can adversely impact the morale of the teams. Moreover, silos are also an impediment to systems thinking, which is absolutely necessary at leadership level for enhancing agility.

Enablers for enhancing agility

The following factors related to organization structure can significantly help enterprises to enhance agility.

Organize teams around business outcomes

Outcome-oriented teams are teams that are structured in a way to deliver a clearly defined business value or business benefit. Outcomes could be in form of products, services, customer capability (for example, ability to search for a product on an online shopping website), or even a feature (for example, customer loyalty). If an outcome is too large, then it is prudent to break it into sub outcomes, for example, the payment feature may be broken into sub features as payment by credit card, payment through loyalty points, and payment by cash on delivery. Examples of business benefits that should be linked to outcomes include increase in sales, increase in customer satisfaction, and so on.

In many enterprises, the completion of a project is defined as an outcome, as the project is linked to a business case. However, there are potential problems with this approach. A project may be completed, but the business outcome, as set out in the business case, may not be achieved. This may happen due to the project being organized by activities, thereby teams losing sight of the outcome. The chances of this happening are higher when the teams are not empowered or equipped to deal with changing requirements priorities. Hence, if a project needs to be broken down into multiple teams, those teams should be organized as sub outcomes, rather than being organized around components or activities. The issue of funding projects versus outcomes will be addressed in the chapter on governance, namely, *Chapter 10, Governance*. On a similar note, the delivery of predefined scope may not necessarily lead to delivering an outcome.

According to Sriram Narayan, author of *Agile IT Organization Design*:

> *"Outcome realization requires real collaboration between those who understand the problem and those who can fashion various levels of solution for it. Initial attempts at solutions lead to a better understanding of the problem which leads to further attempts at better solutions. This doesn't work where the product management organization is separate from the development (scope-delivery) organization." [iii]*

Outcome/sub outcome teams are by definition cross-functional, that is, these teams have within them all the core skills and capabilities needed to deliver the outcome. This is exactly the opposite of activity or component teams, which have to hand their work to another team, unless it is the last activity in the process. These handoffs create dependencies and blockages, thereby not only creating inefficiencies, but a loss of accountability toward achieving the outcome. It is very much possible that it is not viable to have certain specialist roles in the team on a full-time basis, for example, security. People in such roles may cater to the needs of multiple teams. While this approach does create some level of dependency, "pulling" in people with specialized skills avoids a handoff to a specialized team, who, to make things worse, may have very little "skin in the game" toward achieving the outcome.

Outcome-oriented teams also have another significant advantage of bringing out the best in knowledge workers. Being associated with a broader purpose is one of the critical variables that influences intrinsic motivation. By virtue of outcomes being associated with a purpose, people in outcome-oriented teams are far more motivated than in other types of team structures, and far more satisfied with their work as well.

A necessary precondition for creating outcome-focused teams is to break the silos within the structure, all the way until the functional boundaries are dissolved. A common anti-pattern is to create outcome-focused teams, but continue the functional reporting for people within the teams, for example, a tester in an outcome-oriented team continuing to report to the test manager. The following diagram is a pictorial depiction of activity versus feature/outcome teams.

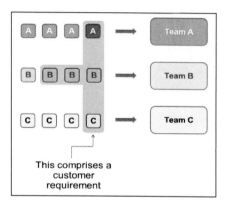

Figure 6.1: A component activity-oriented team

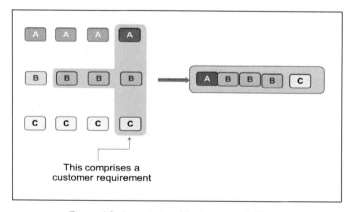

Figure 6.2: An outcome/Feature-oriented team

In the preceding diagrams, the customer's requirement is of a feature that includes functionalities of A, B, and C layers of software. If teams are created based on activities/components, three separate teams will build functionalities of A, B, and C, respectively. These teams would need to integrate the separately built functionalities in order to deliver the customer's requirement.

On the other hand, the outcome-oriented team is a single team that will build all functionalities across the three layers needed to deliver the feature to the customer.

Taking a step further, the outcome-oriented team will also be responsible for deploying and supporting the feature once it is in production.

An outcome-oriented team delivers more than the sum of its parts. This is the result of collaboration between knowledge workers, who are bound together by a common purpose.

Organizing teams, which by definition need to be cross-functional in nature, around outcomes helps to avoid the pitfall pointed out by Conway's law. Conway's law is an observation that the design of any system is significantly affected by the communications structure of the organization that develops it. The law is commonly associated with software development but is considered applicable to systems and organizations of all types. [iv]

The applicability of Conway's law can be seen in the preceding diagrams. The communication structure between the component and outcome-oriented teams will happen very differently, as the component team is not cross functional, but the outcome-oriented team is. The outcome-oriented team will have a more coherent design, that is, design without the inefficiencies of layers, as it does not have barriers to communication being a single team.

Self-organizing teams

Cross-functional teams, as stated earlier, work effectively only when they are self-organizing. Self-organizing teams have the following characteristics:

- ♦ They have clarity on the vision, mission, and strategy of the enterprise, and, more importantly, are able to see the link between the work they are performing and the strategy of the enterprise. They work actively with the sponsors of the work, to understand the value proposition behind the work, and to come with a solution approach with is best aligned to delivering highest value to the customers.

- ♦ They have visibility about the work they need to perform, through a backlog. Based on the prioritized backlog, they "pull" the work to be done, as opposed to being "told" what to do. The team estimates how long it would take to get each piece of work done, and also make timeline commitments based on existing priorities and the estimate for the new work. They share and validate the key assumptions behind the estimates with the relevant stakeholders.

  Should the estimate turn out to be incorrect due to emergence of new information that invalidates the assumptions behind those estimates, they immediately make this visible to the relevant stakeholders and collaborate with them to choose the best possible option for going forward, considering the revised estimate. For example, a team has estimated that a feature would take two months of effort, based on the current size of the team. The team commences development and realizes that the technical complexity involved is far greater than what they had assumed initially, which now results in a revised estimate of four months.

The team would immediately involve the sponsors of the work to share this new information and may provide the following options:

1. A basic version of the feature could be delivered in two months

2. A newer technical approach could be investigated which has potential to bring down the development effort, but the feasibility could be known only after investigation

3. Continue as is and deliver after four months

The sponsors might agree to an option suggested by the team, but may also stop the development of the feature, and take something else which is the next highest priority, as the increased effort on this feature invalidates the business case.

They collectively determine the work allocation among themselves. The work allocation may cut across roles, and it is team which decides when that needs to happen. For example, if the work is closed to being delivered, and the capacity to test is falling short, team members who do not have the role of Tester may be assigned the task of testing, just to ensure that testing does not become a bottleneck toward meeting the delivery commitment made by the team. They ask for help from other teams and leaders, as may be needed. They strive for continuously improving ways of working, and involve the relevant stakeholders to implement innovative ideas.

♦   They have the "Agile mindset."

The following are the influencing factors that enable the teams to become self-organizing.

Coaching

The transition from a hierarchy, silo-based structure, and a command and control style of management is a difficult one for nearly one in any enterprise. Hence, getting people to be a part of cross-functional teams and then expecting them to exhibit behaviors of self-organization can prove extremely challenging for most people. Hence, active coaching may become necessary, without which the teams may not be able to move toward being self-organizing.

Moreover, a group of people put together does not automatically become a high functioning team, especially when they are adopting newer ways of working. A newly formed team will go through all or least some of the initial three stages of the Tuckman Team Formation Model [v], namely, Forming, Storming, and Norming before they reach the fourth stage, that is, Performing. The key takeaway from the model is that a newly formed team, or a team that has many new people coming will take some time before it becomes an effective self-organizing and a high performing team. Having a coach to guide the team can help the team to reach the Performing stage early.

Empowered to make decisions

The teams need to be empowered to make most decisions, such that they do not have to take "approval" from someone higher up in the hierarchy. The team needs to have the freedom to come up with solutions to the challenges they might be facing. They should be able to renegotiate their commitments, if emergence of new information or change in circumstances affect the previously made commitments. The team may involve leaders who are outside the team in decision-making where decisions to be made are exceptional in nature.

Empowered teams make better decisions for two reasons:

1. They are closest to the context
2. The decision-making is a collective effort and therefore multiple perspectives will be taken into consideration before arriving at a decision

Empowerment does in no way imply that the team can "do whatever they want" or should hide information from stakeholders outside the team. The team should be aware of the boundaries of autonomous decision-making. It is pertinent to note that teams that have reached a relatively high level of self-organization and enterprises as a whole which have reached a high level of agility continue to have coaching support provided to the teams. Spotify is one such example. The equivalent analogy is of Olympic Champion or League level champion teams, which have a coach as an integral part of the team.

Empowered teams own their commitments and take accountability for them. The accountability is both at individual and team level. Team members will hold each other accountable for their part of the commitment.

Team chemistry

Just like in the case of successful sports teams, team chemistry, as intangible it may be, is necessary for a team to perform effectively. A good example of the need for team chemistry is to think about bringing together 11 best football players across the globe to create a team, and have that team play against settled teams. It is quite likely that the team with the superstar players may not perform well initially, until some level of chemistry develops within the team. Enterprise should consciously provide opportunities to team members to build informal relationships, which is highly instrumental in building team chemistry.

A group of people coming together becomes a team only after there is chemistry in the team.

Access to needed resources

Also similar to successful sports teams, the team needs to have ready access to all the resources that they need to perform their work. This includes the hardware, software, tools, environments, and the infrastructure needed for communication and collaboration. Lack of needed resources can impede the smooth functioning of the team, thereby impacting the ability self organize.

A negative example of this is a team which has to deliver features for iPhone needs two iPhones for testing those features. This team is provided an iPhone that is two versions old, and to make things worse, moreover just one instrument that has to be shared between the two testers.

It is important to remember that the larger a team gets, the less effective it becomes at self-organization. It is important to find the right balance between the team being cross functional and keeping the team small in size.

The following are the key visible indicators of a well-functioning self-organizing team.

♦ The use of the word *We* much more than *I*

♦ Team members enjoy each other's company at work and outside work as well

♦ Team members willingly share knowledge and information with each other, rather than treat those as sources of power

♦ They motivate each other to improve and excel, as they genuinely care about each other's wellbeing

Self-organizing teams might appear inefficient, and even chaotic during the early stage, but if the enablers are put in place, the team will find its rhythm through emergence and will learn to self-organize.

Stable teams

The "chemistry" within a team, that is, the relationship between the team members which is based on trust, mutual respect, care, and concern for each other, is a huge enabler for the agility of the team, and also for the enterprise. A team is also a **complex adaptive system (CAS)**, albeit on a much smaller scale compared to the business. Hence, healthy interaction between team members is bound to produce value for the team and consequently for companies as well.

As opposed to stable teams, project teams are formed for a specific duration or to meet an outcome by bringing together a group of people with the skills required for the project. The team is disbanded after the completion of the project. Project teams are formed to deliver specific work, while in case of stable teams, specific work is given to the team based on the team's capacity and skills.

Stability obviously cannot be absolute. Some team members will leave the team and new ones will take their place. This limited churn of people is actually very healthy, as new people are able to bring fresh ideas and perspectives to the team. Also, stability does not imply stagnancy. The team will evolve based on team members acquiring new skills, acquiring more experience and getting better at what they do, based on continuous improvement. New ideas and fresh perspectives, from new people coming to the team, will also ensure that there is no stagnancy in the team. The evolution of teams across the enterprise will contribute heavily toward the overall evolution of the business, which is a key indicator of enhanced agility.

Another major advantage of a stable team is that it is well aware of its capacity to deliver on cadence, which is immensely helpful for scheduling work and predicting fairly accurately when that work can get done. Most importantly, team stability is a huge enabler for the team's ability to self-organize.

While controlled movement of people in and out of teams may be necessary and even healthy for the team, what needs to be avoided is "yanking" people from the team to put them on firefighting missions. Such ad hoc and drastic moves are bound to disturb the chemistry and balance of the team and will have an adverse impact on the level of agility of the team, and consequently the performance of the team.

Sometimes it may be necessary to create temporary teams, that is, teams that are formed for a specific event or to deliver a one off specific outcomes, as a project. For such teams to be successful, the team must have clarity on their purpose and the specific outcomes they are expected to achieve, and they must have a strong underlying culture, which acts as a unifier and helps the team to reach the *performing* stage quickly.

Like most things, there are certain disadvantages of a stable team which include a tendency toward "group think" and some level of complacency. However, the advantages of a stable team far outweigh the potential disadvantages and therefore having stable teams, and maintaining them, should be pursued as much as possible.

Flat(ter) structure

As discussed earlier, a "tall" hierarchical structure has the potential to seriously impede agility. Having said this, some level of hierarchy may be necessary/inevitable in an enterprise. However, it is critical that there should be no hierarchy in teams that are organized by outcomes. The lack of hierarchy should not be confused with lack of someone holding a broader role and also with lack of leadership. A team may have a project manager, who is primarily in a customer facing role and always has the big picture view of the project. However, this does not mean that he is the "boss" in the team. Another team may have a scrum master, who has an internal facing role, and can influence all team members individually and collectively.

Again, having a broad role does not mean that the scrum master is the "boss" of the team. If anyone is "the boss" of the team, then it is collectively the team itself. With respect to leadership within the team, it should be situational in nature, based on which role has a greater influence on the outcome, at a given point in time. For example, in the conceptualization stage of a business outcome, the architects and designers have greater influence and should take the leadership role, while in the implementation stage, operations should take the leadership role.

A flat structure should not mean a narrow structure. In order to sense the environment and also be responsive to it, a structure should be flat, but broad, that is, a significant part of the enterprise being directly close to the external environment. The following diagram represents what Niels Pfleaging, author of the book *Organize for Complexity*, refers to as a value creation structure. This is an example of a flat and broad structure [vi]. This, of course, is assuming that the enterprise has "customer first" at the core of its strategy.

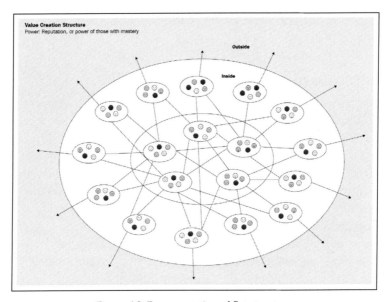

Figure 6.3: Representation of flat structure

In the preceding diagram, the teams in the inner circle represents the leadership and the teams in the outer circle are those which are producers of value and are directly connected with the customers and the external environment. This represents a flat network of teams, which have access to any team and any leader, should they need access to expertise which may not be in the team. The leaders are directly connected with the teams and this is possible as the structure is flat, that is, without a hierarchy. The arrows indicate the flow of value is from inside to the market and environment.

Repurpose the "frozen middle layer"

The term *frozen middle* was invented by Jonathan Byrnes, senior lecturer at **Massachusetts Institute of Technology (MIT)**, while referring to the middle layer of management.

He says:

> *"The essential idea was that whatever initiative top management decided the company would pursue, it would be slowed to a standstill by the unwillingness and inability of the company's middle management team to carry it out." [vii]*

The middle management's role in traditional enterprises comprises of several primary things: the planning, directing, and coordinating of work of people reporting to them and reporting information up their "bosses," who are higher up in the hierarchy. Given that the teams in an Agile business are expected to be self-organizing, as described earlier, the layer of middle managers needs to lean and the role of people who remain in middle management needs to change drastically.

Moreover, managers who previously needed to spend significant time and effort to create dashboards indicating "RAG" status based on percentage completion of items, instead of actual deliveries, will find that their reports are irrelevant and inappropriate in an Agile environment. The middle managers may just have nothing meaningful left to do, unless they adapt their role toward enabling agility.

The question which needs to be asked is, what is the role of a "manager" in an Agile enterprise? Actually, the word "manager" is a misnomer in an Agile environment, as there is hardly anything for someone to manage who is outside a self-organizing team. However, there is a highly impactful role for people who are outside of the teams, who have a wider degree of influence, that is, influence beyond the sphere of a team. The role is that of a "facilitator," who adds value to the enterprise and the team in the following ways:

- Helps the teams to understand the company's vision, mission, and strategy, and also to facilitate their involvement in shaping them as well

- Remove blockers and resolve dependencies, which are slowing down teams

- Share risks and concerns, as seen from a position outside of the team

- Challenge the team to improve continuously

- Coach and mentor team members, to enhance leadership capabilities

Coaching the middle managers to transform to their new roles should be one of the highest priorities in the journey to enhancing agility. Otherwise, this pool of people, which can be a very large number in many enterprises, may become laggards in the journey and can cause a significant drag on enhancing agility.

Enable learning through communities

Self-organizing teams, as autonomous and independent as they may be, cannot operate in complete isolation, as they are part of a larger ecosystem within the enterprise. Teams may need to interact with each other due to dependencies, but they may also interact voluntarily to share and learn from each other. Similarly, individuals with specific skills may wish to interact with other individuals with those skills to share and learn.

People and teams getting the opportunity to interact with each other will unlock tremendous value for the business. People and teams can learn from each other's successes and failures, share innovative ideas and create an informal support system, and build and strengthen informal relationships between individuals. Companies should create a *soft* structure of communities within the overall organization structure, in order to bring people and teams together at various levels of the enterprise. Communities bring significant benefits in business including:

- ◆ Reducing the duplication of work, through the sharing of respective context.

- ◆ Upskilling and on boarding, on specific skills.

- ◆ Creating assets that may be used enterprise wide, for example, a testing community creating a test automation framework or a designer community creating design patterns.

- ◆ Sharing of learnings on successes and failures, helping to amplify successes and avoid further such failures.

- ◆ Huge enabling for breaking silos. While it is easy to get rid of silos on paper, it is much harder to get rid of the silo mindset in people, especially if it deeply entrenched. People coming together across teams and roles to connect, learn and share will tremendously help in breaking the silo mindset.

These communities should be informal and self-managing and should be encouraged to grow organically, based on the value that people and teams derive from these communities. However, leaders have a significant role to play in facilitating the creation of the communities, and in enabling people and teams to sustain them. The Spotify model [viii], as depicted in the following diagram, is a popular model that has communities across teams working in a common domain (for example, mobile), namely, tribes, across skills, and across the enterprise focusing on a capability (for example, leadership, and continuous delivery.

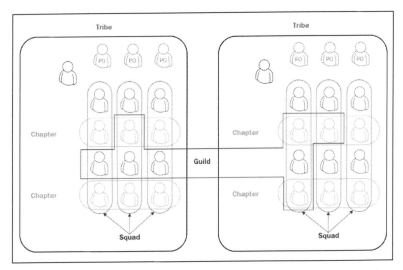

Figure 6.4: The Spotify scaling model

The preceding diagram represents how teams are structured at Spotify. A squad across functional self-organizing team which is responsible for delivering a specific feature/outcome. Each squad is supported by a **product owner** (**PO**), who is responsible for creating, maintaining, and prioritizing the backlog which the team works on to deliver features/outcomes.

Squads that work within a specific business area or a capability, for example, mobile banking and chatbots, are grouped to form a tribe. The objective of creating the tribe is to enable interaction between squads to share learnings. The tribe leaders works toward enabling interaction between squads.

Chapters are created within a tribe as communities where each community is for a specific skill. For example, squads within a tribe may consist of a business analyst, developers, and testers. A chapter can be created for all the testers within that tribe for them to interact with each other to share ways of working and experiences, so that they can learn from each other about improving there are of expertise and use it as a platform to generate innovative ideas.

A guild is a community that spans squads and tribes, which is based on a common area of interest which might span the entire company. For example, test automation and web technologies. Guilds can also be created for non-work related interests and hobbies like trekking, public speaking, and so on.

Delink employee growth from structure

This is actually not really a structure but a people-related issue. However, a change to a lean structure has an important implication from a people angle, and hence this issue is being called out in this chapter. Enterprises that are changing their structure from a tall hierarchy to a lean one should lay particular emphasis on this point. As discussed earlier, in companies with tall hierarchies, employee growth is linked to a rise in the hierarchy. A "promotion" is usually directly linked to a rise to the next level in the hierarchy. There are instances of enterprises that have added layers in the hierarchy only to make room for promoting people.

Another negative implication of growth based on hierarchy is that for someone to go higher up in the hierarchy, they have to compete with their colleagues. This is actually a zero-sum game as for the employee to win, someone has to lose that opportunity. This competition is unhealthy for agility, as colleagues become competitors and individual contribution is seen as the differentiator. As enterprises move to a lean structure, they will need to redefine what "growth" means to people and delink it from hierarchy. Otherwise, there will be tremendous resistance to change in moving to a lean structure

Adhocracy as a decision-making model

There are three common patterns for decision-making model: bureaucracy, meritocracy, and adhocracy. Each of these have a different pivot to drive decision-making. **Bureaucracy** is based on formal authority, and therefore it is not surprising that it is the dominant decision-making model in hierarchical structures. **Meritocracy** is based on the best qualified person/s making the decision. Relevant knowledge and skills and data drive decision-making in this model. **Adhocracy** is based on taking action as quickly as possible. This model tends more toward decision-making based on intuition and "just enough" information, and much less on detailed analysis and documenting the analysis prior to taking action. If there is a dilemma between a *go* and *no go* decision, adhocracy tends toward making the decision and acting on it, rather than spending more time gathering additional data and analyzing it. This is in contrast to bureaucracy, where, when decision makers are in doubt, the decision is referred to the "bosses."

There are two key tenets of adhocracy:

♦ Decision-making processes should heavily involve those closest to the context, that is, people on the "ground"

♦ Early feedback is extremely valuable and hence the bias toward early action

While adhocracy is the preferred model for decision-making, businesses, especially large ones, may have meritocracy and bureaucracy as dominant decision-making models in specific parts of the enterprise. For example, an enterprise may choose to have meritocracy-based decision-making in its R&D department, where knowledge and debate plays a far more critical role than intuition and acting fast.

Adhocracy as a decision-making model is an excellent fit with self-organizing and empowered teams, and teams organized around business outcomes. Hence, introducing adhocracy as teams are being restructured to enhance agility is imperative. It is the most appropriate decision-making model where the environment is fast-changing and unpredictable. If adhocracy is adopted in a hierarchy, it is very likely to lead to slower decisions, which defeats the primary purpose for adopting adhocracy.

Adhocracy, like any other model, is far from being perfect. Some "bets" will be super hits and some are bound to fail. For example, Amazon's bet on Amazon Web Services had paid off big time, but Amazon mobile phone has not been a success. Nonetheless, Amazon continues to have adhocracy as its primary decision-making model.

It is important to remember that what distinguishes the three decision-making models is the relative emphasis on the pivots, as mentioned earlier. Moreover, there will be trade-offs based on the choice of the model. For instance, if adhocracy is adopted, then it is inappropriate to expect predictable outcomes due to following the standard operating procedures.

According to Julian Birkinshaw, Professor and Chair of Strategy and Entrepreneurship at the London Business School, and Jonas Ridderstråle, author of the book, *Funky Business*:

"The demands of the business world often change more quickly than the organizations where we work. Many companies are still moving from the traditional bureaucratic model, which has been around for 100 years, toward a more meritocratic one built around the primacy of information and knowledge. But our analysis suggests that for many companies, this isn't enough. Meritocracy has its benefits, but we believe adhocracy will become increasingly important in the decades ahead. By understanding the benefits of all three management models, you will have a better chance of creating a style of working that positions your organization for future success." [ix]

Supportive tooling

As a business changes its structure from hierarchy style to a lean structure, and from siloed activity-oriented teams to cross-functional and outcome-driven teams, the enterprise must start replacing tools that are based on hierarchy, silos, and tracking activities rather than outcomes. Making changes to the structure is quite difficult in itself, and tools not aligned to the new structure and new ways of working will lead to a significant drag on changing the structure, which will have a cascading effect on the pace at which agility can be enhanced.

Flexible, adaptable, and lean structure

A commonly held belief, albeit a wrong one, about agility is that there is an ideal future state and that it should remain static after attaining. This belief is particularly strong about the structure of the enterprise.

As an example, the Holacracy [x] model has been adopted by Zappos, the online shoe retailer. Zappos themselves struggled to deal with the limitations of this model. An ex-Zapponian has called Holacracy a "social experiment that created chaos and uncertainty" [xi].

The content site, Medium adopted it and abandoned it. Undercurrent tried it and found that it was not suitable for them. Bud Caddel, founder of Undercurrent, has said:

"I found it extremely dogmatic and rigid and overly complex, and it took attention away from our customers."

The conclusion from these instances is that: a) there is no "utopian" structure and b) a structure that has worked for an enterprise may fail in another, thereby implying that copying a structure that has worked for another company is laden with a lot of risk.

While the principles of a structure that enables agility may be common across organizations, each enterprise will have to adopt a structure that is suited for its context, and, more importantly, keep it flexible to adapt to changing circumstances. For example, a sudden crisis, say a regulatory change that poses a threat to the survival of the enterprise, may need to be dealt with by changing into a structure which is more inward facing for a period of time, until the threat is mitigated. An enterprise may choose to optimize on efficiency, rather than on effectiveness during times of severe recession and the structure must be flexible to support the change in objective.

The Lehman Brothers, collapse in 2008, lead to a swift recession, which was particularly severe for many technology and financial services companies. In these extremely challenging conditions, many enterprises had to lay off many people quickly, and shift their focus from growing the customer base to ensuring continuity of existing customers, and to controlling costs diligently. Such major change in focus will invariably warrant a change in structure.

It is fairly obvious that an enterprise will have to modify its structure as it grows in size. An enterprise may start off by offering a single product and may have marketing and sales embedded within that product unit itself. However, as it adds more products to its offerings, the business may feel that it makes sense to centralize the marketing and sales functions to leverage synergies across products.

The challenge is not so much in modifying a structure, but in how quickly the modified structure becomes effective. Hence, flexibility and adaptability of a structure should be viewed from the perspective of how quickly the modified structure becomes effective and can further enhance the agility of the enterprise.

The key to having flexibility and adaptability in the current structure is self-organizing teams, and a lean structure enables the functioning of self-organizing teams. People in self-organizing teams manage themselves, rather than being managed by "bosses." This helps them to build the skills and capabilities needed for decision-making, including developing leadership skills and finding ways through uncertainty and ambiguity. Also, people develop capabilities to respond to the changes in the environment and are therefore become more resilient. Both these factors enable the structure to remain flexible and adaptable. Another factor that enables flexibility is people having *T-shaped skills*. This will be discussed in detail in chapter on people, namely, *Chapter 8, People*. The implication is that people are not totally blinkered by their role but can fit into other roles as needed.

The main characteristic of a lean structure is that all roles in the structure are roles that "produce" value or enable the teams to produce value. This implies that such a structure has no place for non-value adding roles, for example, roles whose primary responsibility is to collect, collate, and provide information, prepare detailed plans and track plans versus actuals, and so on.

Given that emergence is a key property of a complex system, the structure must have the flexibility to accommodate changes arising out of emergence. According to Jim Bright, Professor of Career Education and Development at Australian Catholic University, "Effective structure emerges out of effective relationships and interactions of the component elements of the organization. In this way the form emerges from function. Functional organizations work hard and continually on relationships, and from that iterative process, form emerges, that is intimately tailored to the needs of the particular organization, with their particular staff, and not some abstract, idealized, historic or borrowed examples." [xii]

Summary

In this chapter, we learned that enterprises aspiring for greater agility need to move from an organization structure focused on hierarchy-based decision-making, command and control and optimization of silos and activities to a structure that is aligned to delivering business outcomes in the most effective and efficient way. A flexible and lean structure that empowers and enables the teams to sense, respond and adapt to change will significantly aid in increasing agility.

The next chapter is about the second component of the enterprise, namely, process, and will cover the significance of process, and how to leverage process for enhancing enterprise agility.

References

[i] http://managementstudyguide.com/rise-of-knowledge-worker.htm

[ii] https://en.wikipedia.org/wiki/Knowledge_worker

[iii] https://martinfowler.com/bliki/OutcomeOriented.html

[iv] https://whatis.techtarget.com/definition/Conways-law

[v] https://salvos.org.au/scribe/sites/2020/files/Resources/Transitions/HANDOUT_-_Tuckmans_Team_Development_Model.pdf

[vi] https://medium.com/@NielsPflaeging/org-physics-the-3-faces-of-every-company-df16025f65f8

[vii] https://hbswk.hbs.edu/archive/middle-management-excellence

[viii] https://www.infoq.com/news/2016/10/no-spotify-model

[ix] https://www.mckinsey.com/business-functions/organization/our-insights/adhocracy-for-an-agile-age

[x] https://www.holacracy.org/

[xi] http://fortune.com/zappos-tony-hsieh-holacracy/

[xii] http://www.smh.com.au/business/workplace-relations/why-do-company-change-processes-seem-to-fail-so-often-20171114-gzlizs.html

7

PROCESS

This chapter focuses on the processes of an enterprise. It provides insights on optimizing processes for enhancing agility in an enterprise. A process can be defined as a series of coordinated activities designed to achieve a specific outcome. Going by this definition, anything that needs to be produced/ created should have a process. In other words, a process defines the *how* of production / the creation of output.

Processes are important in all enterprises, including those with greater agility. The difference is that in such firms, processes are designed and modified as needed to serve the needs of the staff and the goals of the organization, not the other way around.

This chapter will explore the following topics:

- ◆ The significance of process in agility
- ◆ Process inhibitors to agility
- ◆ Process enablers for agility

Significance

There is a common misconception that having agility means no processes or that processes are not important. This view comes from the first tenet of the Agile Manifesto, covered in *Chapter 2, From Agile to Agility*, which states, "Individuals and interactions over processes and tools."

What is often forgotten about is reading this tenet in the context of the last sentence in the Manifesto, which states, "That is, while there is value in the items on the right, we value the items on the left more." Hence, the Manifesto is explicitly stating that there is value in processes and tools (the items on the right), and that there is more value in individuals and interactions (the item on the left).

It is important to understand why the creators of the Agile Manifesto gave relatively less importance to processes and tools, in comparison to individuals and interactions. In enterprises that were modelled the mechanistic way, as elaborated on earlier in this book, the focus was largely on optimizing production to maximize efficiency. Most people were "doers" due to the thinker-doer separation, which implied that the knowledge needed to perform activities was embedded in a process. Due to this, anyone who violated a process was punishable. Employees were expected to focus on performing their activities exactly as laid out in the process and the process itself was expected to "bring it all together," that is, integrate the outputs, in order to deliver the expected outcome. Only "thinkers" had a view of the end-to-end process. Any exception, for which the process needed to be "broken," needed prior approval from a senior manager or sometimes even from the **Change Control Board** (**CCB**). A CCB is a group of people who are empowered to make decisions on requests for change.

A broad-based mandate for managers was to maintain the status quo, which meant that process improvement was a sporadic event. Moreover, process improvements were largely suggested and even executed by "experts," who were unlikely to have actually used the process themselves. There was a huge risk that the process would not match the context and hence, people who were associated with these processes lost faith in them.

Companies flaunted maturity model certifications, which were awarded based purely on the extent of compliance with processes. Executing a process became an end in itself, rather than a means to an end. In a trade-off scenario, complying with a process took precedence over delivering value and meeting the needs of customers. The inappropriateness of this approach to processes for knowledge work started to become evident early on.

The following graph shows the plotting of technology projects as successful, challenged, or cancelled for the period between 1994 and 2008. [i] The appalling statistics for failed and challenged IT projects, that is, projects that exceeded the budgeted time and cost and/or underdelivered on scope, as depicted in the following graph [ii], are starkly telling.

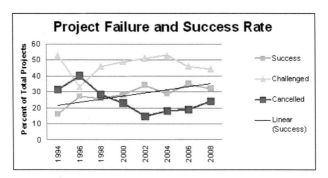

Figure 7.1: Project resolution history

It is more important to look at numbers from the period of mid-1990s to mid-2000s, as most enterprises were then struggling to come to terms with knowledge work and were just seriously beginning to realize the importance of people-centricity. As the Information Age dawned, businesses struggled to deal with the fast pace of change arising from technological innovations. The need to adapt and respond to fast-paced change meant that people, that is, knowledge workers, started to get recognition as being the most important asset for a business.

Heavyweight processes started to become impediments to change, and hence the myth that a well-defined and well-executed process is more valuable than the people who execute the process was being destroyed. Businesses began to understand that rigid, cumbersome, and efficiency-oriented processes are not at all aligned with the six capabilities underlying agility.

This in no way implies that enterprises with high agility should disregard processes. Not having processes, or following ineffective processes, will lead to chaos, just as rigid and cumbersome processes lead to mere compliance. Both of these approaches can become severe impediments to agility. Having processes that are flexible, fit for purpose, evolving based on continuous learning, maximizing effectiveness without compromising on efficiency, and providing scope for knowledge workers to be creative and innovative, will enable the enterprise to remain balanced on the line between order and chaos.

Inhibitors to agility

The following factors related to processes are the key barriers for enterprises seeking to enhance and sustain agility.

Broken processes

A process is deemed to be broken when it is consistently failing or struggling to fulfil the outcome for which it is designed. Typical symptoms of a broken process include long wait times between activities, which leads to unnecessary delays; the outcome/artefact delivered at the end of the process being of poor quality, which leads to a rework; the process having non-value-added activities (for example, an activity to perform manual testing when it is possible and feasible to automate the testing); and team members circumventing the process to get the work done.

The following are some of the key causes of broken processes:

♦ An "expert" designing the process or modifying it, without involving those who execute the process

♦ A structure that forces unnecessary hand-offs

♦ Lack of shared understanding between the owners of the process and the customers about the expected artefacts/outcomes

♦ Modification to the process which results in local optimization, but a suboptimal outcome overall

♦ Customers' needs have evolved, but the process has stayed the same, for example, continuing with paper-based evidence when it is possible to provide the evidence digitally

Broken processes result in unhappy customers and unhappy employees. They compromise on both effectiveness and efficiency. Hence, it is important to identify a broken process as early as possible and fix it by addressing the root cause. Typical anti-pattern reactions to the consequences of a broken process include:

♦ "Throwing" more people at the problem.

♦ Fixing blame on people for those problems, without investigating the root cause. According to the "85/15 rule" [iii], 85% of problems have their source in the process itself.

These measures are not only unhelpful in fixing a broken process, but they can cause serious damage to the mindset of the people involved and consequently damage the company's culture as well.

Processes not being aligned with the company's purpose/outcomes

Processes are often found to be not aligned to the intended outcome. Sometimes, they are even aligned to contradictory outcomes, for example, the outcome expected from a software development process is faster and more frequent delivery into production, but the release management process is designed to maintain the stability of the system. If the release management process owners experience, or even perceive, that fast and frequent software releases are a threat to the stability of the system, then they will resist fast and more frequent releases, thereby nullifying all the optimization of the development process.

Processes not being fit for purpose

Having a single process, without providing for any appropriate variation can result in a process not being fit for purpose, for example, a company has a policy to buy everything, including the most inexpensive things, through their standard purchasing process. So, even if someone urgently needs some stationery, say sticky notes, they need to put in a written request in the specified format to the purchase department, which needs to have the signature of the manager. The purchase department will then order the sticky notes from the preferred stationery supplier. The supplier may deliver this item as per the time-bound cadence or only after the minimum value for delivery is satisfied. The stores department will receive the sticky notes and then inform the requestor that the sticky notes have arrived. This process can easily take a week or more.

As outrageous and trivial as this example appears, this is still a reality in many enterprises, especially large ones. While it is perhaps understandable to have such a process for buying something in very large quantities, or involving huge sums of money, it does not make any sense to have such heavyweight processes for outcomes where speed is critical.

Another type of process misfit is based on the periodic frequency of the process. In many businesses, there are several critical activities, which are, as a process, done annually, for example, performance reviews of staff or allocation of funding for new initiatives. In a fast-changing environment, these processes need to run at a much faster cadence than annually. Many enterprises are yet to adapt their processes to leverage technological advances and the instant availability of information, for example, taking the preceding example of ordering stationery, the process could be modified and made drastically more efficient if ordering was done online. Keeping processes static, that is, not adapting them to make them "fit for purpose," will by default result in broken processes.

Rigid processes

Rigid processes may be effective when the nature of work is stable, done mechanically, and is repetitive. However, most of today's work is complex in nature, which implies that the work is emergent and dynamic, and constant collaboration between stakeholders is a must for delivering valuable outcomes. Under such circumstances, having to follow rigid processes can create severe impediments to agility. Today's era is about being innovative and creative in order to satisfy customers. If any instances of customer satisfaction are examined, then it is almost always because the person serving the customer has bypassed a rigid process.

Striving for 100% utilization

The mindset of striving for 100% utilization of people's time comes from a period when enterprises were aiming to maximize production. In those days, most of a company's workforce was operating machines, and keeping a machine idle meant a direct hit on the bottom line.

Aiming for 100% utilization of people's time perhaps makes sense when repetitive physical actions by the employee, or repetitive physical movements of a machine run by the employee, are directly linked to the mass production of a product. It also perhaps makes sense when external factors are not expected to disrupt the predictable flow of work.

In today's era, the nature of work is mostly knowledge work and the complexity within and outside of businesses has increased significantly. The implication is that work is not repetitive in nature and that it is instead designed and conceptualized in the minds of people. Moreover, true to the core characteristic of **complex adaptive systems (CAS)**, the interactions between employees can add significant value to the work being performed. A lot of work is complex in nature, which means that details will emerge only after an employee has started to perform a task. Recurring unprecedented circumstances and changing priorities mean that the people in teams have to spend time engaging with each other and with external stakeholders, especially as most decisions need to be made quickly and with agreed trade-offs.

A common anti-pattern is to push people to work beyond 100% utilization, when progress appears to be falling behind the plan. This is reflected in people having to work 12-14 hours per day and working over weekends. The core belief behind this push is that extra effort can help to catch up with the delay. The point that is missed is that in knowledge work, extra hours do not always mean additional productivity. In fact, sustained periods of long hours can leave people exhausted, frustrated, and filled with resentment and therefore demotivated.

According to Will Hayes, a senior member of the technical staff at Carnegie Mellon Software Engineering Institute, "This deterministic treatment of an intrinsically variable process may be an artifact of our reliance on manufacturing examples to explain how software project management works.

We behave as if there is a strict algebraic relationship between the micro and the macro, without appreciation for the coupling among the technical tasks or the wide range of engineering talents among the staff (among other things). Packing the schedules of the staff and asking them to multitask under pressure does not result in speeding up the program." [iv]

To make matters worse, some companies make knowledge workers work long hours by paying them overtime, with a belief that more hours will result in more output. According to Jason Lengstorf, a lead developer and architect at IBM, "The thinking behind why managers believe twice the hours results in twice the output is short-sighted and toxic. Companies who regularly enter "crunch mode" forget to consider that their employees are humans — susceptible to fatigue, burnout, resentment, unhappiness — and not robots." He adds, "If she's asked to work extra hours, she *will* produce extra output. But since she's already pretty beat after eight hours, the extra output will be pretty low, and at a high cost." [v]

The problem lies in the way that utilization is measured and thereby enforced. A commonly found method, in some parts of the world, is to monitor how long employees remain logged in to their computers. The ludicrous presumption is that if an employee remains logged out for some time, quite likely due to being in conversation with a colleague or even ideating on a whiteboard by themselves, the logged-out time should be treated as non-working time. Such regressive measures will not only impact the effectiveness of the team but also will have a negative impact on the overall mindset and culture in the company.

Another related anti-pattern is about capacity planning in advance, based on time and the number of people in a team. The critical factors that influence a team's capacity are the skills available in the team and also how proficient people are in their skills.

Other factors include dependencies on other teams, which can lead to the slowing down of the flow of work—to what extent the work units are homogenous and the chemistry between the team members. The true capacity of a team, measured by the velocity of points or number of work units, as recommended by Agile methodologies, emerges once the team has got into the "rhythm" of delivery. The actual throughput by the team is a meaningful indicator of the team's capacity, from a planning perspective. For example, if a team is delivering approximately 20 points in an iteration, and if the backlog remaining is of 100 points, then it is highly likely, assuming that all things stay constant, that the team will deliver the backlog in five iterations.

There are techniques such as *raw velocity* [vi], which is estimated velocity that is not based on actual data, and therefore calculated at the beginning of the project, which can be used for estimation when actual data on throughput is not yet available. 100% utilization, or something close to it, may be theoretically possible. However, the negative consequences of this will negate the benefits, if any, of coming from approaching utilization the manufacturing way. Computers almost stop functioning when CPU capacity utilization nears 100%. There is an inevitable traffic jam when the capacity of a road is 100% utilized. Imagine if an ambulance, with a critical patient, needs to pass through the traffic jam. Keeping the emergency lane free is technically a waste of capacity, but that's simply the right thing to do.

Estimation and capacity planning done by "outsiders"

Another related anti-pattern is about capacity planning that is done by managers, rather than the producers. The best judges of capacity are the people in the team who are expected to deliver the work. Hence, they should be providing the estimates, and revising them based on emergent information if needed, and not someone who is not going to be involved in doing the work.

Recent thought leadership is leaning toward no estimates, with a movement called *#noestimates*. [vii] Those advocating estimation and those wanting to do away with it agree that better predictability is needed for teams, customers, and project sponsors. The *#noestimates* movement leaders believe that predictability can be achieved by keeping teams stable, limiting work in progress, and establishing regular frequency of delivery, which can be supported by collaboration, visibility, and transparency throughout the delivery cycle. The underlying assumption is that if small chunks of work are delivered at regular short intervals, the throughput itself can serve as an estimate for the balance of work.

Enablers for enhancing agility

The following factors related to processes can significantly help enterprises to enhance agility. The enablers suggested are primarily derived from the principles of Kanban, which is a means to design, manage, and improve flow systems for knowledge work. [viii]

Optimize for outcomes

A process produces outputs, which should deliver a valuable outcome to the consumer and the enterprise as a whole as well. However, it is not uncommon that despite the output being optimal, the outcome is still unsatisfactory, for example, a restaurant serving burgers has designed and optimized the process for producing burgers with respect to speed, quality, and cost. However, if the customer is not satisfied with the burger then the outcome is poor, despite the outputs being optimal. If the customer finds the burger lacking in taste or the burger is too messy to eat, then despite the burger meeting the criteria of speed, quality, and cost, it has not delivered a valuable outcome for the customer. The burger has also not delivered a valuable outcome for the business, as the customer may not return again.

The key to bridging the gap between output and outcome is getting feedback from the customer as early as possible, and then tweaking the process to make the necessary changes in the output. Continuing with the burger example, the customer may be willing to pay a higher price in order to get an improved taste with more spices and a patty that is roasted a bit more. The process must be changed accordingly, to deliver the output desired by the customer.

It is clear from the preceding example that a process can be optimized for outcomes only if it includes a mechanism to collect feedback and quickly make the necessary modifications. This is especially important when an enterprise is attempting to introduce a new proposition. The agility capabilities of sense, adapt, and respond are critical for aligning processes for delivering valuable outcomes.

Valuable inputs

A process must be viewed as an enabler for delivering value. This implies that the process can produce valuable outputs only if the inputs are valuable or are in a state in which value addition through the process is possible. Continuing with the example of the burger, if the quality of the bun/wheat flour is poor, then the quality of the burger is bound to be poor, as optimized as the process of creating the burger may be. An example of input hindering value addition in the process is a software delivery process that is optimized to minimize the time to market of a feature, but the feature that is put through the process is so large that faster delivery is simply not possible.

Another key takeaway about this point is that when the quality of the output is below expectations, or the output is failing to realize the expected outcome, the root cause of the problem may be in the inputs and not necessarily in the process. Attempting to fix or optimize a process when the inputs are suboptimal will be futile.

The most effective way to maximize the outcome is to focus on delivering outputs with the highest value. This is possible only if the inputs that have the highest value are put through the process with the highest priority. Obviously, value must be determined based on customer needs. Since the priorities are liable to change quickly, it is important to revalidate the priorities of the inputs just before they enter the process.

"Pull-based" flow

In a "pull-based" process, the person completing a task will pick up an item to work on only when they have finished working on the previous item. This is the opposite of a "push-based" process, where items of work are allocated, usually in a batch, to specific people. There are multiple advantages to the "pull" method:

♦ It keeps people focused, as they are working on only one thing at a time.

♦ It forces the relevant stakeholders to assign priorities to work items, thereby the team gets clarity on the highest priority items which need to be worked upon first. Since the highest value work items are worked on first, the possibility of wasteful work is minimized.

♦ It is easier to cater to changing priorities.

♦ It helps people to work at a sustainable pace.

♦ It eliminates the need for upfront detailed planning.

♦ It helps to keep inventory/work in progress levels in the "sweet spot", that is, not too much and not too little.

♦ It helps with identifying process problems.

The "pull-based" process is far more effective when it is supplemented with **work in process (WIP)** limits at activity/status/stage level in the workflow. WIP limits bring in the culture of getting items to the "done" status in an optimal way.

It forces people to complete the activity and move the work item to the next stage, only after which the next item to be worked upon can be picked up. This, therefore, enables a smooth flow of work, assuming that any work items do not remain blocked for an unreasonable amount of time. It also enables teams to deliver the highest priority items faster than others, thereby enabling the faster realization of benefits, including getting early feedback, accruing from delivering the outcome.

Keeping WIP to a minimum helps to minimize cycle time, which is an excellent indicator of the efficiency of a process. Cycle time is defined as the time taken to complete a task. It is calculated by dividing the total number of items in WIP in the entire process by the throughput, for example, if WIP is 40 items and the average throughput is two items per day, then the cycle time is 20 days. If the WIP drops to 30 items, then the cycle time drops to 15 days. The point is that the cycle time has dropped despite the throughput remaining the same. It is important to keep in mind that some level of WIP is needed to ensure a smooth flow of work, given that activities in the flow take varying amounts of time. The optimal level of WIP and throughput is that which helps the team to consistently deliver value.

The other key benefit of having WIP limits is that the effects arising from the limits provide clear pointers to problems in specific areas in the process. For example, if work items are getting piled up in, say, a "ready for testing" status, then the next stage in the process (testing) needs to be investigated. The problem could be that the testers are blocked from completing the work items on hand due to the non-availability of environments or because the testers are working on multiple items at a time, thereby leaving them unable to complete any item early or the testing function is falling short on capacity.

A "pull-based" system is appropriate only when the work units arriving into the work pipeline are controllable. It is not appropriate when units arrive randomly, for example, customers coming into a supermarket.

Make it visual

In manufacturing, the production line is visible and hence the flow of work is also visible. However, knowledge work is intangible, so the flow of work is not visible and therefore it is harder to spot the problems in the flow. In order to make the flow visible, discrete work items should be abstractly represented on a Kanban board [ix], against their respective stage/status. Kanban boards can be created physically and also electronically. The following screenshot is a sample representation of a physical Kanban board for a software development process:

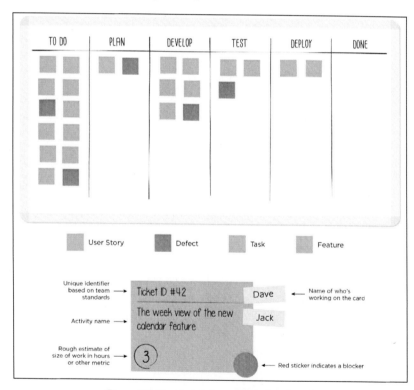

Figure 7.2: Representation of a Kanban board

A Kanban board provides a visual way to track the flow of work by showing the WIP items in the various stages of the workflow. The work units belong to different categories (user story, defect, and so on), each having a distinct visual representation. The board also depicts the information that is tagged to each work unit.

The most significant benefit of making the process, and real-time flow of work, visual is that human brains process visuals 60,000 times faster than text [x]. A Kanban board helps teams to understand status and progress, and spot problems quickly and easily. Moreover, it brings in transparency, which is so critical to agility. The Kanban board creates a shared language that is easily understood not only within the team but also by stakeholders outside the team. Needless to say, the board is valuable only when it is updated as often as needed to display real-time information.

Physical boards are appropriate when the whole or a large part of the team is co-located. However, for teams whose members are distributed an electronic board is necessary, as the board becomes the "single source of truth" for all team members, regardless of location. Enterprises wanting to use a Kanban board at scale may also consider using the electronic version. It must be noted that metrics such as cycle time and cumulative flow diagrams are generated much more easily from an electronic board.

Seize opportunities to automate

Due to technological innovations and viability, it is now possible for businesses to automate repetitive and mundane activities. This includes activities related to data entry, notifications, reporting, systems integration, testing, deployment, and reconciliation. With the emergence of **artificial intelligence** (**AI**), the potential to automate activities that are repetitive, but need human judgement, is enormous. A large bank in India is using AI for matching signatures on cheques issued by customers. Automating such an activity, which needs judgement, perhaps would not have been imaginable just a few years ago.

The advantages of automation are highly significant, as it results in very high efficiency in terms of time and effort. The elimination of human errors provides safety nets for connected activities and, most importantly, liberates the knowledge worker from doing mundane tasks, thereby freeing up the brain power of the knowledge worker to do higher-value activities. Specific examples of benefits for companies are as follows:

- A single-click deployment of software into production, which happens in a matter of minutes. This has enabled the deployment decision to become a business-driven decision rather than a technology-constrained decision. A real instance of this happening concerns a global food retailer, whose CEO would attend the demo at the end of every iteration for a project related to ordering pizza via mobile phones. If he liked the demo of the feature, he would just need to click on the button for the feature to become available in production, that is, to the customers, within a few moments of clicking on the button.

- A release team size being reduced from 100 to a mere two people.

- An unsecured loan being disbursed to an existing customer within just 10 seconds from the customer indicating that they want a loan.

- Frequent code check-ins, due to the automation of unit tests and continuous integration.

If teams are appropriately empowered, then they are highly likely to find automation opportunities and also to develop the tools needed for this. A team at ThoughtWorks created Selenium [xi], in order to automate unit tests. Not only has ThoughtWorks benefited from this tool but it has also been widely adopted across the globe.

Use of enabling tools

The advent of the internet and technological innovations has led to a vast choice of tools being available to perform a wide range of activities. These activities include data entry, data extraction, systems integration, testing, and project management. Tools have been particularly useful in helping to automate mundane and repetitive activities that have led to a significant increase in both the efficiency and effectiveness of processes, for example, the adoption of appropriate tools has helped an enterprise based in the UK, selling train tickets through its digital platform to reduce its DevOps staff from 100 to 2, as stated earlier, and also to reduce the software release cycle time from days to a few minutes.

Using the appropriate tools is critical for optimizing processes. An inappropriate tool can severely constrain a process or render it ineffective, for example, project management tools suited for the waterfall methodology are based on the scope of the product/project being frozen upfront, the micro-level work allocation plan being prepared on day one for the entire project and the estimation completed based on hours/days. Such tools are completely unsuitable for a team using the Agile methodology, in which scope management is carried out based on a backlog, micro plans are prepared just in time, and estimation is done based on story points or on the number of user stories. Similarly, a centralized version control system can severely paralyze the working of a software development team which is distributed across multiple locations.

Another pitfall, which should be avoided, is trying to fit the process to the tool. This is not only in terms of the workflow but also the information captured in the tool. Tools should be used to enable a process and not the other way around. Tools must be customized as needed to fit the process. Sometimes, multiple tools are used within the same process, which can lead to loss of efficiency and effectiveness, for example, customers use tool A to log defects, but the defect management is done through tool B.

If these tools do not integrate properly, then there is the potential for confusion and slippages. Quite often, tools can be constraining for the teams if they are not configured properly. Hence, relevant members from teams should be involved actively when tools are being configured.

Tools should be proactively upgraded, supplemented, and replaced as appropriate. This is because a better version of the tool is available or other tools, which need to integrate with a specific tool, have evolved, thereby creating compatibility issues or there is a change in circumstances that renders the current tool ineffective. An example of this is VPNs, which are a decade old and may not be able to deal with the latest network security threats. Communication and collaboration within and between teams is critical for enhancing agility, and hence relevant tools should be used for these purposes as well. A common misconception is that tools cost a lot of money. Certainly, some tools do but many tools are now available as open source.

Build quality in

The traditional approach to quality has been to have testing as a separate activity towards the end of the process. This approach originated from the mechanistic mindset, where perhaps the hypothesis was that if the quality of inputs into the process was satisfactory, and if the process was optimized to eliminate variability, then the quality of the end product would also be satisfactory. The waterfall methodology, which was used for multiple decades for developing software, took the same approach to quality by having testing as the "gatekeeper" stage towards the end of the process, that is, just before the software was ready to be deployed.

Obviously, poor or substandard quality has a cost for the enterprise. However, it is often quite difficult to quantify the impact of poor quality and usually the cost remains severely underestimated. While some costs, like time spent fixing the defect, may be measurable, others, like impact of customer dissatisfaction, loss of reputation, dip in employee morale, and the opportunity cost of time and money spent on a rework, are quite difficult to measure, if measuring is possible at all. This non-quantification of a negative impact leads to a business not understanding the extent of the negative impact, which often results in minimizing cost and speeding up delivery being prioritized over quality.

Philip Crosby, author of the book *Quality Is Free*, states, "The basic aim of quality management is prevention. Quality control is aimed at detection, finding problems as early as possible, and getting them fixed — and that's a noble thing. But what we want to do is vaccinate the company with the quality philosophy of prevention. So instead of setting up the world's largest smallpox hospital, we vaccinate people and then we don't need a smallpox hospital. That's the same way you have to run a company, by preventing the problems." He adds, "The symbolic way of saying doing things right the first time is zero defects. That's the third absolute, that zero defects is the performance standard, not some acceptable level of defects like six sigma. It means doing exactly what you said you were going to do — that's really the definition of quality." [xii]

In an era where customers are likely to severely "punish" poor quality, the approach to quality needs to shift from "finding defects" to "preventing defects," and the mindset needs to change from quality being the tester's responsibility to quality being the responsibility of not only everyone in the team but also of every person in the organization. Excellent quality has to simply become non-negotiable.

Processes should be designed such that quality is built in right from the start. This is particularly significant for knowledge work, which is emergent in nature. The implication of emergence is that teams will come across new information and unprecedented circumstances while they are performing the work, and therefore they will have to come up with creative ways to deal with emergence. This can often lead to teams deciding and acting "on the fly." It is, therefore, critical to objectify the quality goals, not only for the output but also for the process itself.

An example of objective quality criteria for the output is specifying acceptance criteria [xiii] for every user story, which is a requirements artefact and the primary unit of work in one of the Agile methodologies. These are specific quality attributes for a given requirement, specified from the perspective of the user of the software. Defining the quality criteria upfront enables the customer and the team to be aligned about expectations of quality, with reference to customer requirements. The objectiveness of the criteria makes it easy for the team to estimate the incremental cost of catering to that criteria, which enables the customer to make a conscious assessment about the cost versus value of the solution being able to satisfy that criteria. It is quite likely that a customer may consciously choose to not include a criterion for an edge case, if the cost exceeds the potential value.

While defining quality criteria upfront is the aim, it is important to balance the natural tension between knowing and specifying everything upfront versus being open and adaptable to emergent information. The effective way to manage this tension is to continue having conversations with the relevant stakeholders and evolving the criteria based on the outcome of the conversations. For ensuring the quality of a process, the objective criteria can be specified for each activity in the process, that is, the activity can be treated as *done* only if all the criteria for that activity are met. By doing this, quality is intrinsically built into every step in the process.

Enable teamwork and shared ownership

The value of knowledge work is significantly enhanced through teamwork and shared ownership of the output and outcome. Processes should have built-in mechanisms, as appropriate, to enable communication and collaboration, which leads to better teamwork and shared ownership. For instance, in the software development process, an iteration planning meeting can be built into the process to enable a conversation between the development team and the business stakeholders. This will confirm the priorities and the work planned for the iteration. Similarly, at the end of the iteration, a showcase meeting can be part of the process, in order to get feedback from the business stakeholders/customers.

One of the glaring anti-patterns, which goes against shared ownership of output, is creating work units that are based on activity and tracking progress against the deliverables, based on the completion of those activities. The following is a visual representation of this pattern:

To do	Work in progress	Done
		Feature A analysis
		Feature A UX design
		Feature A development
	Feature A testing	
	Feature B analysis	
Feature B UX design		
Feature B development		
Feature B testing		

Figure 7.3: Activity-based work units

In this scenario, features **A** and **B** have been respectively broken up into four activities, namely, analysis, UX design, development, and testing. Hence, each of these activities is a discrete work unit, which can move through the process, provided that the predecessor activity is completed. Work units created this way are a huge deterrent to shared ownership. In the preceding scenario, feature **A** can be treated as *done* only after the testing activity is completed. Let's assume that the tester performing testing on feature **A** needs help from the analyst, who has moved on to work on the analysis of feature **B**. There is simply no incentive for the analyst to help the tester in this situation, especially if the analyst is being measured based on the speed of completion of each activity. They will be far keener to complete the analysis of feature **B**, rather than to help the tester to complete feature **A**.

Another serious implication of measuring work progress on activities moving to **Done** is that it encourages showing incremental progress based on work which is partially completed, that is, it is not usable by the customer or cannot be moved to the next process, as applicable. Assuming, for the purpose of the example, that all four activities are equal in size, then there is really no value in stating that feature **A** is 75% complete. Work units must be carved out such that, when done, they are valuable in themselves. Hence, when something is said to be *done* at the end of the process, it must be 100% done. *Done* therefore is binary: either a work unit is fully done or it is not yet done. The better way is to set up the process and break down the work is as follows:

To do	Analysis	Development	Testing	Done
			Feature A	
	Feature B			

Figure 7.4: Feature-based work units

In this scenario, the success of the team depends on feature **A** moving to **Done**. Until it gets to "done," the fact that the analyst and the developer have already completed their activities does not become valuable. For the analyst working on feature **B** and also for the team, it is far more valuable at this stage to help the tester to move feature **A** to **Done** over working to complete feature **B**. Notice that there is no separate state in the process for UX design. This could be because the UX designer has a role to play in all the three stages of the process. The tasks due to be completed by the UX designer can be tracked in the exit criteria for each of the stages.

Determine capacity based on throughput

The negative consequences of pushing utilization close to 100% have been discussed. Taking this a step further, it is important to consider the nature of knowledge work when planning the utilization of capacity.

Knowledge work, by definition, is complex. Therefore, knowledge workers need to analyze problems and issues on the fly and often experiment to come up with new solutions. The team may often need to do a *spike* [xiv], which is a timeboxed investigation completed to improve contextual understanding of the problem, to come up with potential solutions or check the feasibility of a solution. Hence, the variability in knowledge work is very high when compared to mechanical work, where variability is highly controllable and therefore predictability is very high. Capacity utilization needs to provide for some slack to handle the variability. Assuming that the nature of work is consistent, then the throughput trend of the past should be used to plan the work, as it factors in the time spent by the team on average on not only handling the complexities of the knowledge work, but continuous improvement activities as well.

Focusing on utilization leads to people focusing on being busy, which can lead to teams paying little or no attention to problems in the process and improving the process. On the other hand, focusing on throughput leads people to become mindful of anything which slows down the flow of work. Hence, work which is blocked, work which is in a waiting state for an unreasonable amount of time due to dependencies, and time and effort that is wasted on reworks are likely to get attention. Enterprises are now beginning to implement throughput accounting [xv], which helps to identify inhibiting factors toward reaching goals, to guide decision-making.

Summary

This chapter focused on how enterprises aspiring for greater agility need to move away from rigid, heavyweight, and activity-oriented processes to having processes that optimize flow, quality, throughput, outcomes, and collaboration. Building processes that are fit for purpose and having agility is not dichotomous. Companies must have processes that serve people and ambitions, not the other way around.

The next chapter is about the third and most important component of a business: the significance of people and how to leverage their capabilities for enhancing enterprise agility.

References

[i] https://ecaminc.com/index.php/blog/item/166-project-failure-bunk

[ii] https://courses.cs.ut.ee/MTAT.03.243/2014_spring/uploads/Main/standish.pdf, p.2

[iii] http://userpages.chorus.net/wmssms/process/3.htm

[iv] https://insights.sei.cmu.edu/sei_blog/2017/12/
agile-metrics-a-new-approach-to-oversight.
html?utm_content=bufferaa541&utm_medium=social&utm_
source=linkedin.com&utm_campaign=buffer

[v] https://lengstorf.com/overtime-hurts-productivity/

[vi] https://info.thoughtworks.com/rs/thoughtworks2/
images/twebook-perspectives-estimation_1.pdf, p. 10

[vii] https://plan.io/blog/noestimates-6-software-
experts-give-their-view/

[viii] https://www.agilealliance.org/glossary/kanban/

[ix] https://leankit.com/learn/kanban/kanban-board/

[x] http://www.t-sciences.com/news/humans-process-
visual-data-better

[xi] https://en.wikipedia.org/wiki/Selenium_(software)

[xii] http://www.industryweek.com/quality/philip-
crosby-quality-still-free

[xiii] https://www.leadingagile.com/2014/09/acceptance-
criteria/

[xiv] http://www.extremeprogramming.org/rules/spike.
html

[xv] https://en.wikipedia.org/wiki/Throughput_
accounting

8

PEOPLE

This chapter focuses on the people component of the enterprise and provides insights on optimizing this for enhancing agility. The onset of the Information Age has been the trigger for businesses to recognize the importance and the value of knowledge. In this era of disruption, arising from fast-paced change, enterprises are realizing that the foundation of their competitive advantage has shifted from mass production to knowledge-based outcomes. The enablers for knowledge-based outcomes are based on innate human attributes: creativity, innovation, learnability, passion, teamwork, and collaboration, to name just a few. In today's era, it is these attributes that are driving the creation of products and services, compared to labor and capital in the industrial era. It is therefore not surprising that enterprises are recognizing the importance of people as critical enablers of agility.

The chapter will explore the following topics:

- ◆ The significance of people in agility
- ◆ People-related inhibitors to agility
- ◆ People-related enablers for agility

Significance

"People are our most important asset" is an age-old cliché. However, a company's level of agility is directly correlated with how the business brings out and nurtures the potential of the people. The underlying capabilities of agility (responsiveness, versatility, flexibility, resilience, innovativeness, and adaptability) are effective and sustainable only when all people, and not just leaders, are able to unlock and utilize their potential to create and deliver valuable outcomes to satisfy customers.

As discussed in *Chapter 3, The Enterprise as a Living System*, people-centricity is the essence of agility. Putting people above everything else, and harnessing their potential capabilities, is absolutely critical in order for enterprises to become a living system.

Inhibitors to agility

The following factors related to people are key barriers for enterprises seeking to enhance and sustain agility.

Mechanistic view of people

Due to the "hangover" of the industrial era, or because management education is yet to come to terms with knowledge work, many enterprises, especially those led by "old school" leaders, continue to show traces of treating people like machines and cogs in a process. The machine in this context is defined in the traditional sense of a closed-ended system, which is incapable of learning on its own.

The most critical difference between a human and a machine is that a machine is cold and impersonal, while a human has emotions. It is emotions that make a human care and feel the need for appreciation and a sense of belonging, dignity, and respect. It is emotions that create a desire to learn.

If there is a problem in the working of a machine, then the exact faulty part can be easily identified and replaced, without impacting the rest of the machine. Humans are far more complex and hence it is very difficult to have a machine-like fix for an emotion-related problem. Another important difference is that humans can think on their own, while machines cannot.

The damaging consequence of treating humans as machines is that they are unlikely to be engaged with their work and with the company as a whole. The consequences of employees being disengaged are very serious. Some prominent consequences are indifferent customer service, employee absenteeism, a higher risk of costly mistakes, curbed creativity, and apathy toward continuous improvement. Moreover, disengagement is highly contagious and can cause the culture to turn toxic very fast.

According to Infosurv Research, "A 2013 Gallup poll for American Express found that 70% of American workers are disengaged, and an ADP study estimated the real cost of employee disengagement at $2,246 per disengaged employee. The total economic impact of employee engagement in the U.S. easily runs into billions of dollars each year, by one estimate over $400B." [i] This cost does not include the impact of disengaged employees on engaged employees.

Some of the important visible signs of this anti-pattern, that is, something that seems like a good approach but actually results in bad outcomes, are as follows:

- ◆ People being thought of as "bodies" that are easily replaceable

- ◆ People don't need to think and just have to rigorously follow the process

- ◆ Micromanagement of how people spend their time at work

♦ Not involving people in decision-making

♦ Lack of empathy and support when people are going through a difficult event/period

Treating human capital like machines is a sure way of destroying enterprise agility.

Lack of trust

Companies, intentionally or otherwise, show mistrust in people when they give more importance to policies and procedures over performance and employee wellbeing. An example found in some parts of the world, even today, is subjecting an employee to disciplinary action for a few instances of coming late to the office. Some enterprises take it even further by monitoring how much time the employee spends in the cafeteria and deducting that time from the stipulated number of hours the employee must work for. Another example, though rare, is asking for documentary proof when the employee takes time off for being sick.

Human beings are varied with respect to their mindsets and their personal circumstances. The problem arises when enterprises introduce rules and processes on occurrences of exceptional behaviors, rather than choosing to treat them as exceptions by having conversations with the specific people involved. This largely happens because the managers and leaders want to avoid having those difficult conversations and prefer to let the process take care of the problem.

The newly introduced process de facto becomes applicable to everyone in the business, even those who have never displayed any negative behaviors or tried to cheat the system, for example, a salesperson was found to be frequently entertaining potential clients at exorbitantly expensive restaurants. When this pattern was noticed by the internal auditor, the company introduced the process of every salesperson needing to get prior approval from their boss for entertaining a client.

Instead of having a conversation with the salesperson who ran up the high entertainment expense bills, the company introduced a process that became applicable to all the sales staff.

According to Tine Thygesen, ex-CEO and co-founder of Everplaces, a mobile technology company:

> *"Process is unquestionably useful to a certain extent, as the counterweight to disorder. For a company to execute swiftly it needs a clear structure of who does what, and when. This will remain a priority. The problem is that many organizations have over-engineered themselves into a setup where standards, scorecards and checklists trump common sense and human thinking."* [ii]

Lack of trust is the biggest people-related impediment to enterprise agility, as it leads to loss of motivation and engagement. Conversely, employees that feel that they are trusted can create a significantly positive impact. According to a survey by HBR and Energy Group, employees who felt that their leaders treated them with respect (that is, trusted them) were 63% more satisfied with their jobs, 55% more engaged, 58% more focused, and 110% more likely to stay with their organization. [iii]

Blaming people

When something fails or has gone wrong, the first instinct of many traditional leaders and managers is "whose neck can I chop for this." The mental model behind this thinking is that the source of problems always lies in people. However, this mental model is wrong in the context of both mechanistic and knowledge work.

In mechanistic and repetitive types of work, the mandate for people is to comply with the process. The reasons for things going wrong in this type of work are almost always related to the process.

According to Dr. W. Edwards Deming, author of the book *The New Economics for Industry, Government, Education*, 94% of problems are attributable to the system and only 6% are attributable to factors like human mistakes, which are outside of the system. [iv] For example, defects related to a manufactured product like a car can be mostly traced back to the quality of a specific part of the car such as an air bag or in the integration of parts, such as, alignment of the wheel. The question to ask is: could the process have been better for checking quality or was there a slip up in someone not complying with the process? In case it is the latter, there has to be acceptance that human beings by definition are imperfect, so inadvertent human errors are always a possibility. The ways to mitigate this are in the process itself, namely, either the repetitive activity can be automated, or an extra step can be introduced in the process to check the quality. The point is that when something goes wrong, a systemic analysis of the process is the right thing to do, rather than instinctively blaming people for the failure, particularly for mistakes.

However, if the root cause is found to be people-related, then the mistake could have been made because an employee simply had a bad day at work or is inadequately trained or has a careless attitude. Each of these reasons needs to be handled in a different way. In the first case, any work that is knowledge-driven, that is, which cannot be automated or delegated to a machine, should involve interaction with other people, preferably as part of a team. So even if one team member is having a bad day at work, the team should be able to compensate for it. In case the person needs training, the action to be taken is obvious. An attitude issue needs to be dealt with through conversations with the manager and if that does not work then perhaps the company needs to let the person go.

Unlike mechanistic work, knowledge work has much greater variability. This type of work needs human judgement and human skills such as analysis, communication, and creativity. While processes are important, blindly complying with processes is completely inappropriate for this type of work. Whether something has gone wrong can only be determined based on whether the work has created the expected outcome/impact or not.

In knowledge work, while there may be patterns of good practices, there is usually no single best way. Given this, blaming people when the outcome has not met expectations is not the solution to improving the outcome. What is needed is fast feedback about the outcome/impact and the ability to learn from what has not worked well. Blaming people makes the staff feel threatened. Feeling threatened leads to disengagement, which is one of the biggest impediments to agility. Blame destroys motivation and makes people focused on self-interest alone. It's akin to "shooting the messenger," which in no way helps to identify the root cause of the problem. The focus must always be on "what went wrong" rather than on "who went wrong." Only then will people be encouraged to take responsibility for their decisions and contribute toward identifying and solving the underlying problems.

Feeling of "being used"

Similar to the impact of blaming people, giving employees the feeling of "being used" leads to disengagement and therefore this is a huge impediment to agility. Typically, this feeling is linked to the actions and behaviors of bosses and leaders, where the message being conveyed is that employees are a means to an end, which can lead to the feeling of being exploited.

A typical example is when people are laid off citing financial compulsions and at the end of that financial year, the senior executives are rewarded with bonuses for positively impacting the bottom line. Other examples of damaging leadership behaviors include being asked to work weekends, while the bosses appear to be taking the weekend off; the company backtracking on commitments, favoritism toward "yes" people, and using people as "pawns" to settle scores with peers. Any behaviors from leaders that are perceived as self-promoting at the cost of others are highly likely to create the feeling of "being used."

Lack of appreciation

According to John E. Groberg, author of the book, *Spiral Up Yoga*:

> *"Appreciation is the deepest need of our ego, deeper even than love (at least what the ego thinks of as love). The ego craves appreciation and it will go to great lengths to find it from outside itself. If it isn't feeling appreciated in a job or in a relationship, it will soon start seeking a new job or a new relationship where it thinks it can find more appreciation. We have the power to give our ego the appreciation it craves, but all too often we think that appreciation is something that comes from outside us from others."* [v]

The preceding quote underscores the need for appreciation in the workplace. Appreciation, expressed through recognition, increases job satisfaction, motivation and engagement, and lack of appreciation result in exactly the opposite outcome. According to a study by OfficeTeam, feeling appreciated often makes the difference between a worker staying and leaving the enterprise.

The findings of the study were that 66% of employees would "likely leave their job if they didn't feel appreciated." This is up significantly from 51% of employees who felt this way in 2012. The percentage is higher for millennials at 76%. [vi]

The "that's not my job" attitude

This attitude is actually a symptom of a problem that has its roots in setting expectations at the time of hiring for using a specific skill, having a tight job description, and being encouraged to work in silos. More importantly, it is also a symptom of disengagement. This attitude gets reinforced when people see their leaders reflecting this attitude.

Bad attitude is a huge impediment to agility as the focus is not primarily on creating value for the customer, but on ensuring self-interest and local optimization. The negative impact of this is particularly severe when people who are directly facing customers display this attitude. Using authority to make people fall in line might appear to work overtly for a while. However, it does not address the underlying problem of disengagement and actually is likely to make things worse.

The "yes boss" mindset

According to the Cambridge Dictionary, a "yes person" is "a person who agrees with everything their employer, leader, and so on says in order to please them." [vii] The fear of displeasing the boss and/or the desire to remain "in the good books" of the boss has several negative implications. Firstly, the boss may be more interested in furthering their own interests, at the cost of the interests of the enterprise. Challenging the boss on actions that may not be in the best interests of the business may result in falling out of the "good books" of the boss.

Secondly, even when the boss and subordinate are thinking about the interests of the enterprise, it is possible that the subordinate may have a better idea, but will be afraid to state it, due to the fear of this difference in opinion being seen as dissent by the boss. The opportunity to have a healthy debate, thereby deriving value from the interaction between "agents", is simply lost. Moreover, it discourages accountability as, if something goes wrong, it was the boss who made the decision.

The suppression of thinking and having to follow "orders" without being able to express a counter point of view leads to frustration, resentment and disengagement. Another highly toxic impact is that such a culture creates the wrong type of competition among people, who are striving to please the boss and get ahead.

The root of this culture lies in the boss being the sole decider of the salary increase and promotion of the subordinates. Typically, the boss is given a fixed sum of money that they have to distribute between subordinates and the subordinates compete among themselves to keep the boss happy, so that they can maximize their rewards.

Louisa Devadason, an editorial associate at Leaderonomics, has summarized how "yes boss" syndrome impedes agility. She says:

"If a company has cultivated a yes-man culture, they have unwittingly bred a culture of people who are either too afraid to say anything or just shut up and collect their pay cheques. A corporate landscape and a leader that does not welcome some opposition and moreover collaboration, is doomed to be stuck and risk the business being bogged down." [viii]

Competition among individuals

Most enterprises encourage competition among individuals, overtly or otherwise, with the intent that it will spur people to be the best, leading to increased productivity. Direct competition is encouraged through means like performance-linked bonuses from a fixed pool of money, while indirect competition is encouraged through forced ranking systems. [ix] While healthy competition can spur people to better themselves, more often than not competition turns unhealthy, which results in consequences that are detrimental for the people and consequently the business.

Often, the essence of competition is based on comparison between people. People who are judged as comparatively better than others are rewarded more than those who are seen as relatively worse performers. Competition leads to the promotion of self-interest over the interests of the company and even the team. Typical signs of competition turning into rivalry between people include softer aspects like an unwillingness to collaborate, to harder and more visible aspects like bullying. When competition turns into rivalry, it becomes a zero-sum game for the enterprise, as the person who has not "won" will be perceived or will perceive themselves as the "loser." This can lead to low morale, high stress and resentment for the "loser."

By definition, competition involves judgement and the possibility of being judged as a failure leads to fear and the erosion of trust. According to Evan Rosen, author of *The Culture of Collaboration*, "Perhaps the most significant way that internal competition derails collaboration involves trust. How can we trust one another if we're competing in a dog-eat-dog culture? Instead of trust, fear prevails." [x] Sometimes, people can go to extremes to compete. At Wells Fargo, for example, employees delivered higher sales numbers by secretly creating millions of unauthorized bank and credit card accounts—an unethical path toward results that has very high long-term costs. [xi]

One of the commonly used techniques in appraising the performance of people is the Bell Curve [xii], which induces competition among people, to fight for a place on the right side of the curve. The main problem with this method is that it is based purely on categorizing people based on relative performance. Hence, even if the entire group has performed well, individually and collectively, the curve forces the manager to identify relative underperformers. To make things worse, salary increases and promotions are decided based on the placement of the individual on the curve, which can be utterly unfair to those who have actually performed well but are judged as relative underperformers. This can severely impact morale and lead to disengagement. Granted, outstanding performers need to be rewarded more, but a forced comparison is certainly not the appropriate way to do it.

Another serious problem with the system of forced rank comparison is that it is highly detrimental for team spirit. Enterprises and teams are complex systems, and therefore collaboration between people and team spirit produces value that is greater than the sum of individual performances. Competition, which leads to the erosion of collaboration and team spirit, is therefore a huge impediment to agility.

Differential treatment for contractual employees

Organizations hire employees on contracts for reasons ranging from tiding over a temporary capacity shortage, to the ease of firing them if they do not perform, to having the leverage of reducing the headcount during times of recession. For example, in Italy it is common to have the majority of the workforce on contract employment, as opposed to permanent employment, as the labor laws make it extremely difficult to fire an employee, even if the employee is a poor performer. The amount of evidence of poor performance that the enterprise needs to build to prove poor performance is absolutely daunting.

The mistake that many businesses make is to treat contractor employees differently than the permanent employees, after they are hired. Some of things that companies do are so blatantly differentiating that they lead to low morale among the contracted employees. This could be not including them in fun events and team outings, preventing them from participating in training that the entire team needs to go through together and keeping them away from "sensitive" internal communications, which are shared only with permanent employees. There are meetings where only permanent employees are invited, followed by another meeting where everyone, including employees on contract, is invited. Not only is this wasteful, but there is a risk that everyone did not get the same message.

This type of differential treatment creates an "us versus them" divide, which is a huge barrier to being engaged with the team and the business. The disengagement creates a vicious circle that feeds into justifying the differential treatment meted out to contractors. To make things worse, the disengagement can even impact how permanent employees treat contract employees, with aggressive and disrespectful behavior being seen on occasion. The divide between permanent and contractor employees destroys the team spirit.

"Forcing" people to become managers

Enterprises that define the growth of a person based on climbing the levels in the hierarchy, that is, people have to become managers to grow, create an impediment to agility. The pitfalls of a "tall" hierarchy are discussed in *Chapter 6, Organization Structure.*

If the only path for this person to "grow" is to take a promotion to become a team lead and the next promotion to become a manager, this is taking them away from their craft and becomes a double whammy for companies. Firstly, the company has lost a person who excels in what they do.

The impact is no different than the person leaving the company. Secondly, the worker may not have the skills to become a manager, that is, to lead a group of people, and also may not have any passion for the role. Without the right skills, aptitude, and passion for the manager role, the chances of the employee becoming an effective manager are minimal.

So why does this person agree to take this career path? It is simply because they have no other option and are "forced" by circumstances to take this path. Their salary will rise meaningfully only if they get promoted. If they stay in the same position for a long time, they might be perceived as lacking competence and therefore not being worthy of promotion. Lastly, a junior may rise in the hierarchy to become the "boss."

An organization structure that is based on separating the thinkers and doers, complemented by HR policies that do not appreciate what growth means in the context of knowledge work, forces people to take on roles that are unrelated to their core capabilities. Not only does this deprive people of the opportunity to build their core capabilities, and thereby foster excellence, it makes them a misfit in the roles that they are forced to take because they have no option but to do so, for the sake of growth.

Enablers to agility

The following factors related to people can significantly help enterprises to enhance agility.

Psychological safety

People feel "safe" in the work environment when they are able to express themselves freely, that is, without fear of being judged. This includes expressing new ideas, disagreements, and alternative points of view. People are not afraid to be vulnerable, even in presence of their "bosses," and therefore become more open to expression, when they feel safe.

Safety increases creativity, teamwork, and engagement, which are huge enablers for self-organization and effectively responding to change, thereby helping to enhance agility.

According to a survey of Google employees, which was carried out to find out what makes teams effective, the number one factor identified was psychological safety. Google has defined this as "can we take risks on this team without them feeling insecure or embarrassed." [xiii]

According to Laura Delizonna, an instructor at Stanford University:

> *"Ancient evolutionary adaptations explain why psychological safety is both fragile and vital to success in uncertain, interdependent environments. The brain processes a provocation by a boss, competitive coworker, or dismissive subordinate as a life-or-death threat. The amygdala, the alarm bell in the brain, ignites the fight-or-flight response, hijacking higher brain centers. This "act first, think later" brain structure shuts down perspective and analytical reasoning. Quite literally, just when we need it most, we lose our minds. While that fight-or-flight reaction may save us in life-or-death situations, it handicaps the strategic thinking needed in today's workplace." [xiv]*

Lack of psychological safety leads to a feeling of being threatened and therefore this is the primary cause of the fight-or-flight instinct in the workplace. The onus for creating and sustaining psychological safety primarily lies with the leaders of the enterprise. Leaders must not only reflect safety in their own expressions, but also behave with teams in a way that encourages creativity and freedom of expression among people.

When there are disagreements, the leaders, in their role as facilitators, must encourage the discussion to move toward finding a win-win solution or coming to an agreement on a "middle ground".

Through demonstrated behaviors and coaching, as applicable, the message must be consistently sent out that disagreement does not mean conflict but is something that should be used for better collaboration and improved outcomes. This approach is critical in making people aware that in case of disagreements, each person's point of view must be handled with empathy and respect. Even if a person's point of view is not accepted by the team, that person must feel appreciated for the contribution and should not be treated as if they have a lack of competence.

Psychological safety becomes even more important in today's environment, where achieving positive outcomes is driven by experimentation and creativity. Perceived safety is therefore a huge enabler for enhancing agility.

Competency-driven people development

Not too long ago, when the pace of change was slow and stability was the norm, businesses focused people-development efforts around improving the skills needed for a person in a specific role to perform their job. However, given the frenetic pace of change, skills are becoming obsolete very fast. Some skills become generic due to wider adoption, for example, word processing. Some skills are not needed because better options are created, for example, software programming languages. In fact, the emergence of unprecedented circumstances makes the need for new skills necessary, for example, in machine learning and artificial intelligence.

Competencies, on the other hand, are much broader than skills. Competencies include skills and also include individual abilities and knowledge/experience. Examples of abilities include analytical thinking, interpersonal relationships, initiative, and adaptability.

Abilities come naturally to individuals and can be improved only up to a certain limit through external intervention. Knowledge and experience can be gained through study and practice, for example, a knowledge of the global business environment and experience in working with international clients. The key is to put the individual with certain competencies in the appropriate role and context, to be able to leverage these competencies to the maximum.

In knowledge work, there is a combination of the three elements of competency: skills, individual abilities, and knowledge/experience, which are necessary to perform effectively, especially when the nature of work is complex. It is competencies, and not merely skills, which will enable people to collectively build the six capabilities underlying agility.

Talent management must therefore focus not only on enhancing competencies, as opposed to only skills development, but also on ensuring that a team has people with the relevant set of competencies within it. Job descriptions must be based on competencies, so that people have better clarity on what is expected from them and, more importantly, what is needed to succeed while working in a complex environment.

Intrinsic motivation

Motivation is something that makes a person want to take a specific action. Motivation can be of two types: extrinsic and intrinsic. Extrinsic motivation is based on the desire to get a certain external outcome, regardless of whether the person enjoys doing what it takes to achieve that outcome, for example, a rise in salary, promotion on the job, and becoming popular among colleagues. Anything done to avoid a negative outcome also falls under extrinsic motivation, for example, arriving at the office at a specific time due to fear of a reprimand from the boss. On the other hand, intrinsic motivation is based on doing something that gives joy and fulfilment to the individual, for example, playing a musical instrument or a sport, solving problems, and so on.

It fuels the desire to do what the individual feels passionate about and therefore is critical for achieving excellence. Moreover, intrinsic motivation is the glue that keeps people engaged with their work, as it provides meaning to the work being done.

According to Daniel Pink, the bestselling author of *The New York Times* and *The Wall Street Journal*, an individual gets intrinsically motivated when the following needs are satisfied:

♦ **Autonomy**: The desire to feel in control and drive your own work

♦ **Mastery**: The urge to better yourself at something that matters

♦ **Purpose**: The desire to do something meaningful or something that makes a difference. [xv]

Autonomy

This can be enabled by sharing expectations about desired outcomes and letting the teams and individuals have the freedom to figure out the best ways to achieve the outcomes. People should be encouraged to come up with new ideas, and, if found viable, given a chance to experiment with them.

Mastery

The key to enabling individual-level mastery is to provide opportunities for people to not only get better at the skills they wish to master but also to display and use the mastered skills. A career path should be provided for people to grow as specialists, rather than forcing them to become managers. Conscious efforts should be made to provide opportunities for people to work on projects/products that can leverage their skills. If staff show thought leadership in their specialization in the form of positive impact through new ideas, these ideas and the concerned people should get appropriate visibility and recognition. Support and encouragement should be provided to people to learn and share at relevant conferences.

Purpose

People are more inclined to associate with and take ownership of purpose when they believe that they have a say in defining it and influencing it. This includes purpose at the enterprise level, namely, mission and goals, down to the objectives at the team level, which should be derived from the goals of the enterprise. Employees should be provided with opportunities to work directly with customers, thereby being able to actually experience the value that their work has created for the customers and consequently for the business.

Perception of fairness in compensation is the most common impediment for boosting intrinsic motivation and is one of the primary reasons for people parting ways with their employer. Hence, enterprises must work toward not only being fair in their compensation policy but also ensuring that people believe that they are being paid fairly. In an extreme case, some businesses such as Sahaj Software are completely transparent about their salaries.

According to Akash Agrawal, co-founder of Sahaj:

> *"We came to the conclusion that salaries were a hidden means of control. It creates a boss and junior setup. That made us decide to be open about the salaries. Everyone's salary, including the director's, is on the Intranet today." [xvi]*

He further goes on to add that salary revisions are decided by everyone working there together and even the director's salary review was done in this manner. Some other organizations share salary bands for all the grades and ensure that not only new hires fit into those grades, but existing employees get salary corrections, if they are falling behind in parity.

Engagement

An enterprise's level of agility almost entirely depends on its people being able to assess the circumstances and respond and adapt to those circumstances. People need to do this constantly in circumstances emerging from fast-paced change. The human qualities of creativity, ownership, commitment, judgement, and accountability are necessary for employees to assess and effectively respond to change. The critical factor that brings out the best in people with respect to these qualities is their level of engagement with the business. Most of the inhibitors to and enablers of agility discussed in this chapter are about increasing people engagement. However, this factor is so critical that, at the cost of duplication, it is still worth a separate and specific mention.

According to Kevin Kruse, author of *Employee Engagement 2.0*:

> *"Employee engagement is the emotional commitment the employee has to the organization and its goals."* *[xvii]*

He further adds that happiness and satisfaction at work are not necessarily indicators of employee engagement.

Engagement is about how people feel about the enterprise and their colleagues, and their emotional connection with both. Engagement is reflected in how much people care about their work and the goals of the business. Essentially, the feeling of being engaged at work is akin to the feeling of being an entrepreneur. The engaged person cares about the work and will strive to do their best to achieve the best outcomes, without being hung up about the additional time and effort that they may need to put in. There is no need to enforce discipline when people are engaged. Companies need to take the following measures to build and nurture people engagement:

◆ The enterprise must have a clear vision and purpose, which has to be bigger than merely making money for the stakeholders. Unless the business has a larger purpose, it is unlikely that it will appeal to the employees for them to identify with it. The company must be open to broadening its purpose, mission and vision and must involve as many people as possible in giving them shape. People need to believe that they have "a voice on the table," with respect to influencing the purpose, mission, and vision. Involvement of people is critical for creating a sense of ownership. Engagement cannot happen without a sense of ownership.

◆ People must be empowered to decide how best to achieve the goals linked to the company's purpose and supported with the necessary resources to deliver the outcomes for achieving the goals. The team must be cross-functional, having the appropriate mix of capabilities needed to deliver the outcomes. People must be trusted that they will do the right thing. Needless to say, empowerment and accountability must go hand in hand. Expectations on outcomes must be explicitly set and agreed upon.

◆ People must be able to clearly understand and visualize how their work is contributing to achieving company goals. For this, staff need to be aware of the "big picture" and be able to drill down the value stream to understand how their work is adding value to the customer and the enterprise.

◆ People must receive continuous feedback, in the form of appreciation, recognition and constructive suggestions for improvement, from peers and leaders.

People engagement is about valuing employees and bringing out the best in them because they feel valued. Engagement leads to feelings of ownership and it is only when staff feel valued that agility can be enhanced and sustained.

Ability to have fun at work

Organizations need to support their people by creating an enjoyable workplace. The nature of knowledge work is such that people need to take periodic breaks to rejuvenate themselves and spending some time on fun and recreational activities can help a great deal. In today's era, where the definition of productivity pivots around creative thinking and collaboration, as opposed to producing output that is directly correlated to the time producing it, having some fun at work actually helps staff to perform better.

A study by BrightHR found that employees who have fun at work are less likely to take sick days and more likely to report feeling creative at work and committed to their organization. In another study, the University of Warwick measured the impact of happiness on employee productivity and found a 12% spike in productivity among happy workers and a 10% drop among unhappy workers. [xviii]

Having fun at work need not be dichotomous with the primary purpose of coming to work, namely, to create value for the enterprise and its stakeholders and be accountable for it. The key lies in people being responsible enough to not misuse the privilege of having fun at work. The potential for misuse is significantly higher when people's engagement with their work and with the company is low. A mistake that many businesses make is that they offer a plethora of recreational activities, for example, table tennis, pool, music room, and many more to a largely disengaged workforce, with the hope that having access to recreational activities will create employee engagement. A disengaged workforce is highly likely to prioritize having fun over performing their work and therefore such measures should be treated as a way to enhance engagement, not as a way to create it.

An important positive outcome of fun activities at work is that they improve bonding between people, as most fun activities involve the need for people to interact with each other.

Some of the fun and recreational activities that businesses can offer include the following:

♦ Access to indoor sports activities

♦ Happy Hour and a games evening at the end of the week

♦ Allowing employees to have flexibility with their work schedule, subject to them spending an agreed number of hours co-located as a team

♦ Opportunities to devote time to philanthropic causes

♦ Birthday celebrations

♦ Periodic budget for team outings

♦ Themed dress days

♦ Birthday breakfast with the CEO

♦ Meetups for people with specific interests and needs

All such activities must be completely voluntary, without any pressure to participate. It is important to note that the definition of fun will vary at every company and for every person. Hence, a fun workplace should be created by seeking ideas from people on the ground and also by involving them in implementing and sustaining them.

Hiring for diversity

New employees entering the organization can provide significant leverage toward a culture change, if they are aligned with the purpose, values, and target culture of the enterprise. Hence, organizations need to invest adequate time and effort into the hiring process to significantly increase the chances of hiring people with the "right fit" with the desired culture.

Obviously, people will come in with their own opinions and fresh ideas about ways to achieve the objectives of the business. These differences of opinion, arising from diversity of thought, will lead to healthy friction, which should be leveraged by the organization.

It is also important to hire in way in which the workforce itself becomes as diverse as possible. Diversity should be aimed for across multiple parameters including gender, age, ethnicity, variety of educational backgrounds, variety of experiences, and many more.

According to Ekaterina Walter, author of the bestseller *Think Like Zuck*:

"Diversity breeds innovation and innovation breeds success."

She cites several studies, including those by the *Harvard Business Review*, McKinsey, and Forbes, which have conclusively proven that diversity leads to an increase in innovation, business growth, problem solving and even financial performance. [xix]

According to Lauren Rivera, a faculty member at Kellogg School of Management:

"For jobs involving complex decisions and creativity,
more diverse teams outperform less diverse ones. Too
much similarity can lead to teams that are overconfident,
ignore vital information and make poor (or even unethical)
decisions." [xx]

Another critical reason to invest in hiring the right people, which is often overlooked, is that quality of colleagues is an important variable that determines employee satisfaction. People who are passionate about work and who strive for excellence find it highly fulfilling to work with people who are similar to them in this regard.

The following points are excellent enablers in significantly increasing the chances of hiring people suitable for a culture aligned to agility:

- The recruitment team should provide training on the fundamentals of Agile and Lean, and periodically they should get some exposure to projects and initiatives involving work related to clients. Agile ways of working require people to have stronger communication and collaboration skills, a keenness to learn, a greater sense of ownership and accountability, among other things. The recruitment team must be sensitized about the importance of these skills and trained on spotting them during the recruitment process.

- People who are on the "bench" contributing toward candidate interviews.

- Assessing beyond technical aptitude. Candidates should be evaluated holistically to get a much better feel for their fit with the culture of agility. Besides the skills stated here, some of the other key aspects to specifically examine include the following:

  ○ Passion for their respective craft

  ○ Ability to think on the spot, in a pressured situation

  ○ Humility

Assessing these attributes will necessitate multiple rounds of interviews. The time and effort spent on assessing suitability must be seen as an investment toward building/creating a culture aligned to agility and not as a wasted expense. Examples of some questions to help evaluate fit with an organization are as follows:

- Elaborate about an instance when you debated on an opinion different from yours and explain what the outcome was.

♦ Give an example of something you failed at and what you learned from it.

♦ What is the last book you read and what are your key takeaways from it?

A dedicated round of interviews may be needed to assess something that an organization believes is critical from a cultural perspective, for example, an organization that places importance on contributing toward economic and social justice has an interview round dedicated to assessing whether the candidate has at least an open mind toward such issues, if not a passion.

Some companies like Weebly, which provides a platform to start an online business, put potential employees through a "trial week." They do this at a stage in the recruitment process where usually a job offer is made. Weebly takes it a step further by asking people to work with them for a week and pays them market rate for that time. Around 75% of prospective employees get an offer to join the 300-person team at the end of the week. [xxi]

Holistic and frequent feedback on performance

In a typical hierarchy, it is the "boss" who assesses the performance of subordinates. In such a structure, keeping the "bosses," particularly the immediate superior, happy in order to get a favorable performance rating and to safeguard opportunities for career growth is a huge deterrent to agility. It creates serious behavioral anti-patterns like putting self-interest above team and organizational interest, playing favorites, heroism, and so on. Such an unhealthy concentration of authority and influence over people needs to be changed as a priority.

A no "boss" culture does not imply that people do not have an immediate superior who they report to. What it actually means is that the superior should not be the only person whose "judgement" matters to an individual.

In an Agile environment, which thrives on collaboration between people, every individual interacts with other individuals to perform his/her work and also influences the work done by them. Given this, feedback on performance should come from those people with whom the individual has worked with and their supervisor should be just one person among those providing the feedback.

The performance appraisal process needs to change in order to move away from relying on "boss-only" feedback, to considering feedback from all pertinent stakeholders, in order to determine an individual's level of performance. The frequency of providing feedback on performance needs to be higher than just once a year, thereby people get feedback regularly. A few enterprises are moving toward quarterly performance reviews.

Learning culture

With the business environment changing at breakneck speed, and consequently companies experiencing constant change as well, people need to keep upgrading their capabilities to deal with the impact of fast-paced change.

A learning culture is a set of organizational values, conventions, processes and practices that encourages individuals—and the organization as a whole—to increase knowledge, competence and performance. [xxii] In an enterprise with a learning culture, people are eager to learn and take every opportunity to share their knowledge. For example, reading an interesting and relevant article found on social media and sharing this with colleagues, conducting *lunch and learn* sessions, and creating, nurturing, and actively participating in communities of practice, which are groups of people who voluntarily come together for collective learning. A learning culture is organic and hence making people attend training programs, as necessary as they may be, should not be confused with a learning culture.

In a study by Bersin & Associates, titled *High-Impact Learning Culture: The 40 Best Practices for Creating an Empowered Enterprise*, companies with strong learning cultures tend to significantly outperform their peers in several areas:

- They are 32% more likely to be first to market
- They have 37% greater employee productivity
- They have a 34% better response to customer needs
- They have a 26% greater ability to deliver quality products
- They are 58% more likely to have skills to meet future demand
- They are 17% more likely to be market share leader [xxiii]

In order to create and sustain a learning culture, leaders must become role models by demonstrating their keenness to learn and share. Moreover, across the enterprise, people's efforts toward learning new things, applying them in the workplace, and sharing their learnings with others must be recognized and rewarded. Encouraging people to create and become part of communities of practices, as mentioned in *Chapter 6, Organization Structure*, can go a long way in strengthening the learning culture. People can also be encouraged to earn **Professional Development Units (PDUs)**, through attending internal and external training based on the identified capability development needs. Considering the immense benefits arising from a learning culture, enterprises must look at the time and effort spent on learning as a necessary investment, rather than an expense.

Tala Nabong, a campaign service specialist at SAP, has aptly said:

> *"Developing a learning culture is no longer just another fanciful idea. It is becoming more imperative."* [xxiv]

Summary

In this chapter, we learned that people, by far, are the most critical element of the enterprise in the knowledge era. A company's ability to hire the right people, to unlock their potential, to nurture and grow their capabilities, and to create conditions whereby they feel engaged with the work and with the business will determine the extent to which the organization can enhance its agility.

The next chapter is about the fourth component of the enterprise, namely, technology and its significance. The chapter will also explore how to leverage technology for enhancing enterprise agility.

References

[i] http://www.infosurv.com/real-impact-disengaged-employees/

[ii] https://www.forbes.com/sites/tinethygesen/2016/06/06/how-lack-of-trust-is-demotivating-employees-and-costing-business-dearly-and-what-to-do-about-it/#7d348175e6f9

[iii] https://www.forbes.com/sites/tinethygesen/2016/06/06/how-lack-of-trust-is-demotivating-employees-and-costing-business-dearly-and-what-to-do-about-it/2/#

[iv] https://blog.deming.org/2012/10/appreciation-for-a-system/

[v] http://www.selfgrowth.com/articles/our_egos_deepest_need_appreciation.html

[vi] https://www.forbes.com/sites/victorlipman/2017/04/15/66-of-employees-would-quit-if-they-feel-unappreciated/#160a824d6897

[vii] https://dictionary.cambridge.org/dictionary/english/yes-man

[viii] https://leaderonomics.com/business/lose-yes-men

[ix] https://www.slideshare.net/dhiraj2hrd/bell-curve-appraisal

[x] https://www.forbes.com/sites/work-in-progress/2015/07/08/competition-at-work-positive-or-positively-awful/2/#

[xi] https://hbr.org/2017/03/the-pros-and-cons-of-competition-among-employees

[xii] https://www.slideshare.net/dhiraj2hrd/bell-curve-appraisal

[xiii] https://rework.withgoogle.com/blog/five-keys-to-a-successful-google-team/

[xiv] https://hbr.org/2017/08/high-performing-teams-need-psychological-safety-heres-how-to-create-it

[xv] http://www.danpink.com/drive-the-summaries/

[xvi] https://yourstory.com/2017/05/sahaj-celebrates-transparency-individuality-greatest-asset-people/

[xvii] https://www.forbes.com/sites/kevinkruse/2012/06/22/employee-engagement-what-and-why/#3b4fa6e27f37

[xviii] http://www.qnnect.com/blog/how-fun-at-work-can-increase-productivity-and-employee-engagement

[xix] http://www.forbes.com/sites/ekaterinawalter/2014/01/14/reaping-the-benefits-of-diversity-for-modern-business-innovation/#24c7b9bb6476

[xx] http://www.nytimes.com/2015/05/31/opinion/sunday/guess-who-doesnt-fit-in-at-work.html?_r=2

[xxi] https://www.businessinsider.in/Why-a-300-person-San-Francisco-startup-doesnt-offer-anyone-a-job-until-theyve-undergone-a-trial-week/articleshow/56743225.cms

[xxii] http://www.oracle.com/us/chro-docs/june-2013-chro-deck4-1961622.pdf

[xxiii] http://www.oracle.com/us/chro-docs/june-2013-chro-deck4-1961622.pdf

[xxiv] https://www.trainingindustry.com/articles/strategy-alignment-and-planning/creating-a-learning-culture-for-the-improvement-of-your-organization/

9

TECHNOLOGY

Until not too long ago, businesses across most industries viewed technology as a support function only. However, in today's digital era, technology has become one of the most important components of an enterprise, regardless of the industry to which the enterprise belongs.

Technology is now critical even for traditional industries such as banking, as indicated by Ralph Hamers, the CEO of ING Bank, who said:

> *"We want to portray ourselves as a tech company with a banking license."* [i]

In the digital era, it has become imperative for businesses to have technology as an integral part of their strategic objectives. This is even more critical now that consumers have become technology savvy and expect businesses to create value for them by leveraging technological innovations. Technology needs to be at the core of a company, in order to enable the enterprise to leverage the fast-changing environment to enhance competitive advantage and to achieve customer satisfaction.

This chapter explores the following topics:

- ♦ The significance of technology for enterprise agility
- ♦ Technology-related inhibitors of enterprise agility
- ♦ Technology-related enablers of enterprise agility

Significance

The importance of technology as a component for enhancing enterprise agility is primarily due to the disruptions that are happening as a result of rapid technological inventions. If a new tech invention suddenly seems to appear from nowhere and gains mass adoption, this could threaten the survival of well-established businesses. Kodak going out of business due to digital cameras, Amazon becoming a serious threat to physical retail stores across industries, and Airbnb shaking up the hospitality industry are just a few examples of the swift and hard-hitting impact that technology is having on organizations.

The role of technology has rapidly changed from supporting a business to being at the core of the business, thereby becoming the driver for creating and sustaining competitive advantage. The following diagram shows the progression of how technology has moved closer to the business world:

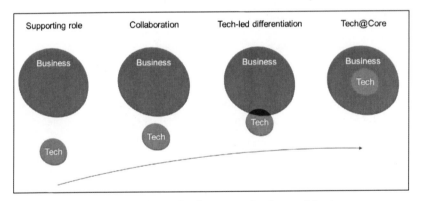

Figure 9.1: The relationship between technology and business

Any enterprise not giving strategic importance to the agility of technology is making itself seriously vulnerable and will likely experience a threat to its survival. Consumers are now seeking direct engagement with businesses. They are engaging with companies through multiple digital channels and expect a top-class user experience across all channels.

Technology has become such an integral part of the lives of people across the globe that Google and Uber have become verbs in the common vocabulary.

The life cycles of technologies are getting shorter by the day. The technology function needs to be nimble enough to adopt newer and better technologies and phase out those which are becoming obsolete. The role of the technology function has changed from maintaining stability to not only becoming responsive to change but also enabling change as well.

The breadth of technology is rapidly expanding, which, if not leveraged, can mean loss of competitive advantage for the business. The breadth of technology now includes data, machine learning, and artificial intelligence, which present several untapped opportunities for enterprises to create additional value-driven offerings for their customers.

Inhibitors to agility

The following factors related to technology are key barriers for enterprises seeking to enhance and sustain agility.

Treating the technology department as a cost center

Enterprises that are yet to realize the importance of technology in their businesses continue to treat the technology department as a cost center, which is associated with technology being a support function. A cost center's primary goal is to optimize on costs, as the function is viewed as a "necessary evil." The cost-center approach severely limits the capability of the technology function in the following ways:

- ◆ It creates barriers to investing in new technologies. The budget constraints force the function to maintain status quo in times when technology is changing at an exponential rate.

♦ It discourages experimentation, as the risk of failure is inherent to experimentation and innovation. A cost center cannot afford to lose money on failures, as the cost incurred on experimentation cannot be justified in isolation, should the experiment fail.

♦ It incentivizes getting into cost-driven contracts with vendors, rather than outcome-driven ones. The relationship with the vendors is based on cost optimization, thereby creating a huge deterrent toward building value-driven partnerships with vendors. The vendor is often forced to compromise on the quality of solutions and services, as capping costs upfront leaves no room to deal with uncertainty.

♦ It becomes extremely difficult to attract good talent, not only because the compensation offered may not be at a level that will attract the best people, but also because the company is unable to offer exciting work opportunities to employees, who are given the mandate to merely play a supporting role and maintain the status quo.

♦ It sends a message to the people in the technology function, particularly to the leaders and managers, that they are not integrated with the mainstream business of the enterprise, and therefore are not responsible for company performance. The performance of a cost center is judged purely from an accounting perspective, while ignoring the impact perspective.

This phenomenon is seen even more prominently in how **Offshore Development Centers (ODCs)**, also known as **Global In-house Centers (GICs)**, are treated. Most of the ODCs/GICs are developing solutions that are business critical for the enterprise and are directly interacting with end customers. Their potential to deliver value is being severely crippled by treating them as cost centers.

In times when organizations have no option but to leverage technology for strategic effectiveness, treating the technology function as a cost center will invite a threat to the survival of the enterprise.

According to Mary Poppendieck, author of multiple books, including *Lean Software Development*:

> *"Startups develop their software in profit centers; they haven't learned about cost centers yet. And in a competitive battle, a profit center will beat a cost center every time."* [ii]

The "stepchild" treatment of the technology function

Another grave fallout of continuing with the mindset of the technology function being a support function is the stepchild treatment given to the function. A common pattern is that the technology department is physically located in some corner in the back of the building, or in a separate building that is run down, thereby being completely out of sight. This creates a huge barrier to collaboration, as there is simply no incentive for the technology team to interact with people across the rest of the company, especially business stakeholders and vice versa. The technology department is remembered only when there is a problem that only it can solve.

Seemingly insignificant gestures, which clearly bring out the "us versus them" attitude within the enterprise, can severely dent the morale of the people in the technology function. For example, an online business in the UK has the senior executives and business people based in a separate building, which is a few meters walk in the open from a building where the technology function is based. People have to often deal with rain and cold winds to walk from one building to another.

The extent of the divided mindset was clearly evident when Christmas decorations were put up in the building where the senior executives were based, but not in the building where the technology function was based. Such blatant discrimination severely impacts the morale of the people who are at the receiving end.

Often business people treat the technology function as a separate service-providing entity, which is seated on the "other side of the table." The mindset usually is, "I am spending money on you (technology) folks to deliver the solution, so don't bother me with any of your problems and come back to me only when you are ready to deliver." The business insists on converting initial estimates into commitments, without appreciating the fact that technological solutions cannot be accurately estimated upfront and that emergent information throughout the development process can completely invalidate the initial estimate. It is quite common to see people in no-technology functions calling it a day after putting in 8-9 hours of work, but the technology team slogging away relentlessly for 9-12 hours a day, or even more, and also some working on weekends. By not giving an equal seat at the table to the technology function or worse, making the function feel like a "second class citizen," enterprises are killing the potential for technology to become a strategic business enabler.

Obsolete legacy systems

Wikipedia defines a legacy system as "an old method, technology, computer system, or application program, "of, relating to, or being a previous or outdated computer system." Often a pejorative term, referencing a system as "legacy" means that it paved the way for the standards that would follow it. This can also imply that the system is out of date or in need of replacement." [iii]

The preceding definition implies that legacy systems are obsolete and hence should be phased out at the earliest opportunity. The counterpoint to this is that the system is tried and tested, and therefore highly reliable, stable, and predictable under most circumstances.

Most companies in traditional industries such as banking are heavily reliant on their legacy systems to deliver their core offering to customers and for the transaction processing of internal functions such as finance and HR. Deciding the way forward on legacy systems is one of the most difficult issues that leaders in the technology function have to grapple with. Replacing a legacy application has the risk of disrupting the business, as well as the internal operations of the enterprise. However, sooner or later, the costs of continuing with these systems will clearly outweigh the benefits. The utility of legacy systems must be evaluated regularly in order to determine the optimal time and manner in which they are replaced.

Legacy systems can severely impede agility due to the following reasons:

♦ They are usually built as monolithic applications, thereby they are highly complex, that is, having spaghetti code [iv], making changes to the code extremely risky.

♦ Due to lack of modularity, even small changes to the application can be very costly in terms of both time and effort.

♦ The skill sets available to maintain the application are very scarce and are fast fading out. This also creates very high dependency on a few individuals.

♦ Integrating digital solutions with legacy applications is highly complex and results in subpar end user experience, due to fault lines in the integration.

♦ They usually lack real-time reporting capabilities, which is a basic requirement for both employees and customers in the digital era.

♦ The cost of migrating them to the cloud can be highly prohibitive.

Besides time and cost, additional key factors include the risk of business disruption, the impact on operational efficiency and effectiveness, and the impact on relationships with the concerned technology partners. The critical issue is to plan the replacement before the legacy system becomes a serious impediment to agility.

Silos within the technology function

Silos, as discussed in *Chapter 6, Organization Structure*, create a mindset of local activation, as the focus is on optimizing activities rather than outcomes. Silos in the technology function get created primarily due to the following reasons:

- Applying a traditional engineering mindset to technology, for example, the architect creates the architecture diagram for the proposed solution and is largely hands-off once the construction starts. Moreover, the architecture largely remains frozen once done.

- Optimizing for efficiency according to specialization. There is no consideration of the value that gets unlocked due to collaborating as a team, for example, in a product development division of a multinational engineering company, testers in a team are purposefully seated on another floor from where the rest of the development team is seated, so that the testers can do the testing with an independent perspective and not get influenced by the developers. Sometimes, the silos can have conflicting objectives, which severely impedes the creation and delivery of value, for example, the mandate given to the development team is to deliver fast to improve time to market, but the mandate given to the release team is to maintain stability. While the intent is to not treat these objectives as dichotomous from a systemic perspective, the silos will result in treating these objectives as contradictory.

♦ How the boundary for the technology function is defined, for example, some enterprises draw the boundary for technology around delivery and keep operations and maintenance functions outside of the technology function. These boundaries lead to silos and, consequently, "works on my machine" syndrome. [v]

Lack of engineering practices

It is quite common to see delivery teams supposedly making excellent progress toward creating the solution until it reaches 90% completion as per plan. If continuous integration as a practice has not been adopted, the integration of the software typically happens very close to the delivery date, with a very high probability of integration failures, resulting in serious defects being discovered very late in the development process. This often leads to a lot of rework under very high time pressure to deliver. The delivery pressure often leads to compromising on quality, which can have serious consequences not only for customers being unhappy, but precious time and effort being wasted in subsequent reworks to fix the defects. This is just one example of how a lack of engineering practice impacts agility negatively.

Engineering practices done right are a huge enabler for agility in the following ways:

♦ They enable fast feedback, thereby significantly increasing the confidence of the team to make changes to the software. The fast feedback spans changes detected through unit tests, which can break a design contract or integration-related problems that are nipped in the bud by integrating continuously.

♦ They force thinking through of exactly what the code is supposed to do, which leads to better design.

- They facilitate safe refactoring, due to changes arising out of new and modified requirements.

- They eliminate the need for technical documentation to a large extent, as the tests for the unit level, which also explain what the code is about, are part of the code itself.

- They help to avoid creating technical debt, as only as much code is written and maintained as is needed. This helps in building quality not just for today, but also for tomorrow.

Adopting engineering practices is a huge enhancer of technical agility, thereby significantly enabling enterprise agility. Conversely, not adopting engineering practices makes change more difficult and negatively impacts quality, thereby creating a drag on enterprise agility.

The bimodal approach

Bimodal is the practice of managing two separate, but coherent, styles of work: one focused on predictability, the other on exploration. *Mode 1* is optimized for areas that are more predictable and well-understood. *Mode 2* is exploratory, experimenting to solve new problems and optimized for areas of uncertainty. [vi]

While Gartner introduced the bimodal IT concept in 2014, technology functions in some businesses were already practicing it. This practice was largely a reaction to the difficulties and challenges of quickly and significantly improving the agility of the technology function, in response to the pressures felt by the business in dealing with rapid technological disruptions.

The technology departments identified the technology offerings for which businesses needed significantly higher speed to market and responsiveness to change and focused on those specific teams and areas within the function to enhance their agility. All other offerings continued to be optimized for predictability and stability, which was the mandate for the technology function when it was largely in a supportive mode.

The model is inherently flawed, as the premise is that it is okay to have a part of the technology function that is less or not aligned to enhancing agility. A part of the enterprise having less or no agility, particularly in the technology function, which has now become the core component of the company and a business enabler, will create severe headwinds for the agility of the enterprise. If the enterprise needs greater agility, then the technology function in its entirety must have even greater agility.

According to Martin Fowler, chief scientist at ThoughtWorks:

> *"The (bimodal) separation is based on software systems rather than business activity. If you want to rapidly cycle new ideas, you are going to need to modify the back-office systems of record just as frequently as the front office systems of engagement. You can't come up with clever pricing plans without modifying the systems of record that support them." [vii]*

The implications of a bimodal approach are that it can lead to a part of the technology function being "stuck" in a culture that is not an enabler for agility. Like a bad apple, this can lead to the entire technology function regressing to the traditional culture, thereby negating whatever little benefit this model potentially provided.

COTS products for core capabilities

An enterprise whose business-critical processes and operations are driven by **commercial off-the-shelf** (**COTS**) [viii] solutions runs the risk of these solutions becoming impediments to enhancing agility. There are several factors that can lead to this negative outcome. If the COTS solution is a few years old, it is likely to have the same issues as legacy software, which impede agility.

Moreover, by definition, these solutions are standard solutions and hence they are unlikely to be fully aligned to the enterprise's processes. Quite often, there are limitations to the extent that these solutions can be customized for the unique context of the enterprise. This often results in the company having to modify its processes, and sometimes even critical ones, in order to "fit" with the solution. As the license of the COTS is owned by the technology partner, the enterprise is forced to depend on the partner for customizing and enhancing the solution. Due to this, the effectiveness and efficiency of the changes may be severely impacted.

Another challenge is if a COTS solution needs close integration with another COTS solution, especially if the solutions belong to different partners. There may be tremendous challenges in integrating the solutions. The business logic may need to reside in the integration pipes, thereby introducing a lot of rigidity in the processing and response capabilities of the solutions.

Finally, the COTS solution may not have been built to support critical non-functional requirements to the extent needed, for example, it may not have the extent of security-related features that are needed as of today or it may not be easily scalable beyond a particular volume of transactions or data. Modifying the solution to cater to the enhanced non-functional requirements may be extremely difficult or just not possible. The enterprise may have to wait until the partner is able to cater to these requirements in the next version and also until the partner and the enterprise are both ready to upgrade the solution.

The quantifiable benefits of COTS, as compared with building a bespoke solution, usually turn out to be a mirage in hindsight. Moreover, there are several potential non-quantifiable factors, as stated earlier, which can impede agility. While opting for COTS solutions, or even deciding to continue with that option, a serious evaluation of the potential risks to agility must be done. As a general rule, the preference should be for bespoke development of solutions that are driving business critical outcomes and that enable the **unique selling proposition** (**USP**), while COTS may be considered for functions like HR and finance, where processes are largely standardized, for example, if a retail business has dynamic pricing as one of its competitive advantages, it is best that this functionality be built in-house, to the exact specifications needed.

Infrastructure vulnerability

Enterprises and their customers are now so dependent on technology that 24/7 system availability is an absolute must for most applications. However, a system outage causing severe inconvenience to customers, or a loss of revenue to the enterprise, is not uncommon. While systems often go down due to their inability to handle increased "traffic," outages due to infrastructure-related issues are also common and are largely preventable.

The system outage that impacted British Airways in 2017 is a classic example of an accidental mistake related to IT infrastructure that had a very severe negative impact for the airline and its customers [ix]. The outage was purportedly caused by someone accidentally switching off the power supply at the data center. This led to the cancellation of over 800 flights and a potential compensation payout of over 50 million GBP. The intangible, but perhaps bigger, impact was the loss of confidence in the infrastructure and network capabilities.

A preventive measure could be using a tool such as *Chaos Monkey* to intentionally create outages and test how the infrastructure responds to the outages. *Chaos Monkey* is a tool invented in 2011 by Netflix to test the resilience of its IT infrastructure. The tool works by intentionally disabling computers in Netflix's production network to test how remaining systems respond to the outage. [x]

Enablers to agility

The following factors related to technology can significantly help enterprises to enhance agility.

Business-technology alignment and collaboration

Given that the technology function needs to play a critical role in driving business outcomes, it is imperative that business and technology functions must be completely aligned, not only about the outcomes but also about how to achieve them.

In most enterprises, technology and business functions have historically dealt with each other with a "throw it over the wall" attitude. This has led to issues like the business treating initial estimates as firm commitments, delivery teams expecting business stakeholders to specify all their requirements upfront to the last level of detail, resistance to change in business requirements during the development phase, project management success based on adherence to the "iron triangle" [xi] regardless of the extent of value delivered and customer satisfaction, quality issues "pushed under the carpet" under pressure to deliver on a specific date, no appreciation for the delivery team who slogged long hours for days at a time, and so on.

While Agile methodologies have contributed significantly to improving collaboration between business and technology functions, through both principles and practices, often these are not enough to bring them to "one same side of table."

What is needed is alignment of the mindset between business and technology functions, to work collaboratively to achieve the goals of the enterprise.

The following specific measures can help to align mindsets across the business and technology functions.

Shared measures of success

Both functions must have common metrics to define success (for example, customer satisfaction). These common metrics must supersede metrics that may be specific to functions, in terms of relative importance, for example, business-specific metrics can be monetary revenue and technology-specific metrics can be the cycle time of a feature delivered.

Business appreciating the nature of technology work

The company must understand and appreciate that creating technology-driven solutions is creative and complex work, unlike mass production which is repetitive and predictable. This implies that there is always a possibility of "unknowns" lurking around when estimates about time and cost are provided to the business by the solution delivery teams. Not only should the delivery and business stakeholders agree on the primary assumptions made during estimation, but also learn to accept the new reality when the unknowns surface subsequently. It is in the best interests of the enterprise that the stakeholders across both functions together find the most optimal way forward, given the emergence of a new reality. For example, if the delivery team has provided a time estimate of two months to deliver a feature, but subsequently discovers that the work is far more complex than assumed, the stakeholders could together come up with the following options:

♦ Deliver the most valuable functionalities that are possible to deliver in two months and take a call on continuing to deliver the remaining functionalities later

- Add additional capacity to the team, so that the team can deliver in two months

- Explore an alternative technical approach, which might have lesser complexity

- Revise the estimate and the plan to reflect completion of delivery in four months

- Drop the feature and stop work on it, as the business case for the feature was based on two months of effort, and pick up another feature for delivery in those two months

The key to discussing options and choosing an appropriate solution lies in understanding that any technology issue that impacts a business outcome is a problem that everyone concerned needs to come together to solve, and that is not a problem only of the technology function.

Visibility and transparency

Building trust between functions that must work closely together is highly critical for meaningful collaboration and alignment. Given that visibility and transparency are huge enablers for building trust, both functions must consciously strive to practice visibility and transparency at all times. The starting point for this should be that both functions must have access to data, which is the single source of truth. Sometimes, teams "dress up" information to paint a good picture, when the reality is pointing otherwise, for example, the delivery has a slippage, but an attempt is made to hide this bad news. Another example of two versions of truth is when delivery teams add buffers to estimates, without discussing with the business sponsors whether there is even a need to add the buffer and, if so, how much is needed.

Early visibility of problems helps a great deal toward effective problem resolution, before it is too late. Taking further the example of the two-month estimate for the feature, imagine the frustration of the business stakeholders if the delivery team gave them the news about the need for increased effort closer to the end of the two months. It would just be too late by then to choose any of the options stated earlier, which could help to deal with the circumstance in the most effective manner.

Direct exposure to customers

People in the technology function should be given opportunities to interact with, if applicable, the current and potential customers for whom they are building solutions. They will get very meaningful insights through the first-hand interaction, which can be huge enabler toward creating solutions that satisfy customers.

Understand that change has a cost

A common misconception among the business function, about Agile ways of working, is that it is free to change requirements and priorities at any time. While Agile methods allow this privilege to the business stakeholders, given the fast-paced change happening in the external environment, the business function must work closely with technology delivery teams to understand the impact of change and decide the best way forward jointly. Business stakeholders must understand that while Agile practices help a great deal to lower the cost of change, there still may be a cost to the change in terms of refactoring the solution or even junking a part of the existing code. Change may also lead to costs related to context switching.

Speak in a common language

Business and technology stakeholders must speak with each other in a common language, that is, in a language that both sides can understand and relate to. Examples of this include explaining the impact of delaying refactoring of a piece of code in technical terms and business stakeholders using finance-domain-related terms and acronyms when explaining requirements. A better way is for the technology team to explain the impact of delaying the refactoring in terms of potential business risks and business stakeholders providing the necessary orientation/training session to explain the basics of the finance domain to the technology team.

Make the business self-reliant

The technology function must endeavor to make the business function as independent and self-reliant as possible, with respect to configuring and using a solution. It is frustrating and distracting for the technology team when business people come to them for even minor changes to system configuration. Often, end users of a system encounter problems due to improper configuration and they log that problem as a defect. However, the technology team has to spend effort to uncover the cause of the defect. Frustration and resentment come in when everyone realizes that the problem could have been avoided by configuring the system properly. Similar to domain knowledge training for technical people, at least some of the business people must be trained on independently configuring the system and understanding the implications of wrong configuration.

Going forward, given the rising importance of technology in the business, it is highly likely that technology and business functions will cease to exist as discrete functions, with delivery teams formed around business outcomes and having all the needed cross-functional skills. However, until business and technology functions retain their separate identities, ensuring alignment and collaboration between both these functions is critical for enhancing enterprise-level agility.

Agile and DevOps

Over the past decade, the adoption of Agile and DevOps practices in the technology function has been a significant enabler for some businesses to leverage technology for creating competitive advantage.

According to Kishore Sengupta, a professor at INSEAD and Andrea Masini, a professor at the London Business School:

> *"Stated in an extremely simple way, IT agility is all about reconfiguring or replacing your information technology systems when new marketplace realities change the way you have to do business." [xii]*

Adoption of Agile and DevOps practices in the right way has resulted in the accrual of the following game-changing outcomes for companies:

- Ability to manage changing business priorities
- Continued visibility into project progress, thereby impediments and risks becoming visible early
- Speed to market
- Improved collaboration between business and technology functions
- Quality of software

Adopting Agile and DevOps is not merely about adopting new ways of working. Technology functions limiting themselves to only adopting new ways of working are unlikely to get meaningful and sustainable benefits that are substantial enough to have an impact on enterprise agility. Meaningful agility in the technology function can be achieved by doing the following, in addition to adopting the relevant practices:

- All the sub/supporting functions must adopt Agile. These include architecture, infrastructure, operations, and maintenance as well.

- The foundation of Agile is a culture that is value-driven, customer-focused, people-centric, and encourages experimentation and learning. This culture must uniformly exist across not only the technology function, but the enterprise as well.

- A **project management office** (**PMO**) must move to governing technology delivery and outcomes based on Agile values and principles.

- Agile must prevail across the entire "concept to cash" cycle. It is critical to leverage Agile not only for the effectiveness of the *how* of the delivery but also for *what* is to be delivered as well.

According to Pearl Zhu, the author of the *Digital Master* book series:

> *"The purpose of building an Agile IT is to pursue an optimal way of running IT, to enable business innovation and transformation via taking advantage of the organization's resources and cultivate a set of necessary and unique business capabilities to gain competitive business advantage." [xiii]*

Culture of technology artisanship

Using technology to create solutions, to fulfill a need or to solve a problem, be it related to the business or an individual, is as much an art as a science. Moreover, the solutions, being assets, will be in existence for a period of time and therefore must be created in a way in which they can not only be maintained easily but also be easily scaled and enhanced, as needed.

Enterprises must, therefore, encourage and nurture the capabilities related to art, that is, artisanship (the word *craftsmanship* is commonly used in this context, but is not being used to avoid any indication of gender bias) of technology, through a culture of experimentation and learning.

Technology is the most potent resource that businesses can use to create change, by coming out with innovative offerings that can disrupt the market and thereby create competitive advantage for the enterprise. Hence, the company must create a culture where the technologists are encouraged to craft innovative offerings using technology, which by itself is a commodity.

The first step toward creating such a culture is to hire people who are passionate about technology and about using that technology to come up with innovative offerings to solve challenging problems. These people need to be nurtured and motivated through the intrinsic motivators, such as autonomy, mastery, and purpose, which have been discussed earlier in the book.

Rather than creating a separate center of innovation, where only a privileged few can get opportunities to explore new technologies to come up with innovative offerings, the opportunities to explore new technologies should be provided to anyone who has an interest in doing so. In fact, exploring the latest technologies must be made part of the job for the people in relevant roles.

Businesses can dedicate specific time-boxed periods to let people work together to come up with innovative products. Hack nights [xiv] and FedEx days [xv] are popular examples of such initiatives. Building and nurturing a culture of technology artisanship needs tremendous conviction and commitment.

According to Sanjay Dubey, a senior director of engineering at LinkedIn:

> *"Craftsmanship can be very difficult to practice, especially when it comes at a big cost. When your deadlines are staring you in the eyes, it takes a lot of courage to make the trade-offs that are sub-optimal in the short term but optimal in the longer term. Craftsmanship is not something that individuals will consistently practice unless it is part of the DNA of the organization. You can't build something amazing on top of poor quality building blocks. Nor can you delay that release by a few weeks to get better craftsmanship if your boss does not support it. Craftsmanship is something that either is in the DNA of the organization or does not exist."*

For an enterprise that sees technology as being at its core, having a culture of technology artisanship is a necessity and not a choice.

Portfolio management

An enterprise can have a large number, even in the hundreds, of technology projects running across business units, functional areas, and geographies. Many of these projects may require additional investment that goes beyond the original budget and fresh investments are needed for upcoming new projects. While the average investment per project may not appear significant, the sum might add up to a very large amount. Companies must have a mechanism to periodically evaluate all technology projects with respect to alignment to business strategies and goals, and the whether they have the potential to deliver value that can justify the incremental investment in them. Slowing down or eliminating running projects may create additional risk for the organization and the enterprise must make incremental investment decisions based on the risk-return tradeoff.

This approach is very similar to managing a portfolio of financial assets. Projects can be clustered across life cycles to ascertain if there is too much concentration of projects in a particular stage of the life cycle. The portfolio approach can provide the ability to view risks simultaneously at project and portfolio levels, thereby providing significant insight to guide decision-making about continuing or stopping further investment or even phasing out the project.

Moreover, an enterprise-level view of technology assets and investments can help to uncover duplication of solutions and opportunities for consolidation. For example, an enterprise using different CRM solutions in two geographical areas, licensed from different partners, can look to adopt a single CRM solution globally and thereby not have to deal with multiple partners. The portfolio approach can also help to cluster the applications according to the technology stack, thereby providing insight into how concentrated or dispersed the technology landscape is. It can also help in ascertaining whether an investment that was classified as strategic, when initially made, has remained so or has now become transactional in nature. The "big picture" view provided by the portfolio approach can help business and technology leaders to have a common frame of reference to evaluate the alignment of investments in technology to business strategies and goals.

Portfolio-level data of investment in various areas of technology, namely, strategic, informational, transactional, and infrastructure, can be compared to industry-level aggregates of the same classification of technology areas, to understand if the enterprise numbers are significantly deviating from industry averages and, if so, this might influence the incremental investments. A portfolio approach to technology, supported by feedback mechanisms to measure value and impact, can significantly enhance agility by providing guidance to leaders on how to align technology choices and technology investments to business outcomes.

Evolutionary architecture

Traditionally, the architecture for software solutions was mostly defined upfront to the last level of detail. The architecture was created based on information about functional and non-functional requirements known at that time and some assumptions were made based on past experience. However, in an era where not only is technology changing very fast, but also it is extremely difficult to predict the future, a fully-designed architecture may become highly constraining about accommodating both business and technology-related changes.

The unpredictable and dynamic nature of requirements necessitate that the architecture be evolutionary and created based on the Agile principle of "last responsible moment." Last responsible moment is a strategy of not making a premature decision, but instead delaying commitment and keeping important and irreversible decisions open until the cost of not making a decision becomes greater than the cost of making a decision. [xvi]

According to Neal Ford, director at ThoughtWorks and Rebecca Parsons, CTO at ThoughtWorks, a few of the characteristics of evolutionary architecture are as follows:

♦ Modularity and coupling, that is, the ability to separate components along with defined boundaries

♦ Organized around business capabilities, inspired by domain-driven design

♦ Experimentation, through several variations of a service existing at the same time [xvii]

To make the evolution of the architecture more effective, the architects should get a hands-on feel of how the architecture is being implemented by the designers and developers. The best way to get this feel is for the architects to themselves write some code, while pairing with developers. The learnings and feedback from this will help immensely in the effective evolution of the architecture.

Build core capabilities internally

For an enterprise that has technology as a core competency, that is, at the core of the business, the critical technological capabilities must be built and nurtured in-house. These capabilities are direct drivers of competitive advantage and investing in them has the potential to further increase that advantage. There is too much risk of losing these critical capabilities, if they are outsourced to contractors and partners. The company must not only invest in internal human capital to build these capabilities, but also foster a culture of learning and knowledge sharing to nurture these capabilities.

Non-core capabilities, on the other hand, do not drive competitive advantage, but are more "hygiene factors." Examples of core capabilities are those which relate to platforms, user experience, and analytics, while non-core capabilities could be in the areas of telecommunications and network infrastructure.

T-shaped skills

The concept of T-shaped skills, or T-shaped people, is a metaphor used in job recruitment to describe the abilities of people in the workforce. The vertical bar on the T represents the depth of related skills and expertise in a single field, whereas the horizontal bar is the ability to collaborate across disciplines with experts in other areas and to apply knowledge in areas of expertise other than one's own. [xviii] People with T-shaped skills are also known as **generalizing specialists**.

Having people with T-shaped skills is a huge enabler for teams to be cross-functional, collaborating, and self-organizing. It increases the flexibility of the team to focus on priorities that are critical, for example, if the software developers have completed the development and the testing capacity is falling short, the developers who have some testing skills can also help to complete the testing faster.

The vertical bar of the T can be looked at from two perspectives. It can represent some expertise in another hard skill, for example, a tester also having the skills to carry out business analysis. It can also represent soft skills such as problem-solving and interpersonal skills. Making people develop T-shaped skills requires a long-term commitment. The additional skills can be developed through a combination of training and on-the-job learning by pairing with the expert in a given skill.

According to Cutter Consortium:

"In the 21st century, being able to focus employee attention as quickly and efficiently as possible on important issues will be a differentiator. Each of us gets 60 minutes in an hour that we can use, and organizations that understand how to use employee insight and capabilities more effectively will have an advantage. Automating the events that are well understood and minimizing disruptions will be important. Those individuals that have not only depth, but also the breadth of skills and knowledge to take advantage of the improved information flow will stand out. All these changes are demanding a new breed of IT professional: the T-shaped IT professional." [xix]

In terms of the need for having T-shaped skills for technology professionals, Cutter Consortium says:

"Globalization is in full swing; unprecedented opportunities are being made possible every day at the confluence of big data, analytics, the IoT, mobile computing, and social media; and cognitive computing enabled by complex pattern recognition is a growing trend. So while the T-shaped concept has been around for more than two decades already, it is now more important than ever for IT professionals to assess how they are creating value and to focus on higher-impact activities." [xx]

Platforms

In the digital era, in which the rate of technology churn is very high, multiple applications and services have to be seamlessly integrated to provide a superior user experience, and partners and customers are an integral part of the enterprise's ecosystem, companies need to move away from standalone products and services toward platforms, in order to enhance technological capability of the business.

The clichéd success stories of the digital era, such as Amazon and Google, are examples of enterprises that have successfully moved from products to platforms. Google started off with a search engine product. Today Google is a platform that has Gmail, Docs, YouTube, and Maps among the many offerings on its platform. Amazon started by selling books and is now a fully fledged e-commerce player.

Platforms are a huge enabler of agility in the following ways:

♦ They enable connecting external entities, such as partners and users, to form a cohesive system within and around the enterprise, and therefore present opportunities to leverage the strengths of the "agents" in the ecosystem.

♦ They can help to scale the offering very quickly. Apple offered many apps on iPad and iPhone and generated billions in additional revenue in a short time period.

♦ They encourage innovation, as they make it easy to plug in and, if needed, plug out products and services.

♦ They encourage a culture of embracing change and evolving with it.

♦ They help to exploit business opportunities, as they make it easier to create offerings across verticals, for example, Apple's offerings extend beyond telecommunications into music, education, e-commerce, and media.

Platforms, while being enablers, are not a solution to reviving poor products or fixing dysfunctional mindsets and culture. While moving to the platform model, priority should be given to those capabilities within the technology function that are most critical for the business. Gartner suggest that enterprises should examine the potential for platforms in five key areas:

♦ **Information systems platform**: This supports the back office and operations such as ERP and core systems.

♦ **Customer experience platform**: This contains the main customer-facing elements such as customer and citizen portals, multichannel commerce, and customer apps.

♦ **Data and analytics platform**: This contains information management and analytical capabilities. Data management programs and analytical applications fuel data-driven decision-making, and algorithms automate discovery and action.

♦ **Internet of Things (IoT) platform**: This connects physical assets for monitoring, optimization, control, and monetization. Capabilities include connectivity, analytics, and integration to core and **operational technology (OT)** systems.

♦ **Ecosystems platform**: This supports the creation of, and connection to, external ecosystems, marketplaces, and communities. API management, control, and security are the main elements. [xxi]

Diagrammatically, the preceding five areas are represented as follows:

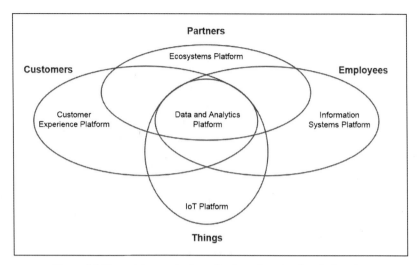

Figure 9.2: Potential areas in the technology function for platforming

Platforms can enhance and unlock value in the technology function by providing a flexible and nimble structure that can keep pace and also evolve with rapid technological change, providing leverage for these changes to enhance competitive advantage as well.

Summary

In this chapter, we learned that fast-paced change in the external environment is led by technology-driven innovations. Hence, the technology component needs to be at the core of the enterprise and should be treated as a creator of value and not as a cost center. The primary drivers for the technology function must be to generate value for the customers and to enable the company to respond to change effectively, by aligning and closely collaborating with business stakeholders and customers. Moreover, given the fast rise of technology obsolescence, enterprises must implement platforms that will allow for "plug and play" style integration of applications and services, and also create architecture that can evolve with the changing technology landscape.

Using technology to come up with innovative offerings for customers is both a science and an art. Hence, companies must invest in building the core technological capabilities in-house and also nurture a culture of technology artisanship. The potential opportunities presented by emerging technologies are open to all. The organizations that have the capabilities to quickly identify this potential, and harness it effectively, will emerge as winners in the marketplace.

The next chapter is about the fifth component of the enterprise: governance. The chapter will cover the significance of governance and how to leverage governance mechanisms for enhancing enterprise agility.

References

[i] https://www.ing.com/Newsroom/All-news/We-want-to-be-a-tech-company-with-a-banking-license-Ralph-Hamers.htm

[ii] http://www.leanessays.com/2017/11/the-cost-center-trap.html

[iii] https://en.wikipedia.org/wiki/Legacy_system

[iv] https://en.wikipedia.org/wiki/Spaghetti_code

[v] https://dzone.com/articles/works-on-my-machine

[vi] https://www.gartner.com/it-glossary/bimodal/

[vii] https://martinfowler.com/bliki/BimodalIT.html

[viii] https://en.wikipedia.org/wiki/Commercial_off-the-shelf

[ix] http://www.independent.co.uk/news/business/news/british-airways-system-outage-it-worker-power-supply-switch-off-accident-flights-delayed-cancelled-a7768581.html

[x] https://en.wikipedia.org/wiki/Chaos_Monkey

[xi] https://en.wikipedia.org/wiki/Project_management_triangle

[xii] https://www.london.edu/-/media/files/publications/bsr/it-agility-striking-the-right-balance.pdf?la=en

[xiii] http://futureofcio.blogspot.com/2016/04/cio-master-book-preview-chapter-9-it.html

[xiv] https://www.smashingmagazine.com/2010/07/hack-nights/

[xv] https://www.scrum.org/resources/fedex-day-lighting-corporate-passion

[xvi] http://www.innolution.com/resources/glossary/last-responsible-moment-lrm

[xvii] https://www.thoughtworks.com/insights/blog/microservices-evolutionary-architecture

[xviii] https://en.wikipedia.org/wiki/T-shaped_skills

[xix] https://www.cutter.com/article/t-shaped-new-breed-it-professional-492976

[xx] https://www.cutter.com/article/t-shaped-new-breed-it-professional-492976

[xxi] https://www.gartner.com/binaries/content/assets/events/keywords/symposium/esc28/esc28_digitalbusiness.pdf

10

GOVERNANCE

At the enterprise level, governance is about aligning the resources and the capabilities of the organization with its highest-priority objectives and initiatives, to deliver maximum value outcomes for the stakeholders of the business. Governance in today's era is challenging, because the fast-changing environment means that the capabilities and initiatives of the enterprise are also changing. This implies that governance must contend with "moving goal posts." Hence, the challenge of achieving alignment between the resources and capabilities of the organization and its objectives and initiatives is much greater today than in the stable environments of the past.

A business that is modeled as a living system, that is, modeled for enhancing agility, needs to be governed very differently than a mechanistically modeled company, which is modeled to optimize efficiency, predictability, and certainty.

This chapter explores the following topics:

♦ The significance of governance for enterprise agility

♦ Governance-related inhibitors for enterprise agility

♦ Governance-related enablers of enterprise agility

Significance

In the period until the dawn of the Information Age, which was dominated by manufacturing, the focus of enterprise-level governance was more on managing constraints and optimizing efficiencies, rather than about maximizing effectiveness and creating value. In times of fast-paced change, where a company's survival hinges on satisfying customers through innovative offerings, continuing with the traditional governance approach is guaranteed to impede agility. Governance must enable the building and sustaining of the underlying capabilities of agility.

While governance is built into team-level Agile practices, such as daily stand-up meetings and sprint reviews, enterprise-level governance is a different "ball game" altogether. While team-level governance is based on the primary principles of visibility, transparency, and fast feedback, company-level governance not only encompasses these principles but is also about balancing the paradoxes such as order and freedom, short-term and long-term and effectiveness and efficiency. How effectively the business can balance these paradoxes has a direct bearing on the agility of the enterprise. Governance is also needed at the portfolio and program levels, to ensure that the strategic objectives are properly translated into team-level objectives, and that the teams work and collaborate in alignment to fulfill the strategic objectives.

Governance in an enterprise also reflects the mindset and behavior of leaders, and therefore it has a significant influence on the culture, and consequently the agility, of the enterprise.

Inhibitors to agility

The following factors related to governance are key barriers for enterprises looking to enhance and sustain agility.

Optimization of silos

Companies that are organized around functions usually treat each function as a cost center or a profit center, thereby budgets are allocated per functional area. Organizing vertically, according to functions, carries a huge risk of strategic objectives being broken down into parts, which not only may not add up to the whole, but may end up being misaligned with the strategy. This can happen as each functional area chooses to narrowly interpret the strategic objectives, that is, from the perspective of specific functions. For example, if the strategic objective is to use technology for competitive advantage, the priorities of the technology vision might not align with the priorities of the marketing division. The technology team may consider allocating most of their budget toward replacing an outdated ERP system, but the marketing team may want investment to be made in digital channels to improve customer experience. Often, the functions are not able to reach an agreement on their priorities, which can lead to suboptimal outcomes. In the preceding example, the marketing function could, using their budget, engage external partners to build digital channels, which might be a misfit with the current technology landscape.

Another serious consequence of operating in silos is that people in the enterprise find it hard to establish the link between the work they do and how it contributes to the purpose and strategic objectives of the business. This results in disengagement, which leads to low morale. Moreover, a cost center approach leads to measuring success based on controlling costs and adherence to the budget, rather than based on delivering valuable outcomes. Finally, this approach leaves no incentive to experiment and innovate.

Relying on misleading and non-actionable metrics

Metrics serve two primary purposes, from the perspective of governance:

- To guide decision-making through these:

    - Tracking progress toward outcomes

    - Providing a trend to extrapolate what might happen in the future

- To influence behaviors

A common anti-pattern in governance is to track and set targets on metrics that are not aligned with the preceding purposes or are even at crossroads with these purposes. Most of these metrics are either misleading or non-actionable or both. Some such categories of metrics are explored in the following subsections.

Watermelon metrics

Watermelon metrics are metrics which, like watermelons, are green on the outside but red inside. In other words, these metrics superficially mask the grim realities by portraying outwardly that things are fine or are on track. Some examples are as follows:

- **Average call duration**: A lower average call duration does not necessarily imply more efficiency. In a bid to keep the call duration short, some customer servicing staff may not be focused on completely resolving the customer's problem. This may be resulting in more calls coming in, as customers may be calling again and, more importantly, the customer satisfaction levels may be dropping.

- **Test coverage**: Unit tests may be written for each component, without having any unit tests at the code level. It is so easy and yet completely misleading to claim 100% test coverage, based purely on writing a single test for every component.

- **Revenue**: Increase in revenue could be due to relaxing credit terms for risky customers or offering a higher rate of discount.

- **System availability**: A high system availability/uptime percentage, say 98%, is no indication of the reliability of the system. The 2% failure may relate to failure happening when it hurts the most, for example, for an online retailer, the website crashing on Black Friday [i], due to much higher traffic levels, can be disastrous.

- **Utilization**: A high utilization percentage, which is used as an indicator for how busy people are at work, is no indicator of the quality of work or the value that is being created. The utilization may be high due to rework and non-value-added work, which are essentially a waste.

In a similar way, summary dashboards, which show green as **RAG** (short for, **red, amber, green**) status could also be watermelons. Moreover, averages, particularly the mean, could be misleading if looked at in isolation, for example, the average sales per customer may be skewed because only a few of the customers have very high sales.

Vanity metrics

Vanity metrics capture things that can be measured, but which have little or no correlation with value-driven outcomes. They give a false sense of success and are of no help in guiding decision-making. Consider these examples:

- Number of people signed up for a newsletter. It does not provide an indication of the level of meaningful customer engagement.

- Number of website views. It may have no correlation with customers who actually purchased something and provide no insights on which customer segments are visiting the website and why.

- Amount of pre-approved loans. It may have little correlation to actual drawdowns by the borrowers.

Lagging indicators

A lagging indicator metric is one which reflects an event after it has taken place, for example, revenue is counted after the product is sold to the customer and cost is counted after it is incurred. They are output-oriented and therefore easy to measure.

However, these indicators do not provide any insight into what might be influencing them and therefore they fall under the category of non-actionable metrics. If the percentage of defects resolved within the **service-level agreement (SLA)** of 72 hours is 70%, it provides no clue on why 30% of the defects did not get resolved in the SLA period. Leading indicators, which measure the variables that influence the outcome, can provide clues to taking specific action. For example, if the average backlog per agent who resolves the defects is greater than the three-day capacity of the agent, it points toward taking the action of adding more capacity or increasing the agent's productivity or both.

Metrics that drive wrong behaviors

Metrics play a very critical role in influencing how people behave. The following are examples of metrics that can drive behaviors that are not aligned to agility:

- A tester is measured on the number of defects found. This discourages the tester from working with others in the team to prevent defects from happening in the first place.

♦ A fixed sum is given away as a bonus to salespeople, where the salespeople get more bonus if they do better than their peers. This discourages the salespeople from helping each other. If someone needs to "win" at the cost of someone else, collaboration will not happen.

♦ A manager is measured on maximizing the percentage utilization of people reporting into them. The manager is unlikely to allow any time to be spent on learning and sharing.

♦ A senior executive is given a bonus as a percentage of net profit of the division/enterprise. The executive is highly likely to drive enterprise transformation only from the perspective of maximizing cost reduction.

When people are rewarded based on targets that do not align with agility, it leaves very little incentive for people to do what is right to enhance and sustain agility.

Sunk cost fallacy

A sunk cost is a cost that has already been incurred and that cannot be recovered [ii]. The moot point about sunk cost is that the cost is irrelevant for future decision-making and therefore should not be allowed to influence rational decision-making. For example, a person buys a movie ticket and five minutes into the movie realizes that the movie is terrible. The person at this point has two choices: to continue to watch the terrible movie or to get out of the theatre at that point and do something more valuable with the time saved by not watching the rest of the movie. If the person stays back to watch the movie just because they paid for the ticket and therefore want to recover the cost, while there is an option available to spend their time in a better way, this person has fallen for the sunk cost fallacy. A gambler continuing to bet more money, with the hope of recovering money lost, is also an example of the sunk cost fallacy.

The sunk cost fallacy is also known as "throwing good money after bad money." A well-known example in the corporate world is in the banking industry, where an additional loan is often given to a defaulting customer, to avoid treating the bad loan as an **NPA** (short for, **non-performing asset**).

Even though the perils of the sunk cost fallacy are very evident, it is not uncommon to find enterprises falling prey to this fallacy, for example, the business case for a new product is based on a spend of $5 million in one year, with expected return of $10 million in two years. Assume that after spending $3 million, the enterprise takes the basic product to the market after six months but gets feedback that the product is not accepted by the market. At this point, the company has a choice to write off the $3 million already spent and stop the development of this product, thereby having the choice to invest the remaining $2 million earmarked for this product in a potentially better opportunity. However, if the business continues to invest the remaining $2 million in the product, knowing that the feedback on the product is not encouraging, but still hoping that the additional investment will rescue the product, it is a victim of the sunk cost fallacy.

Another example is when an enterprise has spent significant money to enter the market, but a competitor has quickly grabbed market share by coming out with a value-added offering at the same price, offering a distinct competitive advantage to the competitor. If the organization continues to be in that market with that offering, with the hope of recovering the money already spent, it has fallen to the sunk cost fallacy.

Leaders become victims of the sunk cost fallacy for multiple reasons:

- It is psychologically proven that humans have a stronger preference for avoiding loss than for acquiring gains [iii]. This tendency for loss aversion makes it difficult for leaders to "bite the bullet."

♦ Leaders become emotionally invested in the initiative, which makes it extremely difficult for them to cut it short and more importantly to accept that it is not realizing the intended outcomes. Most start-up entrepreneurs experience this syndrome when they realize that they have no choice but to shut down or sell the business.

♦ Leaders fear a loss of promotion or drop in bonus and therefore try to push the pain forward by continuing to invest in an initiative that should be stopped. They buy time, hoping that this initiative may turn around or they can get an opportunity to create a success story in that time, which can make them look better in the wake of the *failed* initiative.

♦ Recognizing sunk cost means stopping further investment in that initiative, thereby having to write off the investment and taking a hit on the profit and loss account. Leaders may want to postpone this loss for reasons related to shareholder expectations about profit and taxation. They will therefore continue investing in the initiative just to keep it alive.

Sunk cost fallacy leads to waste, often enormous, of time, effort and money, which could have been used for initiatives that produce greater value.

Speed at the cost of quality

Teams are often governed and measured based on how fast they deliver. While speed to market is critical, often teams are seen to be compromising on quality for the sake of speed. When the team is under pressure to deliver fast, the mindset often is: "We will worry about defects if and when they arise." Given that the time and effort spent on fixing defects is essentially rework, and therefore a waste, compromising on quality, knowingly or otherwise, is simply not an option.

The impact of poor quality, as hard as it may be to quantify, can be very severe. A website crashing during peak loads, leading to loss of revenue, a drop in customer satisfaction and damage to brand image are some of the consequences that can prove extremely costly for an enterprise.

Moreover, treating quality as relatively less important than speed will inevitably result in technical debt, which can prove very costly. Achieving high quality with high speed of delivery is not a paradox. Making quality the responsibility of everyone in a team, such that quality is built in from the beginning, following good engineering practices, and inculcating a mindset of "quality not just for today, but for tomorrow" are critical to achieving high quality, without compromising on speed of delivery.

Annual budgeting

The practice of annual budgeting at the enterprise level is created on the primary premises of predictability and stability in the external environment and within the company, and success being associated with the ability to manage constraints. However, in an era where business priorities need to keep pace with a fast-changing environment, making major financial decisions once a year is almost certain to impede enterprise agility.

The following are some of the major issues with budgeting on an annual basis, in today's era:

- ◆ Funds are allocated based on a business case, which is prepared primarily on a set of untested hypotheses and driven by the budget deadline.

- ◆ Since most, or all, of the budget for the financial year is already mostly, or fully, allocated at the beginning of the financial year, there is little room left to allocate funds to new initiatives and opportunities that may come up during the year.

To make things worse, funds are usually earmarked on a department or function basis, thereby encouraging local optimization and discouraging collaboration across departments. This makes it hard to bring together coherent offerings, which are greater than the sum of the parts. Moreover, the silos make it easy for unscrupulous executives to manipulate the numbers in their reporting on budget-related outcomes.

◆ The annual budget is largely inflexible to adjust to changes in assumptions, which can either strengthen or invalidate the business case, thereby falling short of funds where they are most needed or wasting money on a lost cause respectively. The budgets do not have any mechanism to link incremental spending to the achievement of intended outcomes. Moreover, annual budgets are often created based on percentage increase over previous spends. It therefore encourages leaders to spend the budgeted money, even when it may not be necessary for creating value. The budget, therefore, may be out of sync with the current opportunities and challenges that the business may be facing.

◆ An enterprise has gone to the extent of penalizing their executives for even spending below the budget, the rationale being that if the amount had been budgeted correctly, the unspent amount could have been allocated to another initiative.

◆ It leads to most initiatives for which the budget is approved starting around the same time, thereby creating unnecessary execution strain on the enterprise.

Setting a budget in stone creates rigidity across the enterprise, which is a huge impediment to agility.

Governing for compliance and documentation

The traditional mindset is that if people strictly follow the process and produce detailed documentary evidence of having done so, the project/initiative will succeed. The emphasis is to minimize variations (which is a hangover from manufacturing and made worse by six sigma-driven quality control) and even eliminate them. If there are variations, these are treated as exceptions and must go through a heavyweight change control process. Rather than spending time to work closely with teams, project managers are fully tied up preparing reams of documentation to provide evidence for getting the approval to pass through the "gate." Moreover, the enterprise can have a process that has multiple such checkpoint gates, which actually are a drain on people's time and energy. There are specific roles created for people in the **project management office (PMO)**, whose full-time job is only to check and ensure compliance by examining detailed documentation and verifying the evidence provided in the documentation. The project managers are often treated as "guilty until proven innocent". These people who mind the gates are empowered to reject the evidence even for the slightest slip up or discrepancy, which can seriously hurt the project's progress and lead to a lot of waste. Moreover, these people are seldom held accountable for their decisions and have unilateral veto power to stop the project from progressing forward, for example, an enterprise has a monthly release cycle for all software projects. For a flimsy documentation or compliance mistake, the release may have to wait an additional month for that project.

The message that such a type of governance sends to the delivery teams is that they are accountable only for complying with the process and producing the documentation, and not for project outcomes and value creation. Of course, process and documentation are necessary to the extent they add value, but enterprises need to seriously think about how much of that is good enough. They should be adequate enough to enable the creation and delivery of value, and not impede it.

If they are adding value, then they should be given as much priority and capacity as given to developing a feature. Blind compliance to a standardized process shouldn't be encouraged in times where speed to market can mean the difference between survival and extinction of the enterprise, especially when it comes to experimentation-oriented projects and initiatives where fast feedback from the market is extremely critical.

Projects/initiatives delinked from strategy

Enterprises often take up projects and initiatives that may appear to be benefitting the business, but may not actually be doing so. Sometimes projects are taken up in a hurry, in order to gain the first-mover advantage, without adequately evaluating whether the project is in alignment with the enterprise's business strategy. Occasionally, the business case is "shoehorned" to make it appear that it is aligned to strategy.

The root cause of the misalignment often is that local/silo optimization is encouraged over taking an end-to-end organization-level approach. It can therefore result in departments like marketing and technology attempting to optimize the respective functions, rather than value aligned to strategy. Moreover, projects below a certain value may not go through the rigor of ascertaining alignment with strategy before being launched. However, small projects across the enterprise can add up to a significant number, for example, a large business in the UK had 24% of its yearly spend allocated to projects that were disjointed from the strategies of the enterprise. This is acceptable only if there is a conscious decision taken to run projects as experiments in order to seek out strategies. Such projects come under scrutiny only when they are in trouble and need more money, people or time in a bid to rescue them. These projects often get terminated at this point, when the realization dawns that they are not aligned to the overall strategy.

Another reason is that the strategy may not be well understood or may not make sense and therefore people are unable to translate the strategy into something to which they can relate their work to. Projects and initiatives not aligned to strategy can end up wasting precious resources of the company and deprive the enterprise of opportunities to create value.

"Frozen middle"

The frozen middle, that is, the middle layer of management, has been discussed in *Chapter 6, Organization Structure*. This layer is not only an impediment for agility from a structural perspective but also from governance perspective. Due to this big layer in the middle of the hierarchy, the governance structures become heavy at the top. This leads to not only a delay in senior executives receiving the information "on the ground," but, more importantly, the information received at the top getting diluted or even distorted by the middle managers to hide bad news or to make themselves look good. The vertical flow of information and decisions through the hierarchy, which is significantly "taller" due to the frozen middle, significantly impacts the timeliness and quality of decisions, thereby reducing the responsiveness of the enterprise.

Enablers to agility

The following factors related to governance can significantly help enterprises to enhance agility.

Value-driven prioritization

The fast pace of change is creating pressure on enterprises to create new offerings, take them to the market as quickly as possible and keep enhancing them continuously. Due to this, most enterprises are in a situation where there are many initiatives that the organization would like to do, but there are constraints around people and monetary resources that they are able to allocate to these initiatives. Many enterprises make the mistake of treating all initiatives as equally important.

As Patrick Lencioni, the author of the book, *The Five Dysfunctions of a Team* has aptly said:

> *"If everything is important, then nothing is." [iv]*

Lack of prioritization, that is, everything is treated as important, leads to fights among initiative sponsors for getting the people and money for their respective initiatives, which often leads to the more critical initiatives being understaffed and under-resourced, thereby not only impacting the speed to market of the critical initiatives, but also creating higher work in progress, which has a carrying cost.

People and money, which are perennially in limited supply, can be optimally allocated only if the enterprise can prioritize initiatives based on those which have the potential to, and are actually proving to, deliver the highest value. Moreover, enterprises must set priorities at both strategic and operational levels, that is, at strategy level and within each strategy at initiative level, and within each initiative at feature level, within each feature at epic level and so on.

Prioritization helps to create alignment about the strategic and operational priorities of the enterprise. The alignment leads to the matching of people with the appropriate capabilities to initiatives, especially the higher-priority ones. Moreover, clarity in priorities enables the teams to make better decisions, without having to always rely on the leaders to do so.

One of the prioritization techniques is prioritizing features by the **WSJF** (short for, **Weighted Shortest Job First**) [v] method. This method helps to bring objectivity in determining which feature, or any other work unit for that matter, should be given higher priority for completion.

The original formula for calculating WSJF is as follows:

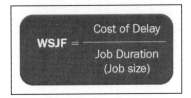

Figure 10.1: The WSJF formula

The item with the highest WSJF value is the item that should get highest priority. It is important to note that job duration/size, being in the denominator of the formula, has a significant influence on the WSJF score. Given everything else being the same, the smaller the job duration/size, the higher the WSJF score will be.

The cost of delay is calculated as follows:

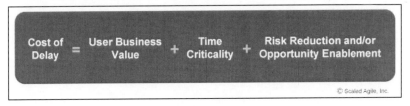

Figure 10.2: The cost of delay formula

Scaled Agile Inc., the creator of the SAFe framework for Agile, defines the cost of delay elements as follows:

> *"User-business value — Do our users prefer this over that? What is the revenue impact on our business? Is there a potential penalty or other adverse consequences if we delay?*
>
> *Time criticality — How does the user/business value decay over time? Is there a fixed deadline? Will they wait for us or move to another solution? Are there Milestones on the critical path impacted by this?*
>
> *Risk reduction-opportunity enablement value — What else does this do for our business? Does it reduce the risk of this or a future delivery? Is there value in the information we will receive? Will this feature open up new business opportunities?"* [vi]

While Scaled Agile Inc., suggests using the relative sizing [vii] technique to assign values to all base variables in the equations, real values, if known, can also be used. Joshua Arnold, managing director of Black Swan Farming, which is in the field of product development consulting, suggests using a modified version of WSJF. According to him, if expected value is zero, then time criticality should not matter. The modification that he makes is to multiply value by urgency and not add them. The revised formula for cost of delay, therefore, is as follows:

Cost of delay = (user or business value + risk reduction and/or opportunity enablement) × (time criticality) [viii]

Since prioritization is based on a set of assumptions, especially about business value, it is important to periodically ascertain whether those assumptions continue to be valid, or if they need to change based on feedback. If so, changing the priorities of the initiatives may become imperative.

Continuous validation of value

The traditional approach to governance makes a fundamental assumption that leaders and managers are able to predict outcomes. It is therefore not surprising that once a project or initiative is approved, the business case is seldom revised. The focus is on monitoring variations in projected versus actual numbers, with the implicit assumption that the projected numbers are valid.

However, in a complex environment, where fast-paced change is the norm, it is important to validate the projections and the underlying assumptions at short intervals. Changing customer preferences, a competitor coming out with a new offering, finding additional complexity in the project that invalidates a part or all of the business case, are some reasons that reinforce the need to verify whether changes are needed to the project or even whether it should be discontinued. The focus and effort on validation may taper off as the backlog of features is delivered. The key takeaway here is that validation and delivery need to happen in parallel and not sequentially.

The following diagram depicts the dual-track approach of simultaneous validation and delivery:

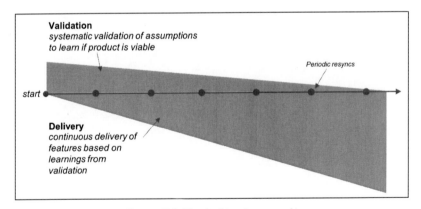

Figure 10.3: The dual-track approach

Validation can be effective only if the following conditions are fulfilled:

- Knowing what to validate
- Short feedback loops, which enable the team to quickly gather the relevant information needed for validation
- The ability to act quickly, based on learnings from validation

Incremental funding

In a complex and fast-changing environment, predicting outcomes with a high level of certainty is futile. The value propositions, based on which funding decisions are made, are mere hypotheses, which need to be validated periodically to ascertain whether the cost-benefit equation continues to be favorable. Moreover, committing the entire funding needed for an initiative can deprive the enterprise of opportunities to invest in potentially more valuable initiatives, which can come up at any time.

Companies must align their investments to value streams where they see the highest potential to generate value, rather than commit upfront to funding a project or an initiative. The critical enablers for effective funding are periodic releases of highest priority features and getting feedback on actual realization of value. A *go* or *no go* decision must be made after each release about continuing to create the next highest priority features in the backlog or stopping the initiative in favor of investing in another initiative, which has the potential for creating more value.

The following figure highlights the importance of periodic checkpoints for incremental funding, tied to incremental delivery:

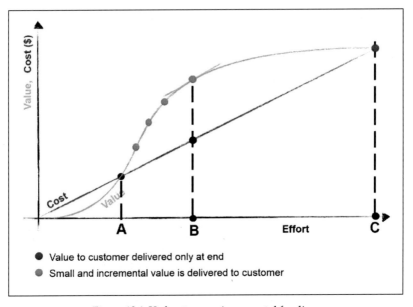

Figure 10.4: Upfront versus incremental funding.

In a "big bang" approach, the realization of value happens only at the end of the project, that is, at point **C** in the plot. If the project is stopped midway, there is no value generated, as nothing has been delivered yet. This means that the entire cost until that point will turn into a loss.

On the other hand, under the incremental approach, the **MVP** (short for, **minimum viable product**) [ix] is delivered at point **A** in time, with funds being committed only until this milestone. At that point, the value generated equals the cost incurred. Assuming that there is potential to generate greater value with the next incremental release, funding is committed to the extent needed for the next release, which is planned for point **B** on the timeline.

The release is made at point **B** as planned and, as seen in the figure, the cumulative value generated is far greater than the cumulative cost incurred until that point in time. If the assessment at this point is that the potential for incremental value is limited, the initiative can be stopped at point **B** itself. The cost not spent on the initiative, which is about 50% of the total budgeted cost, can be incurred on another initiative that has the potential to deliver greater value.

Funding that is linked to the validation of value-oriented outcomes at periodic intervals, as opposed to funding a project, sets the enterprise up for maximizing return on its portfolio of investments. This will lead to a mindset change from "do we have budget for this?" to "will the next milestone generate enough value to justify the investment?"

Balancing of leading and lagging indicators

Effective governance needs to have metrics that are a balance of leading and lagging indicators. While lagging indicators measure outputs and outcomes, leading indicators measure what is influencing the outputs and outcomes. For example, customer satisfaction is a lagging indicator and happy and engaged employees is a leading indicator, as empirical evidence suggests that happy and engaged employees result in higher customer satisfaction [x]. Typically, lagging indicators are much easier to measure and are also more accurate than leading indicators. This is often why leading indicators are not measured.

While lagging indicators are post-event metrics, which are essential for measuring progress toward goals, leading indicators must also be measured, as they are predictive in nature. However, being predictive, they do not provide complete certainty about the successful outputs and outcomes. Hence, deciding leading indicators can be tricky. Often, they are decided based on assumptions, which should be validated until a consistent pattern of positive correlation with the leading indicator emerges.

Sometimes, a lagging indicator for an outcome can become a lagging indicator for another outcome. For example, customer satisfaction, which is a lagging indicator for a marketing outcome, can be a lagging indicator for the company's stock price, which is a finance outcome. Occasionally, leading indicators can be derived from lagging indicators. An example of this is the burn-up chart. The chart is powerful not only because it provides visibility on both leading and lagging indicators but also because it is easy to understand and interpret. Moreover, it can be applied to any initiative or piece of work that is to be delivered over a period of time, and where the scope of work and throughput can be quantified using a common unit of measure like story points. [xi]

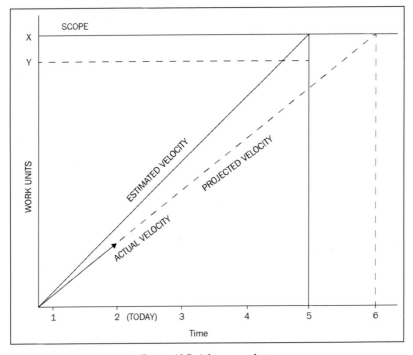

Figure 10.5: A burn-up chart

The preceding burn-up chart shows that *scope* = X is expected to be delivered by the end of time period **5**, based on an estimate of average throughput, that is, velocity, per time period. At end of time period **2**, the actual cumulative velocity (lagging indicator) is below the estimated velocity. If the expectation is that the team's future velocity will be in line with the actual velocity for the past two time periods, the trend line of projected velocity (leading indicator) indicates that the team will be able to deliver the entire scope at the end of period **6**, as opposed to the original estimate of completing delivery at the end of period **5**.

The leading indicator provides meaningful information, which can help the team to take action before it is too late. The decision options are as follows:

♦ To reduce the scope from **X** to **Y**, such that the delivery of scope is completed by time period **5**

♦ To add capacity to the team to bump up the throughput, to get it in line with estimated velocity

♦ To accept the reality that if nothing is changed, the team will need one extra time period to deliver the entire scope

In another commonly found scenario, there is an increase in scope midway through the project. The impact of scope increase on the timeline will become immediately evident, by extending the velocity trend line to the point where it intersects with the revised scope line. William Bruce Cameron, author of multiple bestselling books including *A Dog's Purpose*, has rightly said, "Not everything that can be counted counts, and not everything that counts can be counted." Counting a balanced set of metrics, which includes the relevant leading and lagging indicators, will help significantly toward achieving effective governance.

Attend showcases/demos

While quantitative metrics provide insights about progress toward objectives and information to guide decision-making, mere numbers often don't tell the entire story. Attending team-level showcases/demos can provide additional insights, which are not reflected in the metrics.

Doing a showcase [xii] at the end of every iteration is an integral and critical part of the Agile way of working. The team demonstrates to the business stakeholders what they have created during the iteration, which is typically features and stories planned for the iteration. The team also explains reasons for not being able to deliver anything that was planned to be delivered at the end of the iteration, if any. This is a periodic opportunity for the sponsors and business stakeholders to give feedback to the team in terms of a change in priorities of the product/feature. The feedback provided by the business stakeholders serves as a critical input for adaptive planning for the backlog.

Attending the showcase/demo, as a third-party independent observer, can provide evidence of the morale of the team, how happy the sponsors are with the outcomes, the impediments, and dependencies and blockers that may be hampering the team's ability to deliver optimally. Getting a direct feel for these variables across teams, and abstracting patterns at portfolio and enterprise levels, can guide decision-making from a governance perspective.

End-to-end link between purpose and initiatives

An enterprise with high agility will endeavor to deliver the highest value outcomes that are aligned to its purpose and mission. It is critical to have clarity on how the strategies are defined and refined, such that they meet their purpose and every initiative is contributing toward making the strategy successful. Often, these linkages are weakened due to the churn in strategies and the underlying initiatives, arising from the need to adapt to a fast-changing environment.

Clarity on end-to-end linkage between the purpose of the enterprise and ground-level initiatives is critical to enable employees across the company to remain focused and aligned on outcomes that matter, and not get distracted by doing things that can result in suboptimal outcomes, like optimizing a silo. The effective approach to connecting purpose (the *why* of the enterprise) to strategy (the *what*), and strategy to initiatives, that is, execution (the *how*) is the **lean value tree** (**LVT**).

The LVT structure is as follows:

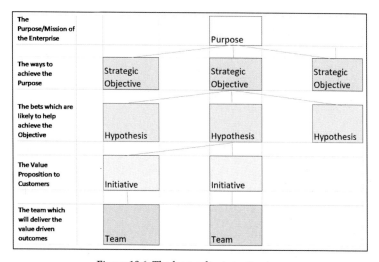

Figure 10.6: The lean value tree structure

The following diagram is a simple example of an LVT, applied at a personal level:

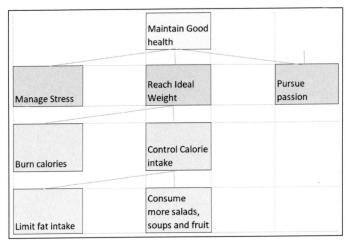

Figure 10.7: An LVT example

It is very critical that for each level of the LVT, namely, purpose, strategic objectives, hypothesis and initiatives, measures of success are defined. For the preceding example, the measures of success at each level can be as follows:

◆ **Maintain healthy lifestyle**: Blood sugar, blood pressure, and cholesterol are within acceptable levels and the person is able to get eight hours of sound sleep every day.

◆ **Reach ideal body weight**: Attain weight of 65 kgs.

◆ **Control calorie intake**: Maximum 1500 calories per day, of which maximum 200 calories from wine

◆ **Limit fat intake**: Maximum intake to be 30 grams per day

In complex systems, the cause-effect relationship is not necessarily linear. Therefore, measuring outcomes at every step is necessary to ensure that the objectives, hypotheses, and initiatives remain aligned to the purpose, for example, despite controlling calorie intake and burning adequate calories, the weight may not go down. It is then necessary to bring in another hypothesis about hormonal balance. The key implication is that all components of the value stream, from purpose right down to initiatives, are subject to being revised. Enterprises must ensure that all initiatives that are ongoing, or still to be started, remain / are aligned to deliver on the strategic objectives that they are associated with.

LVT combined with continuous validation of outcomes, freedom to experiment at the initiative level, and incremental funding of initiatives will ensure that the portfolio of investments is geared to deliver maximum value for the enterprise.

Summary

In this chapter, we learned that governing for greater agility is about optimizing the entire value stream, in order to deliver valuable outcomes aligned to fulfill the purpose of the enterprise. The focus of governance must shift from being on process and compliance, to focusing on inclusiveness and delivering valuable outcomes. The decision-making must be collaborative and must include teams that are directly delivering outcomes. The metrics must enable decision-making by not only measuring progress toward the outcomes but also pointing to variables that can influence the outcomes.

At the company level, governance is about keeping the business on the fine line between order and chaos, that is, on the "edge of chaos" [xiii]. As stated in *Chapter 3, The Enterprise as a Living System*, complex adaptive systems function best when they are on this edge, in terms of enabling experimentation and learning, and therefore are better equipped to respond and adapt to change.

The next chapter will examine the sixth and last major component of the enterprise: the customer, and will explore how best to serve the customer for enhancing effectiveness of enterprise agility.

References

[i] https://en.wikipedia.org/wiki/Black_Friday_(shopping)

[ii] https://en.wikipedia.org/wiki/Sunk_cost

[iii] http://leepublish.typepad.com/strategicthinking/2015/03/sunk-cost-fallacy.html

[iv] https://www.goodreads.com/quotes/10464-if-everything-is-important-then-nothing-is

[v] https://www.scaledagileframework.com/wsjf/

[vi] https://www.scaledagileframework.com/wsjf/

[vii] https://sites.google.com/site/agilepatterns/home/relative-sizing

[viii] http://blackswanfarming.com/safes-cost-of-delay-a-suggested-improvement/

[ix] https://en.wikipedia.org/wiki/Minimum_viable_product

[x] https://www.usatoday.com/story/money/personalfinance/2013/02/19/treating-employees-well-stock-price/1839887/

[xi] https://www.mountaingoatsoftware.com/blog/what-are-story-points

[xii] http://www.agileacademy.com.au/agile/sites/default/files/Showcases%202011.pdf

[xiii] https://en.wikipedia.org/wiki/Edge_of_chaos

11

CUSTOMER

What is the focal point for everything that a business does? Who is even more powerful than the board of directors in influencing the future of a business? Which is the most important entity on whose patronage the survivability of a company depends? The answer to all of these questions is straightforward: the customer. As obvious as this may seem, it is quite surprising that many enterprises overlook or even ignore this blatant fact, intentionally or otherwise. If this seems too extreme, it can at least be said that most organizations see the customer as being "on the other side of the table."

The aforementioned mindset toward the customer can lead to a belief that delivering value to customers and generating value for the enterprise are two different objectives. The potential misalignment between these two objectives can result in trading off one for the other, which will result in an overall suboptimal outcome. A business must view customers as an integral and critical part of its ecosystem. This will enable the enterprise to truly become a "customer-first" company.

This chapter explores the following topics:

♦ The significance of the customer for enterprise agility

♦ Customer-related inhibitors to the effectiveness of enterprise agility

♦ Customer-related enablers to the effectiveness of enterprise agility

Significance

Until recently, most companies, especially well-established ones, served their customers in predictable ways and could largely take their customers for granted. Most product segments had a few established brands and the customer did not have much to choose from. High entry barriers were a huge deterrent for new players, which meant that for most products and services, enterprises were in a market-driving position. Consumers made their buying decisions based on a sequential "funnel" model of awareness-interest-desire-action. The consumer had no other source of information about the products than what was provided by the marketers and, more importantly, the engagement with the consumer was extremely minimal until the "action," that is, ready to buy stage was reached.

Contrast this with today's environment, where the customer has plenty of choice, a new player can suddenly crop up and disrupt the market with a unique offering, there is plenty of independent information available for the consumer to evaluate the product and so on. Consumers now want to engage with marketers at every stage of the buying process, which is now nonlinear and complex. Consumers are seeking to not just have their needs met, but also to be satisfied through exceptional service and innovative offerings. Customers today are not just seeking to fulfill a need. They now expect to get an end-to-end value-driven experience. They are ready to quickly shift loyalties to anyone who offers them a value-driven outcome and experience. An enterprise that fails to anticipate and respond to a change in customer preferences is likely to lose its value rapidly, a good example of which is Nokia, which quickly lost customers to the iPhone, as it offered a superior experience.

The connection between agility and customers is critical. It is obvious that agility is needed to serve customers, for the reasons discussed earlier. Equally important is the fact that the capabilities underlying agility must be effective toward serving customers.

While the other five primary components of the enterprise (organization structure, process, people, technology, and governance) can be leveraged for enhancing agility, the customer component of the business can enable the company to increase the effectiveness of the capabilities underlying agility.

For example, the effectiveness of the innovativeness capability can be increased through better understanding of customer needs and aspirations and aligning the experimentation initiatives to meet the needs and aspirations of customers. Similarly, a closer connection with customers will provide guidance on the best ways to maximize being responsive to them. An enterprise may be very responsive when customers interact through digital channels. However, the customers may be seeking personal interaction with the same level of responsiveness as the digital channels. It is only through a close connection with the customers that the enterprise will gain this insight, thereby improving the effectiveness of its responsiveness capability.

Inhibitors to the effectiveness of agility

The following factors related to customers are key barriers that impede the effectiveness of enterprise agility.

Exploitation mindset

For every business, the only source that generates revenue and profits is the customer. Moreover, every business aims to maximize both revenue and profits continuously. In the zest to increase these numbers, customers are sometimes viewed as resources, which are meant to be exploited. The tactics of exploitation are usually built around the fears and ignorance of customers.

One of commonly found means of exploitation is making false claims about the product. Examples of false claims are many, from food products to cars to social networking sites [i]. Danone claimed that its yoghurt brand, Activia, was clinically and scientifically proven to boost the immune system and regulate digestion. Based on this claim, Activia was priced 30% higher than similar products. A lawsuit filed by a customer resulted in a judgement that these claims were false.

Another such case, which got high publicity globally, is that of Volkswagen cheating on emission tests on its diesel cars [ii]. Volkswagen admitted that 11 million cars sold worldwide had been fitted with a *defeat device*, a software that could detect when the vehicle was being tested, which would trigger a temporary change in the engine's performance.

When such exploitations get discovered, through lawsuits or by law enforcement agencies, the consequences for enterprises are very severe. Not only is the reputation of the business and the concerned brand damaged, but the story gets amplified and spreads like wildfire due to social media, and the company may have to take a severe financial hit, for example, Volkswagen had to pay a fine of $25 billion in the USA alone [iii].

Another form of exploitation is the purposeful lack of transparency. Fees related to the servicing of loans, terms of product warranties, and exclusions in insurance policies are commonly found examples of lack of transparency. Such items may either not be stated in the contract with the customer or could be in such fine print and clubbed with so many other terms and conditions written in legal jargon, that most customers may not bother to read them. Another case of non-transparency, which is still unfolding as the book goes to press and which has affected about 87 million people across the globe, is the Facebook data leak episode [iv], in which Facebook is purported to have shared personal data of its subscribers with third parties, without the consent of the subscribers.

Conscious exploitation of customers is clearly a breach of their trust. While enterprises may think that they can get away with it, if and when they are exposed, the customers are bound to feel cheated and deceived. Slogans like "our customers are our highest priority" and "we exist to satisfy our customers" suddenly sound extremely hollow. The relationship between the business and its customers may be damaged beyond repair or may take a very long time to become normal again.

While it is important to continuously anticipate customer needs, the digital age necessitates that businesses must understand the negative impact of using technology to discover and meet customer needs, for example, **GDPR** (short for, **General Data Protection Regulation**) [v], a law regarding the protection of personal data, is an afterthought which happened because businesses did not take adequate measures to protect the personal data of customers. Measures such as **PBD** (short for, **privacy by design**) [vi], an approach to ensure data protection rights from the outset, must be built by enterprises into product design.

Taking customers for granted

According to Panos Mourdoukoutas [vii], a professor and chair of the Department of Economics at LIU Post in New York:

> *"Of all strategic mistakes the leadership of fast-growing corporations make, one stands out: taking the customer for granted. Blinded by growth, leadership comes to believe that whatever products corporations produce are unique and indispensable, so their customers will always be there to buy them." [viii]*

As elaborated on in *Chapter 3, The Enterprise as a Living System*, this mindset comes from the times of the industrial revolution, when businesses were in a seller's market, as customers had limited product and service options to choose from and the demand for products and services generally exceeded their supply.

However, it is now clearly a buyer's market across most industries, as customers now have a wider choice of products and services, are ready to change their preferences based on offerings enabled by newer technologies (for example, moving from branch visit banking to mobile banking) and due to the widespread availability of information, are much more aware of not only the choices they have but also the opinions of customers who are already using a product or service.

Enterprises that are taking their customer base and customers' tastes and preferences for granted are hugely risking losing their customer base to the competition. Companies must accept the reality that competitive advantage is moving from being sustainable to becoming transient, as customers are willing to dump loyalty if they see the potential for better value in a competitor's offering.

The most common and visible symptom of taking customers for granted is poor customer service. Kate Nasser, The People Skills Coach™, has compiled the 25 worst customer service stories in her article, *The 25 Worst Customer Service Stories to Train the Best CSRs* [ix]. The following are a few of them. They are replies given by customer service representatives:

♦ "There is nothing I can do for you."

♦ "You are not listening to me."

♦ "I am sorry but that's our policy."

♦ "You will have to go online and fix this."

♦ "You are not understanding our process."

Sunny Bindra, a management consultant based in Kenya, sums it up nicely when he says:

> *"Many businesses know they are short-changing customers in terms of service delivery; yet they will still engage in marketing sprees, selling their wares at every street corner, engaging in wall-to-wall advertising. The result?*

*More queues, more congestion, more frustration. Why
do we never factor in the cost of the annoyance we instill in
customers? We are feeding a pool of suppressed ill-will, which
will only become apparent when credible competitors appear;
then, your 'loyal' customers will abandon you in droves." [x]*

Focusing only on linear customer journeys

The word journey implies starting at one point and travelling to
a predetermined point, implying linearity. However, in today's
digital world, a business that restricts itself to linear user journeys,
and optimizing those journeys, is likely to lose customers, as this
forces customers to adhere to predefined journeys.

According to Daniel Taylor, a digital marketer:

*"Every customer is different and has their own set of needs,
wants, preferences and behavioral patterns. Brands need to
see customers as people and appreciate that each relationship
will be different. In the modern age, the journey now has
perpetual motion, with the course firmly in the customers'
hands. By making this change, a brand can start to make
meaningful relationships and making itself more relevant
in the modern, multi-channel world." [xi]*

He adds:

*"Modern customer service isn't 9-til-5, it's a perpetual
engagement machine, where customer-controlled erratic
'journeys' need to be met on the customer's terms, with
the end result being customer satisfaction with as little
effort being exerted by the customer as possible."*

An example of a nonlinear approach to user journeys is the introduction pick-up points by Amazon. For those customers who are unlikely to be home to take delivery of the product, Amazon introduced pick-up points [xii], where customers could collect their parcel as per their convenience. Moreover, Amazon also provided the facility to nominate someone else to collect the package, in case the buyer is not able to collect the package personally.

The challenge is for enterprises to allow flexibility, by which the customer can start and stop the journey as per their convenience. A "boilerplate template" approach is likely to leave a large number of customers unsatisfied with their experience.

According to Jonathan David Lewis, a partner and strategy director at McKee Wallwork + Co. [xiii]:

> *"We're witnessing the rise of what I call "palindrome marketing," a new approach to the customer journey that looks more like a circle than a line. Business is no longer linear, and relevance requires marketers to build programs that are on-demand and self-aware."*

He further adds:

> *"If you want to succeed in our on-demand culture, your business approach must move beyond old conceptions of customer journeys. It must operate as a complete thought, relevant and coherent at every entry point. It must have depth, consistency and anticipate needs far before a prospect realizes they have them. It must be nonlinear." [xiv]*

Make assumptions about customer needs and preferences

Many businesses make the mistake of believing that they understand the needs of their customers and that their products and services are aligned to meet those needs. The needs of the customers are usually derived from market research reports and industry trends, alongside competitor analysis and the opinions of senior leaders in the business.

According to Adam Richardson, the author of *Innovation X: Why a Company's Toughest Problems Are Its Greatest Advantage*:

> *"Most companies are the centers of their own universes. It's a natural enough impression; after all, the products and services they offer are on their minds 24/7. The trap is in those companies deluding themselves into thinking that they are as important to their customers as they are to themselves. This is almost never the case. This delusion interferes with understanding customers and their needs, and frequently leads companies to talk to customers in ways that seem foreign or confusing." [xv]*

The best way to understand the needs of customers is by observing their behaviors, where possible, and by having direct conversations with them. Unfortunately, many enterprises are not investing enough time and effort into getting direct feedback from their current and prospective customers. This applies particularly to senior leaders, who seldom go out and speak directly with customers, for example, the head of marketing of a large online retailer has not met a single customer in the past two years.

Organizations often miss out on speaking with ex-customers and the customers of competitors. Feedback from these groups can provide some hard-hitting insights about the shortcomings of the products and the underlying needs which the product is not meeting. It takes needs courage and an open mind to accept this feedback and to admit to the shortcomings. Many businesses find it hard to accept the harsh realities from feedback and prefer to focus only on the positive feedback.

Moreover, with customers having lots of information at their disposal, combined with technological innovations improving the customer experience, the needs of customers are changing frequently. Unless the enterprise maintains a strong engagement with its customers across all segments, it is likely to miss out on understanding the real needs of its customers.

Ignoring end users

This impediment largely applies to enterprises and **information technology** (**IT**) departments providing software systems that are used at the organization level (for example, ERP system) or even as part of the organization (for example, a CRM solution for customer service).

The requirements for such solutions are usually communicated through a **request for proposal** (**RFP**), and the vendor/partner who is most competitive and perceived as credible is selected to develop and deliver the solution. Sometimes, even the internal IT department could be developing the solution. These RFPs are often created by a team of **subject matter experts** (**SMEs**), who may be out of touch with the realities of the end users that they purport to represent. To make things worse, the RFPs are often given to SMEs outside the organization, with the hope that they will define the requirements based on industry best practices. These outsider SMEs are even more likely to be out of touch with ground realities.

Clients usually put aggressive timelines on the delivery of a solution, once the contract is signed with the vendor/ partner or with the IT department. The vendor that says it will do the most at the lowest price and in the quickest time usually wins the contract. The time pressure often results in the system providers not getting enough or sometimes no time for speaking with and observing the end users. This results in the solution being developed on requirements that may be out of sync with what the end users are seeking in terms of value. Moreover, this realization often happens at the **user acceptance testing** (**UAT**) stage, when it is too late and expensive to take on new requirements. The solutions usually are technically functional but are poor on usability and customer experience and nowhere close to bringing satisfaction to the end users.

End user unhappiness can result in resistance toward adopting the new system. Even if the users are forced to adopt it, they certainly won't be positive about it. This dissatisfaction will ultimately reach those who sponsored this initiative, which can result in a poor reference for the solution provider, if it is an external entity, or creating a divide between the end users and the IT department, if the solution provider is the internal IT department.

While the solution providers and IT departments must work within the budgetary and time constraints of the sponsors, they must engage with the end users to understand their needs and pain points. If the requirements given by the SMEs are not in sync with the realities of the end users, they must work with the sponsors to strike the right balance, such that at least the critical needs of the end users are addressed.

According to Sandy Behrens, a professor at Central Queensland University:

> *"Today's competitive environment requires that IT departments become more sensitive and responsive to business needs. But old ways of relating to end users have made IT staffs insular and unaware of what happens at the front lines of their organizations. IT leaders have to respond by developing a new relationship with their end users. With this new social contract, based on open collaboration, IT departments will be able to respond appropriately with technology to help their organizations survive and thrive." [xvi]*

Enablers to the effectiveness of agility

The following factors related to customers are key enablers that can enhance the effectiveness of enterprise agility.

The "customer-first" culture

As discussed earlier, many enterprises have an explicitly stated policy of "customer first," that is, customer satisfaction being the highest priority. However, often these best intentions largely remain only on paper. Creating a customer-first culture is an imperative for the business to have the agility to retain its customers.

A necessary, but not sufficient, condition, which directly has an impact on customer satisfaction, is happy employees, that is, employees who derive their satisfaction and fulfillment through making customers happy. Southwest Airlines is well known for following the philosophy of happy employees leading to happy customers.

According to Herb Kelleher, co-founder of the airline:

"If the employees come first, then they're happy. A motivated employee treats the customer well. The customer is happy so they keep coming back."

The current CEO, Gary Kelly, gives weekly shout-outs to those employees who have demonstrated customer experience best practice and his internal videos highlight the very best examples of empathetic engagement. In addition, Southwest Airlines makes a promise:

"Employees will be provided the same concern, respect, and caring attitude within the organization that they are expected to share externally with every Southwest customer." [xvii]

Translating the intent to put the customer first and to improve their experience can be hard. According to Dilip Bhattacharjee, a principal at McKinsey & Company:

"Improving customer experience is difficult to get right, because the primary hurdle is translating boardroom vision for a superior customer experience into action at the front line. The additional value that comes from focusing efforts on important customer journeys, rather than individual touchpoints, makes the task of training and deploying effective frontline workers all the more complex."

He adds:

"Many companies are making customer experience a strategic priority. Yet, in our experience, we find that they typically struggle to gain traction with their efforts." [xviii]

Organizations must invest in educating their customer-facing staff about the company/brand's value proposition for the customers and about the importance of customer happiness for the organization and its employees. Leaders must be in regular touch with employees to reinforce the importance of putting customers first and how their work is contributing toward the purpose of the enterprise. As discussed in *Chapter 8, People,* when employees are able to see the link between the work they are performing and the purpose of the company, they will become motivated and energized. They must not only be trained about the offerings to customers and their features, but also be made to personally experience some of the critical customer journeys. This will help the employees to better empathize with the customers' needs and challenges.

A grave mistake that enterprises can make is to follow the customer-first philosophy only until the point of purchase made by the customer. This is particularly common when the product or service being sold is an infrequent purchase, for example, a laptop, or the customer is "locked" into a relationship with the company, that is, a bank that has given a loan. In a bid save on costs, the after-sales customer service is outsourced to a third party and the third party may have its staff in another country, where the wages are lower. These outsourced customer service centers often operate like a "factory," where the customers are likely to be treated as faceless entities and the dealings with them are based on a predefined written script and driven purely based on adherence to process. The customer service representatives are incentivized to maximize the number of customers served, while keeping the call time to as low as possible. In such a scenario, the representatives will have no inclination nor incentive to have any emotional connection with the customers, who are calling most likely because they have a problem that needs resolution. Handling customer problems in an impersonal manner will almost always result in lower customer satisfaction.

Another critical aspect of customer-first culture is to ensure that all the departments that impact the customer journey and experience have access to a single source of data. For example, if a new partner is added to the loyalty program, the information should be immediately available to the customer service team. This can often be a challenge when departments have fragmented systems that are not integrated properly. Instances like customers having to enter profile-related information more than once or the company website showing a new product launch, but the customer service staff not being aware of it are typical examples of poor or no integration of systems across the enterprise. The enterprise must make the necessary investment toward ensuring that the systems and processes are well-integrated, to provide a smooth and seamless experience to the customers. Companies are investing in positions such as customer listening and engagement journey analyst [xix], which bring the customer to the front and center of all decisions. Enterprises can use the **Net Promoter Score (NPS)** [xx] to measure customer satisfaction and loyalty, and thereby the effectiveness of the customer-first strategy.

Aim for customer delight

In today's era, customers are seeking value not only in the features of the product or the service they are buying, but also from all the experiences that they have while interacting with the company. Given this, companies cannot sustain their competitive advantage by merely satisfying customers' needs and must aim to delight their customers at every available opportunity.

Delighting customers is perhaps the best way to make an emotional connection with them. It is the emotional connection that leads to increased brand loyalty and creates the best brand ambassadors.

Delighting customers takes conscious and concerted effort. According to Bhattacharjee:

> *"There's no shortcut to creating emotional connections with customers; it requires ensuring that every interaction is geared toward leaving them with a positive experience. That takes more than great products and services." [xxi]*

He adds:

> *"Our research finds that emotionally engaged customers are typically three times more likely to recommend a product and to purchase it again."*

Keeping customers happy often involves an element of positive surprise and innovations can become huge enablers for giving those positive surprises to customers. According to Sophia Bernazzani, a senior marketing manager at HubSpot:

> *"You need to be constantly innovating your products, your processes and the overall customer experience to truly delight people. Innovation can be large-scale, like a new product or a whole new way to get help with your product. It can also be on a smaller scale, like how you train new employees to handle customer questions or the content formats you' re using to help people see value in your product." [xxii]*

However, delighting customers can also be achieved with simple gestures. A company emailing a customer on their birthday, an airline pilot personally greeting passengers as they board the flight, and a business remembering the specific preferences of customers and catering to them when the next opportunity arises (for example, a customer likes mocha coffee with a bit of cinnamon powder in it) are some examples of simple ways in which customers can be delighted. Even a simple gesture of sending a thank you note usually results in a delighted customer.

Understand what value means to the customer

According to Dr. Robert Woodruff, a professor at the University of Tennessee:

> *"Customer value is a customer's perceived preference for and evaluation of those product attributes, attribute performances, and consequences arising from use that facilitate (or block) achieving the customer's goals and preferences in use situations." [xxiii]*

In simple words, customer value can be defined as removing the barriers, both perceived and real, which may be related to price, time, convenience, and an emotional need, which hinder the customer from achieving their goals. It is important to recognize that the customer derives value at various points in the customer journey and not just at the end of it. For example, when making an online purchase, the customer can derive value from the ease of searching for the item intended to be purchased, the product recommendations made based on the customer's profile and past purchase behavior, and ease of payment, among several touchpoints in the journey.

Companies often have preconceived notions of what value means to customers, in the context of their offerings. While this may be a good starting point to begin understanding what customers value, the value proposition must be validated from the customer's perspective.

An effective approach to understanding customer value is the use of **human-centered design (HCD)**, which is a design and management framework that develops solutions to problems by involving the human perspective in all steps of the problem-solving process. Human involvement typically takes place in observing the problem within its context, brainstorming, conceptualizing, developing, and implementing the solution. [xxiv] The basic steps in HCD are as follows:

- Gain insights about customers' needs and pain points by speaking to them and by observing their behaviors

- Based on the insights, define the customer journey and the potential points at which value can be created

- Ideate on potential solutions and approaches to deliver value and validate their feasibility and viability

- Get feedback from customers on which solution is the best for creating and delivering value

- Develop and deliver the solutions identified in the preceding step

A well-known case study of a company discovering customer value is how the *squish gripper toothbrush* [xxv] was created. In 1996, Oral-B, a brand of oral hygiene products, approached IDEO, a global design company, to design toothbrushes for children [xxvi]. The first thing that the IDEO team said was that they needed to watch kids brush their teeth. The team observed that the way children hold their toothbrush is very different from the way adults hold it. They noticed that kids grab the toothbrush, as opposed to adults, who have manual dexterity, who use their fingers for fine movements. The adult toothbrushes were too narrow for children and hence flopped around in their hands. This led to creating a toothbrush that delivered value for children.

Sometimes, customers do not know that they value something until they see or experience it. Steve Jobs, the co-founder and ex-CEO of Apple, Inc., said:

> *"A lot of times, people don't know what they want until you show it to them."* [xxvii]

However, such an approach is laden with risk, as it is based on a set of assumptions about what customers will value.

According to Chunka Mui, a futurist and innovation advisor at Devil's Advocate Group and strategic advisor to the American Medical Association:

> *"I actually think Jobs was right but only in the very narrow category to which he aspired: where his products, such as the Mac, iPod, iPhone and iPad, either redefined or created product categories. That's not the domain in which most businesses play. Remember also that Jobs backed up his unique insights with an enormously expensive creative process populated by world-class designers. Without Jobs' talents and the unparalleled creative team and processes that he built around himself, you won't get away with doing no market research and not listening to your customers." [xxviii]*

In today's era of fast-paced change, enterprises have the best chance at staying ahead of the competition only if they continue to stay in touch with customers, understand what they value and refine existing value propositions and offer new ones with the aim of satisfying customers. Practices such as developing and validating **MVPs** (short for, **minimum viable products**) [xxix] by following lean principles will help to validate customer value hypotheses and lead to more effective evolution and management of the offerings to customers.

Summary

In this chapter, we learned that today's customer is very different from the average customer from two decades ago. The customer of today is technologically savvy, well-informed of available choices, seeking value-driven experiences over the mere fulfillment of their needs and, most importantly, is ready to quickly shift loyalties to anyone offering a better value proposition.

Given this, enterprises must aim to satisfy their customers through a customer-first culture. Companies need to stay very close to their customers to be able to understand their changing needs and preferences and to validate their value propositions. To do this effectively, businesses must not see the customer as being "on the other side of the table," but as part of the enterprise itself. By doing so, the organization will be in the best position to create value for its customers and, through that, value for itself as well.

This chapter concludes the section on the components of enterprise agility. The next chapter is the first of two chapters about "blind spots" and, specifically, distributed teams. The chapter examines the significance of distributed teams and how to leverage them for enhancing enterprise agility.

References

[i] https://www.businessinsider.in/18-false-advertising-scandals-that-cost-some-brands-millions/Red-Bull-said-it-could-give-you-wings-/slideshow/51630716.cms

[ii] http://www.bbc.com/news/business-34324772

[iii] http://fortune.com/2018/02/06/volkswagen-vw-emissions-scandal-penalties/

[iv] http://www.euronews.com/2018/04/09/the-facebook-data-leak-what-happened-and-what-s-next

[v] https://en.wikipedia.org/wiki/General_Data_Protection_Regulation

[vi] https://ico.org.uk/for-organisations/guide-to-data-protection/privacy-by-design/

[vii] https://www.forbes.com/sites/panosmourdoukoutas/

[viii] https://www.forbes.com/sites/panosmourdoukoutas/2011/09/16/dont-take-the-customer-for-granted/#5e10d9a250c3

[ix] https://katenasser.com/worst-customer-service-stories-train-best-csrs/

[x] http://www.sunwords.com/2009/07/12/many-big-companies-take-their-customers-for-granted/

[xi] https://www.digitalmarketing-conference.com/customer-journey-no-longer-linear-brands-must-evolve/

[xii] https://www.amazon.com/gp/help/customer/display.html?nodeId=201954990

[xiii] https://www.mckeewallwork.com/

[xiv] https://www.forbes.com/sites/forbesagencycouncil/2018/02/27/you-have-the-customer-journey-all-wrong/3/#2f90e6403939

[xv] https://hbr.org/2012/12/dont-assume-you-know-your-cust

[xvi] https://www.cio.com/article/2438388/it-organization/time-to-rethink-your-relationship-with-end-users.html?page=3

[xvii] https://www.southwest.com/html/about-southwest/index.html, the *Mission* section

[xviii] https://www.mckinsey.com/business-functions/operations/our-insights/the-secret-to-delighting-customers-putting-employees-first

[xix] https://www.ziprecruiter.com/c/Princeton-Information-Ltd/Job/Customer-Listening-and-Engagement-Journey-Analyst/-in-Irving,TX?ojob=4a7638036052a63ee5919cff5ff9bf63

[xx] https://www.medallia.com/net-promoter-score/

[xxi] https://www.mckinsey.com/business-functions/operations/our-insights/the-secret-to-delighting-customers-putting-employees-first

[xxii] https://blog.hubspot.com/service/customer-delight

[xxiii] http://www.intangiblecapital.org/index.php/ic/article/view/389/361

[xxiv] https://en.wikipedia.org/wiki/Human-centered_design

[xxv] https://www.rdhmag.com/articles/print/volume-16/issue-6/departments/product-report/childrens-toothbrushes.html

[xxvi] https://www.usertesting.com/blog/2015/07/09/how-ideo-uses-customer-insights-to-design-innovative-products-users-love/

[xxvii] https://quotefancy.com/quote/757088/Steve-Jobs-A-lot-of-times-people-don-t-know-what-they-want-until-you-show-it-to-them

[xxviii] https://www.forbes.com/sites/chunkamui/2011/10/17/five-dangerous-lessons-to-learn-from-steve-jobs/#55ca59133a95

[xxix] https://www.techopedia.com/definition/27809/minimum-viable-product-mvp

— PART FOUR —

THE BLIND SPOTS

This part of the book examines two blind spots of the enterprise, namely, distributed teams and technology partners, and suggests measures to unlock and enhance the agility of these areas, which will lead to enhancing the agility of the company.

12

DISTRIBUTED TEAMS

This chapter focuses on distributed teams and provides insights on the challenges arising from distributed working and the enablers that can be introduced to address these challenges. A distributed team is one where all members of the team are not co-located, that is, they are separated by physical location and have to work toward achieving a common outcome. This separation could be just being on different floors in the same building or as far as being on the opposite side of the globe.

By definition, distributed working is difficult due to the "tyranny of distance." Despite all the advancements in technology related to communication and collaboration, distributed teams still face challenges, as people are "not in the same room." However, implementing specific ways of working can help a great deal to alleviate the challenges, if not eliminate them.

While a team that is distributed will face challenges regardless of the type of work being performed, the challenges are accentuated for software development, given the highly-complex nature of the work. Hence, while the chapter is largely based on scenarios related to software development, most of the patterns shared in the chapter will apply to any distributed team.

This chapter will explore the following topics:

♦ The significance of distributed teams for agility

♦ Inhibitors to agility

♦ Enablers for enhancing enterprise agility

Significance

In the early days of Agile adoption for software development work, some purists believed that agility and distributed teams could not coexist, going by this principle: "The most efficient and effective method of conveying information to and within a development team is via face-to-face conversation." Distributed teams are a reality that cannot be wished away, and, in most cases, they are a conscious choice due to some very convincing reasons like cost arbitrage, access to talent, and maintaining proximity with clients.

The Agile principle stated here provides a peek into a reality that enterprises must recognize: quality of communication is impacted negatively when a team is distributed. The bigger reality is that distributed teams face many challenges and if these challenges are not addressed, they can become an impediment for the team in enhancing its agility. The challenges are further compounded when two different organizations are involved, for example, the client is in the USA and the supplier/vendor is in India. It is relatively easier to be open, align objectives, and resolve issues when people belong to the same organization.

According to Patrick Lencioni, author of multiple books, including *The Five Dysfunctions of a Team*:

> *"If you cannot avoid working on a virtual team—and plenty of organizations can't—then sit down as a team and acknowledge the inevitability of miscommunication, unintentional politics, and painfully inaccurate behavioral attributions. Be diligent, even a little paranoid, about small misunderstandings, and don't let them get out of hand."*

He adds:

"The truth is, virtual teams can work. But they often don't. That's not because the people on the team have bad intentions or are taking advantage of the fact that they aren't together. It's almost always because they underestimate and fail to take seriously the challenge they face." *[i]*

Inhibitors to agility

The following factors related to distributed teams are key barriers for enterprises that are seeking to enhance and sustain agility.

Cultural differences

Distributed working often involves teams spread across nations and continents. Cultures vary widely across the globe and that creates an additional barrier, which teams must overcome to become "one team." When people are ignorant of culture, even an innocuous gesture, or the lack of it, can cause ill will among people.

An example will illustrate this point. In some countries, it can be quite uncomfortable for many people to directly say "no," whereas in others, it is perfectly acceptable to say this and also expected, rather than providing a mixed response. One can imagine the awkwardness on a telephone conference call, when there is a long silence or an incoherent response, when the person actually means to convey a "no." Such situations could potentially create major misunderstandings, impede the building of trust, and impact solution delivery as well.

Time zone differences

If teams are working in vastly different time zones, for example, San Francisco (US West Coast) and Pune (India), there is a challenge in overlapping working hours. With a view to the teams getting at least some overlapping hours, teams in both locations will need to stretch their days by starting early or ending late. This can impact the work-life balance of people across teams and lead to feelings of frustration and resentment, thereby impacting agility.

Language differences

Another situation that often characterizes distributed teams is when teams are from different parts of the world and their primary language is not the same. A team in China, that speaks Mandarin, will find it difficult to communicate with another team in Brazil, which speaks Portuguese. These teams will have to use a language common to both teams, say English. Given that English will not be the primary language of either team, the ability to communicate clearly and crisply, while keeping a neutral accent, will be challenging.

Even if people across different locations speak English, accents can make it difficult to understand communication, despite speaking in a common language. This problem is aggravated when communication needs to happen through audio/video tools, which can blunt pronunciations.

Lack of the "big picture" view

This challenge typically occurs when some employees in critical roles, such as the **product owner** (**PO**) and **business analyst** (**BA**) in a software delivery team, are in separate locations from the rest of the team. While they may conduct a knowledge transfer session to provide the big picture view, their conversations around the big picture may get ignored, as the team members might just get to see limited pieces of the puzzle and may not be able to relate to them.

The problem is further aggravated when the team's work is managed by stakeholders who are based in a location away from the team.

Misunderstanding of requirements

Another challenge arising from the distance between business stakeholders and a team is that opportunities to elicit and clarify requirements are rare. This can naturally lead to higher documentation for communicating requirements and clarifications done over the phone. This poses a huge risk of requirements being misunderstood, especially if there is no common primary language.

Trust deficit

Building trust between team members is a "chicken and egg" problem. When people are separated by distance, there needs to be greater trust between them, to work collaboratively. Trust cannot be built between people unless they connect in person and spend meaningful time together. Absence of trust leads to a "passing the buck" mindset and finger-pointing when things slip or fail. In this situation, there is a very high risk of negative feedback being given or taken in the wrong spirit.

This is a significant challenge, particularly when teams have a high level of dependencies between them. Even inadvertent mistakes can lead to the erosion of trust. Imagine a day when a team in Pune leaves behind a broken build, just as the other team in San Francisco starts the workday. This will result in loss of productivity for the team in San Francisco. Even if there is every reason to believe that this was an inadvertent slip from the India team, it could cause resentment in the US team, thereby leading to an increase in the trust deficit.

Lack of visibility

While working from a remote location, it is quite difficult to get good visibility of work happening in other locations, as radiation of information across locations is a huge challenge. This can lead to "multiple sources of truth," which can result in misunderstandings and unpleasant surprises, particularly when integrating work across teams.

Low morale

This is typically seen at offshore locations, due to onshore teams having a superiority complex and/or offshore teams having an inferiority complex. When the onshore team members carry the belief that the work done by the offshore team is of relatively low value compared to their work, they seldom appreciate the other team members. This can lead to a feeling of being taken for granted and result in low morale.

Lack of collective ownership

Collective ownership, in the case of software code, means that no single member of the team owns a piece of code, but it is owned by the entire team. This means that the code is up for refactoring for all team members. Implementing this in a distributed environment poses two major challenges. Firstly, unless appropriate tools and a version control system is used, maintaining collective code ownership can be difficult across locations. Secondly, lack of trust between team members can lead to highly negative consequences, like blaming each other, when things go wrong.

Risk of unpleasant surprises when "everything comes together"

When multiple locations are producing work that needs to be integrated at some point, there is a huge risk of things falling apart, unless continuous integration is practiced rigorously. Inconsistencies between locations in types of tools used, an unsuitable version control system and lack of common quality standards can become major impediments toward achieving "surprise-free" integration.

Enablers for enhancing agility

The enablers suggested in the following subsections are largely in the context of software development teams. However, they can be adopted in any context, keeping intact the underlying principle behind each of the enablers. The enablers can be divided into four broad categories: people, processes, tools and infrastructure, and structure.

People

The following factors related to people can significantly help enterprises to alleviate the challenges of distributed teams, thereby enabling them to enhance agility.

Proxy product owner/business representative

Given that the customer/business is part of the team's ecosystem and given that the team's primary objective is to deliver value to the customer/business, the importance of having a PO as part of the team is immense. The PO provides business context to the team, prioritizes the requirements, and signs off the developed features. In a distributed setup, however, the PO is likely to be located remotely from most of the team members. In this scenario, creating a proxy PO role can be extremely helpful.

The proxy PO needs to be co-located with the remote team(s). They need to spend adequate time with the PO to understand the business context, the drivers for the solution, and the key requirements in detail. Most importantly, they need to win the trust and confidence of the PO, so that they can effectively represent the PO in the team. Typically, the BA is best equipped to play the proxy PO role, as this person is in the team anyway and has to work very closely with the PO. The empowerment to make some decisions at runtime is what differentiates the proxy PO from being just a BA.

The proxy PO should be in a position to provide context and clarifications to the team, to a large extent. The proxy PO should shadow the PO very closely on such matters. This will significantly help in building the proxy PO's capabilities quickly, thereby drastically reducing dependency on the PO. It is important that the proxy PO is empowered to make most decisions, in order for the role to be meaningful and effective. In the absence of a proxy PO and the PO being remotely located from the team, an electronic tool should be the single source of truth for the entire team and the PO, with respect to clarifications and changes in priorities. An effective proxy PO will ensure better collaboration with the business, faster decision-making, and an increase in end user satisfaction.

Having a proxy PO does not mean that the PO should be totally disconnected from the team. The PO should participate in key team meetings, such as inception and release planning, as the PO is in the best position to share the big picture with the team, and the PO also gets an opportunity to hear from the team about their concerns and challenges. If possible, the PO should have a short call on a daily basis with the proxy PO and the technical lead, to ensure alignment on important decisions that have been or need to be made during the day.

Cross-pollination

As mentioned earlier, a key to working effectively in a distributed environment is the level of trust between the team members. People meeting face-to-face and spending time together is the first and most important step toward building trust. There are two major anti-patterns, which need to be avoided:

♦ *Having only onshore team members visit the offshore team, which might imply that offshore team members need not visit the onshore team.*

This makes it look like a "one-way street" and will not bring in optimal results. People traveling both ways, that is, people onshore traveling offshore and vice versa, is necessary for cross-pollination to be effective. It gives people, across different locations, an opportunity to understand and appreciate the context and constraints that the distributed team members work in. Moreover, it helps to build stronger relationships amongst the distributed teams. The value lies in people spending time together not only at the office, but also when they socialize together after office hours. That is a huge enabler toward building trust and personal rapport.

♦ *The visits are for a very short period of time, perhaps just a week.*

This is usually a waste of time when people are visiting from very different time zones, as jet lag often has a negative impact on the effectiveness of the visit. On a week-long visit, the first day is spent warming up and getting to know people, while the next two-to-three days are when work momentum begins to gather pace, and the last day is spent on wrapping up and saying goodbye.

Subject to visa and family constraints, the duration of visits should be several weeks, the longer the better. Assuming that the necessary infrastructure, including communication channels, are in place, people traveling should be able to continue their work with minimal disruption while they are on the road.

The main obstacle for people to travel is usually budget constraints. Typically, leaders look at money spent on travel as an expense. In distributed working, the money spent on travel is not an expense, but an investment, which is necessary for people to work collaboratively. The payoff on this investment will almost always be huge.

Cultural sensitivity

When we discussed the challenges of distributed working, we examined how lack of cultural sensitivity can become an impediment toward people working together. It is important to invest the time and effort to educate people who are traveling, especially for the first time, to a location that has a different culture from theirs. These orientation sessions can be carried out by external experts or even by those within the organization who are well-traveled and have had good exposure to the particular region in reference.

It is also crucial to hold cultural awareness sessions in general, across locations, to orient team members about cultures in other locations. Culture will come into play when people communicate. For example, many people in India nod their head in a particular way to communicate a "yes," which might be very different from how people nod their head in many parts of the world for the same reason. If, for example, a team is distributed between India and the USA, it is advisable to educate the employees in the USA about this behavior in India. Conversely, it is important to make the India team aware of how this movement can be misinterpreted by people in the USA.

Feedback culture

Feedback is one of the key elements of agility, and it becomes even more important when the team members are distributed. Positive feedback to team members helps a great deal in strengthening relationships and creating a feeling of oneness, while feedback on what is not working helps to avoid misunderstandings and resentment. Team members should be encouraged to give feedback, both positive and for improvement, as appropriate, to other team members. The timing of the feedback is critical, as feedback given late loses its effectiveness and impact.

Here is an example of how feedback on a seemingly trivial but important matter helped a team. The team was distributed between the USA and India and was quite new to working in this manner. During joint meetings, the team members in the USA would sit at a rectangle-shaped table with the telephone in the middle of the table. The team members in India could hear people who were sitting closer to the telephone but could hardly hear those who were sitting at the corners. This not only impacted the effectiveness of the meetings, but also made the team members in India quite frustrated. The team members in the USA were unaware of this problem, until it was pointed out to them. Once they got feedback about the issue, the team members occupying the corner slots started walking up to get closer to the phone or moved the microphone closer to them when they spoke.

It is important to understand why the team members in India did not give feedback to their American colleagues until they were prompted to do so. It could be attributed to "onshore-offshore" syndrome, as mentioned earlier, where the offshore team members have an inferiority complex and the onshore team members have a superiority complex. Alternatively, it could be because it did not strike the Indian team that the problem could be resolved with some very minor adjustments or maybe it was just a cultural issue.

Regardless of the reasons, the team was negatively impacted. If the problem had continued, it might have led to the team members in India feeling even more frustrated and also perhaps resentful toward the American team members.

Working agreements between onshore and offshore teams, which explicitly state the ways of working and the values and principles that all team members agree to abide by, can help in not only preventing unnecessary irritants, but also enhancing the "one team" sentiment.

Leverage effective communicators

It is a fact that working in a distributed environment requires superior communication skills. It is also a fact that not all team members have the same level of proficiency in communication skills. Therefore, it is important that a team takes stock of the communication skills of all team members and ensures that team members with better communication skills lead the conversation/ communication. This is particularly important at these instances:

- The team is new to the distributed way of working
- Trust is yet to be established with team members who are not co-located
- Something unpleasant or negative needs to be communicated

Communication, particularly verbal, is not just about fluency but also about using the right vocabulary and tone. This can become very important in situations like those mentioned earlier. While some people have a natural flair for communication, for others this skill can be developed over time through observation, mentoring, and practice. Team members with better communication skills may take the lead for some time, however, they should consciously help their coworkers to develop their own capabilities.

Process

The following factors related to process can significantly help enterprises to alleviate the challenges of distributed teams, thereby enabling them to enhance agility.

Inception/project kick-off workshop

The importance of an inception workshop, though held perhaps only once in the life cycle of a project, cannot be overemphasized, as some of the key decisions, which impact almost all aspects of the project, are made in this meeting. These include business and technical scope, key project drivers, such as time to market, cost, quality, among others, and the trade-offs among them. Moreover, arriving at a common understanding related to business vision, as-is and to-be processes, end-user journeys, risks, dependencies, and assumptions also happens in this workshop, which can be spread over several weeks. Not to be forgotten is the fact that relationships between stakeholders are cemented in this period, as most stakeholders get an opportunity to spend time with each other during and after business hours.

Obviously, it may not be possible for the entire team to participate in this workshop, due to travel and logistical constraints. The exception would be when the team is small and there is adequate travel budget. Nonetheless, it's absolutely critical that all roles across all locations are represented in this meeting, in order to maximize the effectiveness of meeting the key stakeholders in person. No amount of documentation can be a substitute for the richness of conversations in person and this benefit becomes even more important when team members are distributed. The team members who have attended the inception are in a much better position to pass the context to the rest of team in their respective locations.

Participation of those not physically present via video conferencing should be explored. The time and effort invested in this will definitely pay off. Should the project span multiple releases, the option of those who did not attend the inception workshop now attending release planning meetings should be also be considered. An inception workshop turns a group into a team. This fact should be leveraged to the maximum possible extent, especially when team members are distributed.

Joint stand-ups

The importance of stand-up meetings as an effective working habit of an Agile team is undisputed. The meeting provides an opportunity for the entire team to get together and focus on the work at hand, assess progress toward the goals for the iteration, and discuss risks and blockers, if any. This practice assumes even greater importance when the team is distributed, as the need for the entire team to be aware of who is doing what work, and dependencies and blockers, is critical.

Given this fact, the team has to strive to hold stand-up meetings that include all members of the team. This can be quite challenging if there is a time difference between the locations of the team members. This is one of the main reasons that drives overlapping working hours between the locations.

As much as possible, video-based tools should be used for the joint stand-ups. If the team is dialing in from another office, the use of video conferencing is highly recommended. Moreover, whether the video conferencing actually works must be checked before the meeting, so that previous time allocated to this short meeting is not lost in resolving technology-related issues. Using a teleconference number is obviously the next best option.

Joint retrospectives

Just like with stand-ups, the importance of this practice is heightened when the team is distributed. While analyzing challenges and problems encountered by the team, it is very easy to fall into the trap of blaming the team members who were not part of the retrospective, when it is not held jointly. Even a single instance of this has the potential to lessen the trust between teams. Given that the entire team is not in one location and consequently the nature of communication is complex, the team needs to provide adequate time for the meeting. Complexity often arises due to all team members being required to vote on action items and maintaining anonymity during the "safety check" exercise, which may be done to get a sense of how comfortable people are with discussing problems openly. Strong facilitation skills are also called for, due to the aforementioned reasons.

A tool that helps in exchanging information in real time, and which acts as the single source of truth, is a must for retrospectives of distributed teams. There are several tools available that serve these purposes. Some free examples are IdeaBoardz [ii] and Scrumble [iii].

Maximize overlapping hours

One of the biggest challenges for distributed teams is maximizing overlapping hours across locations. The challenge is accentuated when time zone differences are significant, as they are between India and the US West Coast, and also when onshore team members *push* their offshore counterparts to adhere to what is convenient for them.

It is critical that everyone, regardless of location, is ready to demonstrate flexibility toward maximizing an overlap in working hours. The advantages of synchronous communication, while being at work, far outweigh the compromises, within reasonable limits, which team members would need to make. The goal obviously should be to maximize overlap with minimum sacrifice and compromise by each team member.

Teams can come up with creative ways to do so, for example, some team members, by rotation, coming in early or leaving late or teams across locations taking turns to come in early/leave late and being flexible about taking calls from home. Not only does maximizing overlapping hours help toward improving communication and collaboration, but the willingness to compromise and be adaptable also helps tremendously in creating a "one team" feeling.

Periodic "work in process" showcases/demo

By definition, a showcase/demo is supposed to be done at the end of an iteration to demonstrate working software to the stakeholders. A practice that helps distributed teams to reduce unpleasant surprises, and to build trust and confidence, is for the teams to showcase their work in progress to those who are distributed, without waiting for the end of the iteration. This can be done upon completion of each story, but it need not always be that way. Even showcasing code and interfaces through the use of mock objects [iv], if necessary, adds a lot of value for the entire team. These showcase meetings can be kept short and crisp, and once the teams get into the cadence of doing them on a regular basis, the time taken for these meetings will be minimal and nondisruptive. This practice is particularly useful when iteration length is two weeks or longer. It greatly improves the predictability of iteration end demos.

Tools and infrastructure

The following factors related to tools and infrastructure can significantly help enterprises to alleviate the challenges of distributed teams, thereby enabling them to enhance agility.

Electronic work pipeline

A key challenge faced in a distributed working environment is ensuring that regardless of the location, everyone has a common view of current and upcoming work, team metrics, and so on. As discussed earlier, the electronic wall becomes the single source of truth for all team members across various locations. An electronic work pipeline can be a huge enabler in terms of bringing in shared understanding of iteration progress, blockers, and dependencies. It can also help is ensuring that duplication of work is avoided.

An electronic story card wall is particularly useful in cases where team members are dialing into the stand-ups from their homes. The real time nature of an electronic wall helps to avoid communication overheads and its transparency helps in building trust as well. This applies not only to the development team, but also to the product's stakeholders when the electronic wall is shared with them.

A criticism levelled against electronic walls is that they do not convey information as clearly as physical walls do. There is definitely some merit in this assertion, as the benefits of "information staring you in the face" at all times are immense. However, this limitation of the electronic wall can be overcome by either maintaining a physical wall in addition to the electronic wall or even better, by projecting the electronic wall in the area where the team is sitting. In case the team decides to maintain a physical wall as well, it is imperative that the physical and electronic walls remain in sync at all times. Regardless of whether a team is distributed or not, an electronic wall helps immensely in collecting metrics accurately, with minimal effort.

Electronic build radiator

Similar to electronic walls, the benefits of knowing the build's status, on a software development project, on a real-time basis, are immense. In fact, knowing whether the build is broken prior to checking in [v] code into the version control repository is an absolute must, which can save the team from a lot of rework. Knowing when the build is broken not only prevents check-ins in a broken state but can galvanize the team to resolve the issue together, should someone be struggling with fixing the build. A build monitor also helps to ensure that teams do not "pass the baton" to another location when the build is in a broken state.

Communication and collaboration tools

The most difficult and persistent challenge in distributed working is the barrier encountered in communication and collaboration between people across locations. While nothing can be more ideal than having face-to-face conversations, both individually and as a team, the constraints of doing this are a major limitation of distributed working. Inability to communicate and collaborate face-to-face not only creates a huge strain on team members but also has the potential for serious consequences such as loss of trust.

Hence, it is imperative that distributed teams are provided with appropriate tools for communication and collaboration, with the aim of getting as close as possible to being face-to-face. These tools should facilitate individual as well as group communication and collaboration and should allow for as much online communication as possible. Moreover, to the extent possible, video-based communication should be used, as seeing a person, even if it is via video, greatly enhances the quality of communication.

Examples of such tools include Gtalk or Lync for point-to-point communication between individuals, HipChat [vi] for conversations at team level, Google Hangouts for team meetings, Trello [vii] for any activity requiring collaboration, and many more. Organizations need to find the tools that adhere to their security policies. This can be a challenge if the teams/people in charge of security are not sensitive to the challenges faced by distributed teams. It is important to work closely with the security team to identify tools that don't compromise security and that meet the needs of the distributed teams.

Another meaningful way by which communication and collaboration challenges can be eased is by permitting team members to use their own devices when they are outside the office, for example, when at home or traveling. The organization will need to define and implement a policy for **BYOD** (short for, **bring your own device**), which fits within the boundaries of the organization's security policy. Maintaining a wiki can help a great deal in effective context sharing among team members.

Leaders play a very important role in encouraging the use of communication and collaboration tools. Leaders, as always, are looked up to as role models, and hence leaders must themselves use those tools that they want their teams to adopt. For example, if the leaders want the teams to use a wiki to record minutes of important meetings and critical decisions, the leader must use the wiki actively. If the leader uses emails instead of the wiki, it will set a bad example for the team.

Coding standards

When distributed teams work on a common code base, it is critical for teams across all locations to agree to coding standards and, more importantly, to have the discipline to adhere to them. Nonadherence to coding standards not only increases the risk of defects creeping in, but also becomes a "fly in the ointment" toward common code ownership. This can be a needless cause of breaking the trust among teams.

Source control system

Distributed teams should work with a source control system that encourages trunk-based development [viii] or otherwise minimizes the need for branching. Sometimes, there is a need for team members to maintain source code on their respective machines and make local commits. If this is a valid requirement for the team, the source control system should have the flexibility to support this. Given that distributed teams are a larger unit, the source control system should support check-ins in large numbers, without having to grapple with conflicting pieces of code or juggle multiple versions. Team members should be able to view code changes across locations quickly and give feedback, as needed, before pushing their commits to the central repository. This may be achieved by using local, short-lived feature branches that are shared across team members for testing purposes or by employing the *pull request* methodology when merging local changes to the central repository.

Network connectivity

Network connectivity and bandwidth are actually more hygiene factors than enablers for distributed teams. Teams working across locations, especially across countries, can pose network-related challenges, which may not occur if the team is co-located. It is often seen that these challenges are not proactively anticipated and are usually dealt with in firefighting mode, once they become showstoppers or serious impediments to the functioning of distributed teams. The choice of network, access rights and bandwidth should ideally be addressed before the distributed team begins functioning.

Network-related issues may be magnified when two different organizations need to access a single environment, for example, a client and vendor. Complexities arising out of this scenario must be anticipated and dealt with in advance, to ensure the smooth functioning of teams.

An important aspect that comes into play for distributed teams is network security. This aspect also should be dealt with proactively, as security lapses on the network can lead to devastating consequences. A misconfigured network can lead to leakages of source code, which can be prevented through configuring the security permissions appropriately.

Structure

The following factors related to organization structure can significantly help enterprises to alleviate the challenges of distributed teams, thereby enabling them to enhance agility.

Cross-functional teams

The importance of cross-functional teams has been explained in *Chapter 6, Organization Structure*. This becomes even more important when people are distributed. Roles being split across locations can lead to people becoming activity-driven, rather than being outcome-driven.

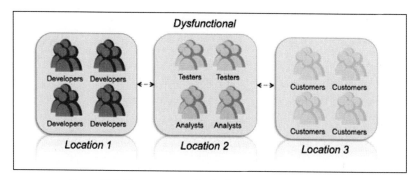

Figure 12.1: The structure of a dysfunctional distributed team

At the other extreme, the most effective team structure will be as shown in the following diagram:

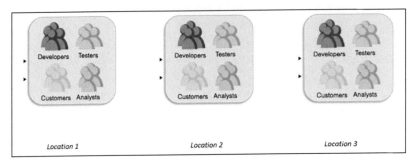

Figure 12.2: An effective distributed team structure

Practically speaking, it is extremely difficult to achieve the preceding most effective team combination across locations, especially since the probability of customer representation being located across all team locations is quite low. However, this limitation can be mitigated by having proxy POs in every location. As far as possible, the other roles should be represented in every team across all locations. This applies to full-time roles within the teams. Specialized roles, like security, may be based in a specific location, but may have to travel across locations.

Conway's law

Conway's law states, "organizations which design systems are constrained to produce designs that are copies of the communication structures of these organizations." [ix] The law is based on the observation that the design of a solution is a function of how the teams that are building the solution communicate. The communication is in turn based on how teams are structured. Therefore, a dysfunctional structure, which will lead to dysfunctional communication patters, will result in dysfunctional design, according to this law. The contrary will also be true: if teams are structured correctly, the design of the solution will be optimal.

Distributed teams must therefore be structured appropriately, keeping the impact of the structure on the design of the system in mind. This is important for distributed teams, as the communication bandwidth between teams that are not co-located is low. There is significant tension when teams need to have high communication bandwidth, for example, to work on a monolithic application, but because they are distributed the bandwidth is low. In such cases, finding ways to split the monolithic application, and structuring the teams such that they can afford to have low bandwidth communication with other teams, will produce better results.

Conway's law reinforces the need for creating business capabilities/outcome-oriented teams, as this will enable the actual design to be aligned with the intended design. If using microservices, every microservice should have only one team responsible for it. On the contrary, if the solution is designed based on business capabilities/outcomes, but the teams are created based on application layers (frontend, middleware, and backend), the actual design will end up being based on application layers and the feature/outcome-based design will remain only on paper.

Creating business capabilities/outcome-oriented teams can be hard to achieve, as all the relevant skills to create a feature-driven team may not be available at all locations. However, striving in that direction will help to minimize the misalignment of intended versus actual design of the solution.

Gene Kim, author of multiple books, including *The Phoenix Project*, has summarized this view:

> *"Done incorrectly, Conway's Law will ensure that the organization creates poor outcomes, preventing safety and agility. Done well, the organization enables developers to safely and independently develop, test and deploy value to the customer."* [x]

Perception of power

An important structure-related factor, which determines how teams perceive power, is the concentration of team members and the location of the leader, especially if the leader is based onshore. If the majority of team members are located in a single location, that location may be perceived as more powerful by both the teams in that location and those not in that location as well.

According to Tsedal Neely, a Harvard Business School professor:

> *"This imbalance sets up a negative dynamic. People in the larger (majority) group may feel resentment toward the minority group, believing that the latter will try to get away with contributing less than its fair share. Meanwhile, those in the minority group may believe that the majority is usurping what little power and voice they have." [xi]*

This perception may get worse if the leader of the team is based in the location with the maximum amount of team members. Leaders need to be sensitive about how teams may perceive power and watch out for the dysfunctions arising from this perception. While it may be often quite difficult to have a balanced number of team members across multiple locations, leaders can minimize the perception of power imbalance by cross-pollinating people, as discussed earlier. Moreover, leaders should aim to spend meaningful time across locations. Most importantly, leaders need to constantly reinforce the message that regardless of location, the company is one team bound by a common purpose and that the leader is available to them at all times. Giving regular attention to teams across locations, by involving them in shaping decisions, appreciating their contributions and calling people on special occasions like major work anniversaries, will help to create a sense of belonging and increase the cohesiveness in the team.

Summary

In this chapter, we learned that distributed working, due to team members being spread across locations, is often a reality that enterprises must endeavor to leverage positively, as this phenomenon is likely to grow further going forward. Distributed working creates challenges related to communication, collaboration, visibility, transparency, and integration. The best way to deal with the challenges is by introducing appropriate enablers related to people, process, structure and tools, and infrastructure. While the enablers may not completely eliminate the challenges, they will certainly go a long way in alleviating them. Leaders must view these enablers as a necessary investment, which is needed in order to maximize the benefits of having distributed teams.

The next chapter covers the second "blind spot": technology partners. It will address how to leverage the relationship with partners and enable them to deliver based on Agile ways of working.

References

[i] https://www.linkedin.com/pulse/virtual-teams-worse-than-i-thought-patrick-lencioni/

[ii] http://www.ideaboardz.com/

[iii] http://scrumble.pyxis-tech.com/

[iv] https://en.wikipedia.org/wiki/Mock_object

[v] https://sliksvn.com/support/subversion-basics-using-check-out-update-check-in-commit/

[vi] https://www.hipchat.com/

[vii] https://trello.com/

[viii] https://www.thoughtworks.com/insights/blog/
enabling-trunk-based-development-deployment-pipelines

[ix] https://en.wikipedia.org/wiki/Conway%27s_law

[x] https://dzone.com/articles/how-to-design-with-
conways-law-in-mind

[xi] https://hbr.org/2015/10/global-teams-that-work

13

TECHNOLOGY PARTNERS

This chapter focuses on technology partners, which is the second potential blind spot in the process of enhancing agility. While most organizations in the technology-driven products and services space have, or at least claim to have, adopted Agile ways of working, it is quite likely that the maturity of the Agile processes and the practices of the business, and those of its technology partners, are not the same. If specific measures are not taken to address this mismatch, it can lead to unhealthy friction between the client and the technology partner, which can become a challenge or even a drag on enterprise agility.

The chapter explores the following topics:

♦ The significance of technology partners for agility

♦ Inhibitors to agility

♦ Enablers for enhancing agility

Significance

Almost all enterprises do at least some outsourcing of **information technology (IT)** work. American research firm Gartner defines IT outsourcing as "the use of external service providers to effectively deliver IT-enabled business process, application service and infrastructure solutions for business outcomes." [i]

Outsourcing ranges from working with a single provider, to having an ecosystem of providers. It is not uncommon to find the number of providers to be in three digits. For example, a large bank in India has 300 different companies for its IT solutions and services providers, and an internal team of over 100 people to manage these providers.

The primary drivers for outsourcing include the following:

♦ Access to specialized capabilities

♦ Cost reduction

♦ Augmenting IT capacity

♦ Focusing on core competencies

♦ Reducing risk

While these benefits are important for every company, collaborating with a technology partner has its own set of challenges, given that the partner is a different enterprise, which has its own distinct culture, vision, and priorities, which may not be aligned with those of the business. It is critical to identify common objectives and success criteria for both companies and maintain alignment with them over the period of the partnership, which is usually a long time. Given the strategic nature and the long tenure of the partnership, the partner becomes a critical part of the enterprise's ecosystem. Hence, if the partner teams that are engaged with the firm are lagging in agility, the partnership can become a severe drag on the overall agility of the enterprise itself. So, it is important to get the partner on board to deliver based on Agile ways of working, as soon as possible.

Whatever the rationale for entering into a relationship with a technology partner may be, the relationship can become a problem for enterprise-level agility if the partner is doing critical work but is lacking in Agile maturity, with reference to the contracted work. One of the key objectives of transforming to Agile is to increase collaboration between technology and the business.

For organizations that are transforming to Agile, this objective should be extended to partnerships as well. In fact, the transformation initiative provides a very good opportunity to re-examine the need and nature of relationships with partners. It is often seen that Agile adoption initiatives begin as being purely internally focused, thereby alignment of outsourcing with the Agile adoption initiative is often ignored until it is too late.

Inhibitors to agility

The following factors related to the relationship with technology partners are key barriers for enterprises looking to enhance and sustain agility.

Resistance and concerns in adopting Agile ways of working

For an enterprise to be able to enhance its level of agility, it is critical that the technology partner also be equally mature in Agile ways of working. There could be several reasons why the partner may not be willing or able to adopt and improve on the Agile ways of working:

♦ To adopt Agile ways of working, investment might be needed to train and coach the relevant people. The partner may not be willing to make this investment.

♦ The business model of the partner may be based on billing per staffed person, but the client may seek an outcome/value-driven model. Such divergent expectations can be hard to resolve, thereby leaving one or both parties feeling that the contractual obligations are detrimental to them.

- The quality of training and follow-through coaching may not be up to the mark. Hence, while on paper it may appear that the partner teams have undergone Agile training and coaching, the Agile ways of working in practice might be highly ineffective.

- The partner may be uncomfortable with the visibility and transparency that comes along with Agile ways of working.

- The partner may not be ready for the extent of close collaboration needed with the enterprise.

- The partner may be uncomfortable with the possibility of disruption resulting from a different way of working in a part of its organization.

- The partner may not have the technical capabilities and/or the mindset to deliver working software at the end of short timeboxed iterations.

Whatever the reason for the gap in the maturity of Agile ways of working between the enterprise and its partner, the gap can hit the business in a bad way and can cause tension in the relationship with the partner. For example, the company might be expecting the partner to write unit tests in order to ensure a high-quality solution. However, if the unit tests are written poorly, that is, not to the standard that the enterprise is expecting, and if there is a defect found in production, it might lead to an unnecessary blame game.

The business and the partner must work together to find a way to build and sustain the necessary Agile-related capabilities within the partner's organization. Otherwise, the relationship is highly likely to create obstacles, if not becoming an impediment to the agility of the enterprise.

Transactional relationship

The transactional relationship mindset toward the partner, or vice versa, is a huge anti-pattern in a relationship where the stakes are high for both the enterprise and partner. Often large partners, especially those with very strong brands, arm-twist companies to get them to buy additional products and services from them. They gradually, but purposefully, get the business into a position where exiting a relationship with that partner becomes extremely expensive and risky. The enterprise, as the customer, does not any longer have a voice in the relationship. The partner begins to take the client for granted as a result. Conversely, if the client tenders work on a fixed-cost or a cap-on-cost basis, the partner will have very little incentive to maximize value for the client. Moreover, changing partners just because another partner is offering a lower cost contract leads to a transaction-driven mindset.

Many enterprises get swayed by the partner's sales pitch and enter into a relationship with them thinking that they are entering a strategic relationship. Enterprises often choose large, well-known brands as partners, with the hypothesis that a known and established brand is less risky than a lesser-known one. After all, if things were to go wrong, nobody would get fired for engaging with a well-known and established brand.

According to Ross Pettit, a director at ThoughtWorks:

> *"Partnership implies equivalency. Yet the commercial world is full of alleged "partnerships" that are superior-subordinate, making them inherently unbalanced. Companies stay in condescending or even abusive relationships because they're afraid of the uncertainty of the alternative. Sellers do this because suckling at the teat of easy revenue is far easier than hustling new business. Buyers do this because they feel held hostage by a supplier. Even though it comes at a high commercial cost (squeezed margins) and high human cost (second class status and compromised careers for those involved), such business "partnerships" can last for a long time." [ii]*

Given the critical importance of the technology function, especially in today's era, enterprises must be extremely conscious about two things. Firstly, they must ask why critical capabilities are being outsourced and why they are not being developed inside the business itself. Secondly, they must ensure that the partner is aligned and committed to upholding the strategic interests of the enterprise. Should a relationship that began on the right note show early signs of turning transactional, the enterprise needs to recalibrate the relationship with the partner, even at the cost of enduring short-term pain. A dominating partner, who has primary control over critical technology functions and with whom the business is in no position to have an influence, is a huge impediment to agility.

Sometimes, the client lacks the skills to engage with the partner, to take the relationship from a transactional level to a strategic level. The people engaging with the partner are either not aware or are not sensitive to the needs and challenges faced by the partner and may lack the maturity to bridge the differences between the two organizations. In such scenarios, the relationship will remain transactional, that is, as a client-vendor relationship and may not morph into a partnership.

Frozen contracts

Frozen contracts, that is, where time, cost, and scope are fixed upfront with technology partners, are a "lose-lose" proposition. The client is interested in getting in as many requirements that they can think of, without having validated them with market needs, as they cannot add requirements post the contract. However, in hindsight, a large number of requirements turn out to be non-value adding and therefore a waste. The partner will add risk premium in terms of time and cost buffers, as not everything can be known upfront when creating software, and additional complexity and scope is discovered post the requirements-gathering phase. To make things worse, these contracts usually also include a penalty clause, thereby putting the partner completely on the defensive.

Frozen contracts are inappropriate for Agile ways of working. They violate the core value of Agile, which is customer collaboration over contract negotiation, and are an indication of lack of trust. When additional scope and complexity are subsequently discovered, the consequences are almost always negative in terms of poor quality and intentional misinterpretation of requirements, which are of little or no value for the customer. The result of a frozen contract is typically that both the parties in the contract are unhappy when it ends. Such an outcome causes a significant drag on agility.

Enablers for enhancing agility

Assuming that the partner is not co-located with the client, all the enablers related to distributed development, as mentioned in *Chapter 12, Distributed Teams*, will apply to the client-partner co-delivery program as well. Moreover, given that the co-delivery is with two different organizations, the following additional enablers may help.

Ways of working

Adopting the following ways of working can be an enabler for enhancing agility for both the client and the partner.

True spirit of partnership

For a meaningful, mutually beneficial relationship with the partner, the nature of the relationship needs to become a partnership in the truest sense. The following are some questions to answer in this regard:

- ◆ Does the partner's leadership believe in the revised objective of the relationship, that is, collaboration over contract negotiation?

- ◆ Can a shared objective success criterion be defined and agreed upon between both parties?

◆ Does the partner commit to working in an Agile way, at least for the work that is outsourced, regardless of how mature the rest of its organization may be with respect to adopting Agile? For example, does the partner agree to invest in and practice continuous integration, if it is determined that the risk of delayed integration is high?

◆ Most importantly, is there potential to build a relationship of mutual trust?

Ross Pettit has aptly summarized the essence of a meaningful partnership. He says:

> *"Partnership, then, encompasses more than just a relationship of need, but a relationship worth it to both parties to make sacrifices to sustain. When we partner, we each agree to ebbs and flows in the relationship — "in sickness and in health" — and that we will not merely tolerate but accommodate. A seller that has to roll somebody off a team because they can't travel; a buyer that has to reduce the amount they spend. In these situations, a partner sets aside the short-term impairment for the long-term benefits of continuity and consistency." [iii]*

Outcome-focused partnership

Since IT is a critical business enabler, IT-related outcomes are critical for the enterprise. Hence, the partnership for outsourcing should be driven by outcomes and not activities.

According to Sriram Narayan, author of *Agile IT Organization Design*:

"Outsourcing along outcomes is better than outsourcing along activity lines—that is, consider outsourcing application A to partner X, B to partner Y, and C to partner Z rather than handing development of A, B, and C to partner X, IT operations to partner Y, and maintenance to partner Z."

He further adds:

"The feedback loop is badly constricted at contractual boundaries. Designing formal, service-level agreement (SLA)-driven protocols of communication between business, development, IT operations, and maintenance is a recipe for bureaucracy and indifference." [iv]

As opposed to activity-driven partnerships, outcome-driven partnerships ensure that both parties are committed to achieving the same outcome.

Agile contracts

While customer collaboration is more important than the contract, a contract that does not support the Agile way of working will surely derail the partnership, regardless of best intent from both sides to work in an Agile way. Traditional contracts are typical characterized by outcomes based on milestones, defining detailed requirements and freezing them upfront, and heavyweight governance around changing requirements. Often, the traditional contracts stretch to extremes like "fixed bids," where scope, cost, and time are frozen upfront. Such contracts are absolutely not suitable for the partner to adopt Agile ways of working, which requires dealing with uncertainties and change in scope due to a change in business priorities.

A contract to enable Agile ways of working must support flexibility in changing requirements, iterative development, incremental delivery, and stopping the project that is not deemed to be adding incremental value. The types of contracts best suited to Agile ways of working are **time and materials (T&M)** and/or outcome-based contracts. However, the key enabler to even have these contracts in place is trust. Leaders across both organizations need to already have trusted relationships built or believe that an environment of trust can be created and sustained.

According to Justine Johnston, a healthcare expert, and Sam Bunting, an Agile expert, both at PA Consulting, which is an innovation and transformation consultancy, there are multiple variables that can have a bearing on the contents of Agile contracts. They say:

> *"The first step in determining the most appropriate commercial approach is to ask the questions that will ensure you understand the project conditions that you will be operating under. Are you working with a partner who you have a strong transparent relationship with and who you trust will behave reasonably as requirements emerge and change? What level of changes in scope over the course of your project are you expecting? Are you and the partner familiar and comfortable with the proposed architecture and technology set? These types of conditions will impact the type of commercial approach you adopt. For instance, a poor relationship with a partner may indicate a greater level of upfront requirements specificity might be helpful; if you are working with a new technology set, you may endeavor to address uncertainty via prototyping in initial cycles prior to entering into a long-term contract with a partner."* [v]

Instances of switching to an Agile way of working without revising the earlier waterfall-driven contract can lead to distressing consequences, as in the case of the BBC's failed Digital Media Initiative project. [vi] In order that the contracts be redrafted to capture the essence of agility, the lawyers who draft the contracts must be educated on the values and principles of agility, and these can be leveraged by both parties to create a mutually beneficial partnership.

Sara Cullen, the managing director of Cullen Group, has aptly called out the essence of Agile contracts. She says:

> *"Agile contracts are based on a flexible but driven mindset rather than a contract-driven, power-based one. The former can maximize results in fluid environments, the latter merely intensifies the potential for conflict and failure."* [vii]

She adds:

> *"Agile contracts have neither recourse nor variations. A project should be killed as early as possible if it is not going to work. Often this is the first gate — to test the kill switches. Fail fast is a mantra of an Agile approach. If something might not work, this is explored in an early sprint. If the entire project might not work, the first sprints determine this. The project is then either re-imagined or killed before any large expenditure is made."*

Success story

A success story, which both partners can feel happy and proud about, is a huge enabler to building trust and confidence among the partners; also it is a huge enabler toward creating the appetite for adopting the Agile way of working, especially if the partner is new to it.

Some of the key considerations for choosing the initial functionality to be delivered include tangible and realizable business value, being realistic, that is, neither too simple nor complex, and being based on the delivery model agreed between the partners. As a guideline, priority to deliver should take precedence over perfecting the adopting of Agile practices, so that the success story is created as early as possible. The learnings from the success story, that is, what worked and what did not, especially from a systemic point of view, should be a key input in shaping the scaling strategy.

Agile awareness and training

Regardless of the length and strength of the relationship with a partner and also the level of the partner's Agile maturity, shifting from traditional ways of working to Agile can lead to a lot of confusion and uncertainty in the partner's organization. The chances of this happening are even higher if the partner is relatively new to Agile. To mitigate this, it is important to conduct awareness sessions regarding the shift to the Agile way of working, for people who are directly and indirectly impacted by this move in the partner organization. The departments impacted indirectly may include operations, HR, and even infrastructure. To drive the criticality of this shift and also to demonstrate the shift in relationship, that is, no longer being on different sides of the table, these sessions should be conducted jointly by leaders from both organizations. The three key messages that should be conveyed are as follows:

- The relationship changes from client-vendor type to becoming a mutually beneficial partnership
- Both organizations have the same success criteria for the work being done by the partner
- This change can be difficult but "we are in this together"

The awareness sessions may include some high-level information about Agile and how different it is from the traditional way of working, depending on the level of knowledge already existing in the partner organization. The importance of training on Agile fundamentals, as well as role-specific training, cannot be overemphasized when moving toward adopting Agile. However, in today's environment, where many organizations, large or small, are beginning to adopt Agile (or at least want to be seen as doing so!), the need for training and coaching related to Agile, post the redefinition of the relationship, may seem like a waste of time. However, it is critical that both parties discuss the specifics of processes, practices, and tools, to find out similarities and differences in them across both entities and reach an agreement on whether those differences are significant enough to impact the partnership and, if so, how they will be dealt with. Ironing out these differences is essential to coming up with meaningful working agreements about common meetings, metrics for tracking progress and outcomes, and reporting.

However, if the partner organization has little or no experience with Agile, it is absolutely imperative to arrange for relevant training and coaching for those directly involved in delivery. Who bears the cost of training and coaching can be a contentious issue, but leaders from both organizations need to find a model that will work for both companies.

Coaching

Agile is easy to understand but difficult to apply in a specific context. This is where a coach can be of immense help. Assuming that both organizations are aiming to improve their Agile adoption maturity, having coaches at both ends can have a very powerful and positive impact. The coach based at the partner's site should be positioned as the coach for the program of work and not as the coach for the partner. After all, the client's interest in the partner, in terms of Agile adoption, will be limited to the sphere of work being performed by the partner.

Moreover, the coach needs to act in a way that demonstrates neutrality and fairness toward both organizations and all actions of the coach, including pointing out improvements, should be purely from the perspective of benefitting the program of work. The coach can facilitate the partner to organize the delivery and follow appropriate practices toward delivering the agreed outcome.

Stakeholder map and communication plan

A huge enabler for building trust, which is a critical element in turning a client-partner relationship into a meaningful partnership, is building peer-to-peer relationships across both organizations. Creating a stakeholder map, which identifies the concerned people and their peers across both organizations, is the first step in that direction. The next step is to create a communication plan that specifies the nature and frequency of communication between the stakeholders. At the team level, the plan should be specifying the timing and frequency of the joint meetings, for example, stand-ups and retrospectives. For the stakeholders outside the teams, regular one-to-one catch-ups and joint governance meetings should be planned.

It is often seen that one-to-one peer catch-ups are bypassed, supposedly due to time pressure. However, discipline to have these catch-ups is important, to ensure that is trust is not only built but also maintained, as regular communication significantly reduces the chances of misunderstandings and unpleasant surprises, which can seriously damage trust. The communication should be based on common Agile practices (for example, the showcase/demo at the end of the iteration can also include communication about project progress), instead of status update meetings, which will make communication both effective and efficient. The plan should also have guidelines around frequency of face-to-face meetings of key stakeholders. Face-to-face meetings are a key enabler toward building trust and this should be leveraged, particularly when the relationship is new or is in the initial phase of being redefined.

Social contract

Turning groups of employees into effective teams is a challenge in itself and more so when employees from two or more organizations are involved. A social contract, also known as working agreement, provides a framework that helps to define the norms that the team agrees to abide by. Social contracts can be excellent enablers toward creating a culture of trust, visibility, and accountability, which is so essential for teams to be Agile.

Christine Riordan, a dean and a professor of management at the Daniels College of Business, and Kevin O'Brien, the chair of the Department of Business Ethics and Legal Studies at the Daniels College of Business, both at the University of Denver, published an article in HBR. They said:

> *"To turn groups of employees into great teams,*
> *a powerful first step is to form a social contract —*
> *an explicit agreement that lays out the ground rules*
> *for team members' behaviors. A contract can cover territory*
> *such as how members will work together, make decisions,*
> *communicate, share information, and support each other.*
> *Social contracts clearly outline norms for how members*
> *will and should interact with one another." [viii]*

Social contracts should be simple and should be arrived at based on inputs from team members involved. While leaders may be involved in facilitating bringing out the sentiments of team members, the temptation to influence or mandate the social contract should be avoided at all costs. Social contracts can include behaviors that the team wants to encourage and see more of, for example, saying, "We value diversity of thought and hence everyone has a voice at the table," and "We focus on finding solutions, not faults," as well as those which the team wishes to avoid and discourage. An example might be saying, "Do not criticize a team member behind his/her back."

An example of how a social contract helped a team is a large financial conglomerate in the USA, which was working with a technology partner in India, doing co-sourced product development. Since the time difference between the two locations was 9.5 hours, the partner team in India was often working at least until 9 PM, which was 11.30 AM for the team in the USA. The late evenings began to take a toll on the morale and health of the partner team members in India and the teams agreed to define a social contract. One of the points in the contract was that the teams in the USA and in India would take turns to start late and stay late in the office, to get a minimum of three hours of overlap time between the two teams. Once the teams began following this, the relationship between the client and their partner in India improved significantly.

The social contract should be a living document and team members should update/refine it at regular intervals. The social contract can begin as a simple working agreement, which can be enhanced subsequently to include behaviors linked to values and principles that the team decides to abide by. For social contracts to work, that is, for team members to have faith in them, the team members also need to establish how violations will be handled. Teams need to establish procedures for providing constructive and timely feedback, arriving at a decision despite having disagreements that cannot be easily resolved, and when to get help from outside the team to deal with a violation. While implementing social contracts within a team that includes partner employees may not be easy given the potential cultural differences between the organizations, this can be a powerful tool to create the *one team* feeling despite employees belonging to different organizations.

Alignment on estimation framework and standards

As both organizations have moved / are moving away from time-based estimation of requirements and perhaps are still becoming familiar with point or T-shirt-based estimation, it is important to agree on the sizing framework (story points, T-shirt size, and so on) and also the sizing standards (what story can be a one-pointer, two-pointer, and so on, or small, medium, and so on. These are sizing techniques commonly used in Agile methodologies). The reference stories should be such that teams from both organizations should be able to relate to them. This aspect is critical, as in most cases the output of teams of both companies may get combined for arriving at velocity.

Alignment on the definition of "ready" and "done"

Defining *ready* and *done* criteria is core to the Agile way of working. However, when handoffs are involved between partners, it is critical that the concerned teams reach an agreement on the criteria. This is important to ensure that seemingly incomplete work is not handed off to the other team. The "definition of done" is even more critical in terms of counting points toward iteration velocity, if both parties have agreed to use that metric. In a real-life example, where the client was a bank in Europe and the partner a consumer lending solutions provider based in India, *done* for the purpose of velocity count was initially agreed when the client tested the functionality and found it satisfactory. However, except for fixing defects, if any, the partner's role on that story ended when its team was done with testing on its side. The partner was not happy with the initial agreement on the definition of *done* and was keen to count points toward velocity as soon as testing finished, but the actual incidence of *done*, as good practice, was only when the client tested the story and found it satisfactory.

It took some convincing before the partner agreed to a common definition of *done*, after realizing that the anti-patterns emerging out of having separate definitions of *done* were not worth the "gain" of counting points toward velocity, at best one iteration ahead of time.

Ensure infrastructure and security alignment upfront

On the surface, arranging for the appropriate infrastructure and alignment of security policies of both organizations appears like an inconsequential issue. However, consider the following scenarios:

- In order to use a physical wall at a partner's office for having the "card wall," approval had to be received from its infrastructure management office, which took almost two months to come through.

- Another partner, who was severely constrained for office space, was reluctant to provide any physical space for the card wall, as it feared that the card wall and the meetings around it would disturb its employees not associated with the project. It took some really tough talking by the client to get the partner to provide space for creating the card wall, which ended up being a conference room that as a floor above where the team was located. The outcome was less than ideal, as the team looked at the wall only when they gathered around it for the stand-up meetings.

- As a chat tool, Gtalk was acceptable to one partner, as per their security policy. However, as per the other partner's security policy, Gtalk was not acceptable but Lync was, which was not acceptable to the other partner. After a hard-fought six-month war, one of the partners gave in.

- In a partnership distributed between Australia and India, the staging environment was in India and the users were accessing it from Australia. However, the users were constantly experiencing poor performance and the issue was identified as being the limited network bandwidth in India. The partners agreed to implement a **Multiprotocol Label Switching (MPLS)** network to resolve the problem. However, the security team of both partners raised objections around data security over the network. To make things work, the network operator in Australia stipulated certain conditions that violated Indian laws. It took a full year to amicably resolve these issues.

- A partner's security policy did not allow Skype to be installed on any of their machines, including laptops provided to (selected) employees. However, given the lack of video conferencing facilities, this was the only video conferencing method acceptable to the other partner. Skype calls would happen using the coach's laptop, who was a third party. If the coach was absent, there would be no video call on that day. After a few months, the partner's security team granted permission to install Skype on a limited number of machines, but with a condition that employees should not initiate the call but only receive it.

The key learning from the aforementioned instances is that matters related to infrastructure and security are not trivial, and that the earlier the obstacles are anticipated, the better the chances of finding a quicker resolution.

Risk and issues – identification and management

Distributed delivery between partners can result in additional risks at both team and program levels, and therefore it is important to establish a risk identification and management process early in the relationship. All people directly and indirectly involved across both partners should have the opportunity to raise a risk/issue at any point and to also make it visible using a risk wall. Qualification, classification, and mitigation of risks should be discussed jointly among stakeholders across both partners. Joint efforts are critical for avoiding finger-pointing, should any risk/issue have an adverse impact. Agile practices, such as daily stand-up meetings and retrospectives, should be used as forums to bring up risks and issues as soon as they arise or appear as a "smell."

Governance mechanism for handling escalations

People take time to build trusted relationships when working with partners and until the trust levels are high, there is a tendency to instinctively and immediately blame the "other side" when things go wrong. A single instance of finger-pointing has the potential to cause serious damage to whatever level of trust has been created and also impedes any measures to increase trust. Hence, partners need to sensitize people to not rush to finger-point toward the other side, but to escalate the matter to the concerned stakeholders, who may be in a better position to take an impartial view of the situation and raise it with the concerned partner stakeholder with appropriate sensibilities, to resolve it jointly.

While a culture of people giving direct feedback should be the ultimate goal, giving negative feedback, which may appear like blame, without an appropriate level of trust being established, can cause long-lasting damage to relationships. Hence, until the relationship between partners reaches a high level of trust across people, a mechanism needs to be in place to communicate and resolve issues, by raising them as program-level issues and not as those belonging to one partner or the other.

Lead partner

If the program involves multiple external partners, it may be worth considering having one partner play a leading role with the other partners, on enabling other partners with the capabilities needed for the success of the program. For example, in a core banking platform implementation, the product was from partner A, the testing was done by partner B, and partner C brought in engineering capabilities, like automated build pipelines and continuous integration. Partner C was appointed the lead partner to help partner A and B to deliver the customizations to the product in an Agile way, using the engineering practices mentioned earlier.

Heads up on changes in capacity

Ramping up people capacity at short notice, especially if it is linked to a specific skill set, can be a challenge that most organizations would struggle with. It may involve hiring people from outside, which can be a very lengthy cycle. Once hired and post joining, a lot of time may be spent on training and upskilling these people in order to make them ready for the program. If these numbers are significant, the potential for an adverse impact on the program timeline is immense. It is therefore very critical to maintain constant visibility and transparency on the program plans with partners, thereby giving the partner an opportunity to scale up without feeling rushed or having to potentially cut corners. Short notices can cause resentment among the partner leadership, but the moot point is about the potential negative impact on the entire program itself.

There may be exceptional circumstances that may necessitate that the partner ramps up the program capacity as quickly as possible. In such cases, the issue needs to be examined at a program level and not as the partner's problem. Both organizations should work closely to reprioritize and distribute work and realign people across both organizations, until the partner is able to bring on board the required number of appropriately-skilled people.

Responding quickly to change may also lead to the need for quickly scaling down the program capacity. However, a sudden ramp down, leading to loss of billing, can impact the partner quite severely. Should such a scenario be unavoidable, in the spirit of partnership the client must be willing to take a part of the hit.

Primarily focus on outcomes, not on practices

While it is fair to expect partners to do their best to embrace agility, expectations should be realistic about the extent to which they can not only adopt Agile practices but also how quickly they can move up on the maturity curve of those practices. This may not be just a function of the intent of the leaders of the partner but could be influenced heavily by practical constraints. For example, a stream of work involved a client and three partners spread in multiple locations across different time zones. This led to a lot of difficulties in having a stand-up over video conference or even a conference call. The teams found a solution of a chat group, through which each person on the team provided the update. The team was able to achieve the intended outcome through the chat group, namely, to share individual updates, to examine current and potential blockers, and so on, despite not conducting the stand-up meeting in the way it is usually done. Given the circumstances, insisting on carrying out the stand-up the "right way" would have led to an increase in frustration levels for everyone and thereby could have led to diffused focus on the outcomes.

Phased introduction of advanced Agile practices

Advanced Agile practices, such as continuous delivery, may be critical to the success of a program, and therefore the client may be very keen that the partner should adopt these as soon as possible. However, it is not advisable to rush into *pushing* the partner to adopt advanced Agile practices for the following reasons: a) the partner may not be ready to handle the disruption that may arise through the introduction of the practice, b) the change may need the involvement of other departments of the partner organization and these departments may need time to come on board, and c) the advanced practice may not be set up for success, unless the basic practices that enable it are firmly in place. For example, continuous delivery will be ineffective unless unit tests are written and automated, and the code is checked regularly.

Learning through pairing

Adopting Agile involves learning new practices, as well as a change in mindset. The most effective way to achieve both of these is to pair the inexperience with Agile with those who have the experience. Pairing is one-to-one coaching in its best form and hence it is most effective for achieving the outcomes mentioned earlier as well. Moreover, the subtle, but no less important, benefit of pairing is that it provides a "safety net" regarding the outcome of the new practice being adopted. For example, writing user stories, which is more of an art than a science. Moreover, it also provides a great opportunity to build personal rapport. Pairing can be between people who hold a similar role, for example, a tester pairing with a tester, or across roles as well, such as, a tester pairing with a developer. Pairing should not be limited to pair programming only, which is pairing between developers. While continuous pairing is almost ideal, it may not be possible to pair people across organizations for a sustained period, due to constraints related to travel costs, time spent away from home, and so on. Pairing in short-time spurts, until the inexperienced person has reached the desirable level of adoption maturity, may be one of the solutions.

Moreover, pairing may not be possible for all people in the program from the partner's side and hence the focus should be on pairing with a few people who the partner is willing to groom as internal champions.

Maintain clarity on priorities

Embracing change can lead to frequent changes in program priorities and therefore it is essential to ensure that the changed priorities are understood and also agreed by both partners. The partner should be involved in ascertaining the impact of change and in also determining the cost of the change, if any. It is important to remember that the partner's organization may not be nimble enough to respond to the changed priorities, for example, knowledge of a new domain, and a solution to addressing such constraints must be examined from a program-level perspective, that is, cutting across organization lines.

Given that stakeholders between partners are communicating at multiple levels, it is possible that the team may get a different view of the changed priorities than the stakeholders outside of the team. To avoid any confusion arising from such a situation, the **product owner** (**PO**) should take extra care to ensure that the relevant stakeholders are aligned on the revised priorities.

Continuous eye on quality

Moving from gatekeeping quality toward the end of the development cycle, to building quality in throughout the development cycle is one of the most difficult Agile adoption outcomes to achieve, as it involves a paradigm shift in processes, practices and, most importantly, the mindset. In the enthusiasm to create success stories and demonstrate delivery achievements, it is quite likely that the rigor around building quality in throughout may be given lower priority, even inadvertently.

The risks of not keeping continuous focus on quality include the cost of a rework, impact on incremental development as capacity is diverted toward fixing errors and, most importantly, in the case of development being done jointly, finger-pointing between partners.

Monitor time in wait states post-handoffs closely

Handoffs, by definition, cause friction and create the potential for "cracks" through which work can fall through. This is amplified when a waiting state is created post the handoff. For example, if stories are handed over to the partner, post analysis, and a wait state "ready for development" is created before the partner team picks up the story for development, it is important to watch the time that the story is in the wait state. Of course, the waiting time is only a symptom, but nonetheless it provides a meaningful data point to investigate the potential underlying problem.

Wait states should be created and monitored when different teams are involved on the partner's side, without treating the partner's part of the process as a single "black box." For example, the partner may have a separate team for deployment to the staging area and the wait time should be monitored at this stage of the process too.

Knowledge transfer

In almost all cases, ownership of the work done by the partner needs to be transferred to the organization outsourcing the work and the ownership is incomplete without the knowledge related to the delivery also being transferred. Vinod Sankarnarayanan, a project manager at ThoughtWorks and author of the book *Project Ownership Transfer* [ix], delves in detail into this topic. The following are the key takeaways derived from his book, which should be taken into consideration from a transformation perspective:

♦ **Ownership transfer (OT)** extends well beyond taking delivery of software from the partner. What makes OT even more critical is that it is difficult to do it again if not done right the first time. The same applies to **knowledge transfer (KT)** as well.

- OT should be run like a program within a program and in an Agile manner, for creating stories that track the OT over iterations, evolving the program as more details are understood, and so on.

- Initiating OT toward the end of the project can lead to a poor outcome, as there is usually time pressure to complete it, and therefore OT needs to start early in the life of the project and should be planned to be completed in parallel with delivery work.

- Enhancing the product is as important as maintaining it, and the knowledge needed may be different for both. KT should cater to both.

- KT has multiple dimensions, for example, process, engineering, infrastructure, and so on. It involves transferring not just the end product, but also the "factory that produced it," in order to enable the ability to change the product. This provides a great opportunity to implement appropriate engineering practices for the product, if they were not implemented by the partner.

- Cultural differences play a big role in the OT exercise. Managing these requires heavy involvement of the senior management.

To summarize, OT and KT from partners is not a trivial activity, from the perspectives of size and importance, and is best done by applying Agile principles and practices.

Behaviors

The following behaviors by the client toward the partner can significantly help in creating a true sense of partnership between the two organizations.

Respect their pride

It is natural for employees to take pride in working for their organization and the employees of the client should always be sensitive toward this when dealing with partner employees. The partner organization may have global presence, renowned clients, and a strong track record of delivering projects, among many other things which their employees can and should be truly proud of. The client employees may feel a superiority complex if they believe that their organization is ahead on the agility curve and/or the work culture of their organization is supposedly better than that of the partner organization. This superiority complex can manifest itself in both obvious and subtle ways, and can hurt the pride of the partner employees, thereby causing a lot of resentment.

The leaders of the client organization play a key role in setting the tone for the partner organization to be treated as equal. They should be demonstrating this through words and deeds at all times. They need to educate the stakeholders on their side about the strengths that the partner is bringing into the partnership and how the combining of strengths of both organizations is a critical success factor for the program.

Empathy

Building further on respecting pride, being empathetic toward the employees of the partner organization, particularly toward those directly contributing to delivery, helps a great deal toward creating a sense of meaningful partnership. Change, particularly of the disruptive type which Agile adoption necessitates, can be quite difficult for partner employees and an attitude of empathy goes a long way in facilitating the change. Due to several practices and processes being newly introduced, the partner employees will be forced to work outside of their comfort zone. This can lead to feelings of inadequateness, arising from the skill gap and a fear of being judged. What may worsen the situation is the partner's managers continuing with their command and control behavior, which can be quite disorienting for the team.

Being empathetic also means curbing the instinct to blame people when things go wrong. Barring exceptions, people usually come to work to give their best and something going wrong usually will have its root cause in a systemic issue. The partner employees are best positioned to help to identify the underlying systemic issues and their knowledge of the context should be leveraged for this.

A credible way to demonstrate empathy is by raising systemic issues and constraints being faced by partner employees with their managers. This must be done in a way that protects the employee who has raised the issue/constraint, which is most likely done in confidence. The client employee should look for patterns of such issues/constraints and raise them with the partner management as patterns and/or systemic issues.

Pick your battles

Each organization will have its strengths and flaws and people in the client organization should be careful about picking flaws to be pointed out for improvement in the partner organization. The focus should be on ironing out flaws that are most critical for the program's success at a given point in time. Picking on inconsequential matters, especially those which from the partner's perspective may not be of any consequence at all, can lead to unnecessary resentment. These feelings of resentment are a huge barrier to meaningful collaboration and trust.

To give an example of this, a senior stakeholder of a client in the banking domain was visiting a partner that was replacing its core banking platform and while viewing the physical workflow wall, noticed that a regular piece of paper was being used to highlight blockers. She insisted that the blockers be highlighted using red color post-it notes. While the partner took a note of this, it did not act on it immediately, for good reasons.

The client stakeholder, who was visiting the partner for a few days, did not see the red post-it notes on the last day of her visit and created a scene about the partner not being willing to accommodate such a "small" request. The partner's relationship with that stakeholder was damaged badly and did not return to normalcy throughout the duration of the project.

Summary

In this chapter, we learned that technology partners are a critical part of an enterprise's ecosystem. Enterprises, therefore, must work with partners in the true spirit of partnership to achieve common goals, which include enhancing the agility of the company and also of the partner organization.

For technology partners to become enablers for enhancing agility, or at least to not become an impediment, it is necessary that both organizations, namely, the client and the partner, have shared objectives, such that they create an environment of mutual trust and "win-win" outcomes for both. If necessary, both organizations must recalibrate their relationship, starting from redefining contracts and the deliverables within, adopting, and modifying ways of working and changing behaviors in order to enhance agility and leverage the benefits.

The next chapter is the first of the two chapters in the fifth and final section of the book, which covers putting learnings into action. The chapter provides a framework for creating an action plan to enhance agility, based on the specific circumstances of the enterprise.

References

[i] https://www.gartner.com/it-glossary/it-outsourcing/

[ii] http://www.rosspettit.com/2017/08/partners.html

[iii] http://www.rosspettit.com/2017/08/partners.html

[iv] http://ptgmedia.pearsoncmg.com/images/9780133903355/samplepages/9780133903355.pdf, page 67

[v] https://www.paconsulting.com/insights/agile-projects-need-agile-contracts/

[vi] https://www.computerweekly.com/news/2240213773/The-BBC-DMI-project-what-went-wrong

[vii] http://www.openwindows.com.au/resources/agile-contracts-vs-traditional-contracts-contracting-uncertainty/

[viii] https://hbr.org/2012/04/to-ensure-great-teamwork-start

[ix] https://ptgmedia.pearsoncmg.com/images/9780134181011/samplepages/9780134181011.pdf

— PART FIVE —

THE JOURNEY TO
ENHANCING AGILITY

This part of the book examines how to create an
enterprise-specific action plan for enhancing agility, and
the enablers for facilitating change within the organization.

14

FRAMEWORK FOR ACTION

Just as a person-specific action plan is prepared when an individual's health needs to be improved, in a similar way, each enterprise must prepare an action plan for enhancing agility. Being a **complex adaptive system** (**CAS**), the parts of the organization are not only interdependent but their interactions also lead to dynamic and nonlinear evolution. This leads to each organization being a unique system, and hence the plan and approach to enhancing agility must be created based on the specific context of the organization.

This chapter covers a topic that is worthy of a book by itself. Given the constraints of condensing the material into a single chapter, this chapter should not be treated as a playbook, but as a set of guidelines that can be considered while preparing the enterprise-level plan for enhancing agility.

This chapter explores the following topics:

◆ Leadership alignment on the need for change

◆ Redefining/validating the purpose of the enterprise

◆ Defining the capabilities underlying agility

◆ Translating intent into action

◆ Agility is a journey and not a destination

Leadership alignment on the need for change

While the need for enhancing agility may appear obvious, at least on paper, it is important to explicitly ensure that the leaders of the enterprise are convinced about the need and timing of the change. They must be mentally ready to steer the enterprise through the potential turbulence that the change may cause, and, most importantly, understand how their role will need to change, if the enterprise is to have greater agility.

The path to enhancing agility starts with revalidating or even changing the purpose of the enterprise. Getting this wrong can put the survival of the business at stake. Hence, the decision regarding revisiting the purpose may need the approval of the board of directors. So, alignment about the need for enhanced agility needs to happen at the board level as well.

Lack of alignment at the senior leadership level will send confusing signals and a feeling of tentativeness about the initiative to the entire organization, which is a sure recipe for the initiative to fail. Moreover, leaders have to become role models for the rest of the organization in terms of an Agile mindset, and this is not possible unless the leaders are committed to supporting the change wholeheartedly.

According to Christopher Handscomb, a partner at McKinsey and others:

> *"We have often seen organizations embark on such transformations without first ensuring alignment among the leaders of the organization on the aspiration and value of the transformation. Further, even when there is such alignment, we often see companies that, in the spirit of adopting some Agile principles—such as experimentation and empowered teams—end up creating a burning platform, as different leaders across the organization choose different approaches to implementing Agile, while others dig in their heels to maintain the status quo."* [i]

Leadership alignment should ideally be in place prior to launching the initiative to enhance agility. If the initiative is already launched, it is never a moment too late to have this in place. One of the primary barriers to alignment is the fear of the unknown. Hence, it is worthwhile considering having workshops with senior leaders to understand their concerns and also to educate them on what the journey to enhancing agility might look like.

Redefine/validate the purpose of the enterprise

The purpose/mission of the company defines the essence of its existence. It helps to bring alignment across the enterprise on what outcomes it values most, and therefore is a guiding force for all decision-making in the business. It defines how an enterprise will differentiate itself from its competitors. The criticality of the purpose cannot be emphasized enough, as it is the foundation of the strategies of the enterprise and encapsulates its values.

Enterprises can enhance and sustain agility only if they are an integral part of their surrounding ecosystem. The ecosystem consists of various groups of stakeholders, including employees, shareholders, suppliers, the society at large, and, most importantly, the customers. Enterprises can no longer operate in a vacuum, hence the need to have a mission/purpose that is inclusive of the stakeholders that it is closely connected with and to be able to clearly articulate this as well. However, sometimes this is not easy to do.

According to Simon Sinek, author of the book *Start with Why*:

> *"Every organization on the planet knows what they do. Some know how they do it, the things that you think make you different or special or stand out from the crowd, but very, very few people and very, very few organizations can clearly articulate why they do what they do, that purpose, cause, or belief that drives everything you do.*

And that's really essential. All the great organizations in the world, all have a sense of why that organization does what it does." [ii]

Many organizations have defined their primary purpose as "maximizing shareholder wealth." Having such a purpose caters to only one group of stakeholders, even at the cost of other stakeholders. This narrow and superficial purpose means that leaders are under pressure to report increasing top lines and bottom lines every quarter, which are expected to then have a favorable impact on the share price. The primary focus shifts to managing the expectations of stock market analysts, over running the business. Long-term interests of the business are compromised to protect top and bottom lines in the short term.

Jack Welch, ex-chairman of General Electric has said:

"On the face of it, shareholder value is the dumbest idea in the world. Shareholder value is a result, not a strategy. Your main constituents are your employees, your customers and your products." [iii]

Moreover, maximizing shareholder value can create a serious conflict of interest for senior leaders when their compensation gets linked to the share price. According to Mark Krammer, a senior fellow at the Harvard Kennedy School of Government:

*"The ultimate irony may be that the allegiance to shareholder value has caused the very problem it was intended to cure: enriching senior executives at the shareholders' expense.
Given long enough time on the horizon, the interests of the company, the investors, and the executives would ultimately align. But with an average chief executive tenure of four and a half years, and an average stock holding period of only four months, short-term pressures exacerbate the focus on manipulating the stock rather than building the business.*

The increase in high speed trading and the proliferation
of hedge funds and private equity firms has further increased
the short-term pressure for financial engineering rather than
long-term value creation." [iv]

An organization aspiring for greater agility must become a purpose-driven organization, rather than a profit-driven one. The purpose needs to be inclusive toward creating value for all stakeholder groups connected with the organization, the most important one being customers. Just like the true purpose for someone wanting to become a doctor is to heal and serve people, as opposed to making money, an enterprise cannot have maximizing shareholder wealth as its true purpose. Every business must have a purpose that encapsulates the true reason for its being.

According to John Kay, one of Britain's leading economists:

"The great corporations of the modern world were not
built by people whose overriding interest was wealth, profit,
or shareholder value. To paraphrase Mill: their focus was on
business followed not as a means, but as itself an ideal end.
Aiming thus at something else, they found profit by the way."

He adds:

"So the most profitable companies are not the most
profit-oriented, and the happiest people are not those who
make happiness their main aim. The name of this idea?
Obliquity." [v]

Having a clear purpose is becoming even more important due to the increasing number of millennials in the workplace. According to Karl Moore, a professor at McGill University:

"Fulfillment at work, fulfillment at home...millennials want it all and they want it fast. They are constantly seeking purpose in what they do for a living and at the same time want to know how their job is helping them get to the top. They're constantly questioning where they are going next and why. That is, which position they will hold next. If your organization can't tell them that, they'll seek out another firm that will." [vi]

Some examples of inclusive purpose / mission statements, which extend beyond merely maximizing shareholder wealth, are as follows:

♦ Babylon, a subscription healthcare provider: "Babylon's mission is to put an accessible and affordable health service in the hands of every person on earth." [vii]

♦ Life is Good, an apparel company that is known for putting optimistic messages on T-shirts and hats: "To spread the power of optimism." [viii]

♦ sweetgreen, a restaurant chain: "To inspire healthier communities by connecting people to real food." [ix]

♦ Google, the world's most popular search engine: "Organize the world's information and make it universally accessible and useful." [x]

It is only when people can relate to the purpose of the enterprise that they will be meaningfully engaged with it. For a company to have sustainable agility, meaningful engagement across stakeholder groups is critical. Hence, enterprises embarking on the journey to enhancing agility must redefine their purpose, if needed, to make it inclusive, such that at least the customers and the employees can relate to it.

Satisfied customers and happy employees will lead to maximizing shareholder wealth. More importantly, for the purpose to be perceived as authentic, it must be reflected in the strategic objectives and initiatives.

Simon Sinek, author of *Start with Why*, has aptly said:

> *"When an organization starts with WHY (i.e., the true purpose), they stand for something bigger than any product, result or metric. Their brand has real meaning and true value in the world. They are better able to attract and unite employees, customers and partners. And their people love coming to work." [xi]*

Define the capabilities underlying agility

Every enterprise must have clarity and alignment on what agility means in its specific context and circumstances. The way to give meaning to agility is by identifying the capabilities that are needed to enable the business to be on the journey to fulfilling its purpose, and also defining how each of these identified capabilities helps toward fulfilling the purpose.

As discussed in *Chapter 2, From Agile to Agility*, agility is a set of underlying capabilities. The chapter covered the six underlying capabilities based on the framework created by David S. Alberts, namely, responsiveness, versatility, flexibility, resilience, innovativeness, and adaptability. However, the critical point about capabilities defining agility is that they need not be limited to these six, and enterprises can identify additional capabilities that are appropriate for their context, for example, stability is a capability that some enterprises may wish to have.

While agility is usually associated with speed and responsiveness, there are some parts of the business, or even a part of a component, which may have stability as a primary capability, for example, a bank may wish to keep its technology platform stable for core services such as accounting, and also have the flexibility to add and replace the products connected with the platform. Another example of an additional capability is efficiency. It may be a critical capability for organizations that perform process-heavy and repetitive types of work, for example, **business process outsourcing** (**BPO**) and manufacturing.

According to Wouter Aghina, a principal at McKinsey:

"Coca-Cola's organization structure has integrated dominant geographic units (regions and countries) as the primary axis, and a second dimension around a few strong central functions (marketing, finance, HR, and the like) in a well-understood, and largely unchanging, basic operating model. Adjustments are often made to the specifics as new issues and opportunities arise, but the essence of the matrix structure — i.e., geographic units as the primary axis, intersecting with strong key functions — has remained virtually unchanged for many years." [xii]

Besides identifying the relevant capabilities underlying agility, enterprises must also define the meaning of those capabilities, which is specific to the context of the enterprise, for example, responsiveness may be defined by one organization as a willingness to help customers by providing prompt service, in order to meet and exceed customer expectations. Another may define it as developing products and features based on customer insights and delivering these to customers at the shortest possible lead time. Given the fast pace of change and the emergent nature of a CAS, enterprises must regularly examine the relevance of their agility-related capabilities and the meanings that have been ascribed to those capabilities as well.

Translate intent into action

After having clarity and alignment on the purpose of the enterprise and the agility capabilities that the business endeavors to have, the next stage is about defining and implementing actions to enhance agility. This stage is divided into four phases, as shown in the following diagram:

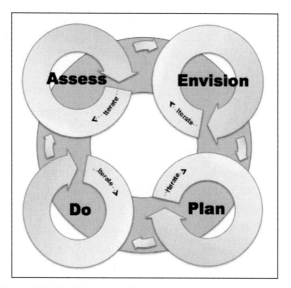

Figure 14.1: The framework for the agility enhancement journey

The first phase of the framework begins with an **assessment** of the current state that considers the entire landscape of the enterprise, which includes its foundational blocks and components. The current state assessment is followed by **visioning** activities that help to identify the goals for any potential changes, with a subsequent adoption **planning** process being applied to develop a high-level approach for introducing change, tailored to the organizational context. The fourth and last phase of the framework is about **executing** the plan, in order to embed the changes across the foundational blocks and components in a phased manner.

The execution plan is adaptive and iterative, including deferred decision-making and inclusive governance, to deal with the complexities of organizational change. The execution phase is also used to ensure that the newly-developed behaviors and practices are fully leveraged and applied at appropriate points within the larger enterprise, in order to make the changes sustainable.

The critical point to note is that each of the four phases, and the cycle of the four phases, are iterative in nature. The approach is based on the "inspect and adapt" philosophy of Agile, which means that each of the four phases in the stage must be performed in a cyclical way, that is, the next cycle must be based on inspecting the results of the previous cycle and adapting the plan for the next cycle based on these results.

Assess the current state

In the journey toward enhancing agility, the first step is to understand where the enterprise currently is. An objective assessment of the current state helps to create the foundation for change in the following ways:

- ◆ Understanding the strengths of the enterprise. Awareness and understanding of strengths is important, as the strengths that are relevant to agility can be leveraged to enhance agility.

- ◆ Identifying the root cause of problems/pain points. It is important to be able to not confuse the symptoms with the underlying problem, for example, a person getting fever could be a symptom of malaria or it could be just a seasonal flu, and the treatment will vary accordingly. Similarly, poor quality is a mere symptom of testing done toward the end of the delivery cycle, technical debt, or a culture that is lax toward quality or a combination of these factors.

◆ Baselining the current metrics. As part of the assessment, it is important to baseline key metrics, so that improvements over the current state can be tracked and measured.

The scope of the current state assessment should at least be one product/service offering of the enterprise. The offering can be in the form of a single product/service or a bundle of them. If a business offers multiple products, the factors to consider while choosing the products for assessment include the following:

◆ Level of strategic importance

◆ Size (revenue and number of people involved)

◆ Representation of stages in the product life cycle, for example, if the enterprise has products in the introduction, growth, and maturity stages, a product from each of these stages should be included

◆ Criticality of pain areas like slow time to market, low customer satisfaction, and so on

If an enterprise is organized by product components, the most critical components must be in scope. If it is organized by separation of platform and services, the core functionalities of the platform and important services, based on size and criticality of pain areas, must be included in the scope. For the offerings selected to be in the scope, the entire value stream of those offerings must be included. The value stream is all activities from ideation, that is, "concept" to realization of value, that is, "cash" and customer support and maintenance activities as well.

Moreover, corporate-level functions, such as marketing/sales, finance, and the **project management office** (**PMO**), which have an influence on the outcomes of the value stream, must also be included, in case they are not included in the value stream. For the selected value streams, the assessment must focus on the following outcomes:

♦ What is working well.

♦ What are the challenges and pain points.

♦ Data related to metrics being currently tracked. If possible, data should be collected for metrics that are usually recommended as good practices, for example, if cycle time [xiii] is not being measured, it should be measured for the current state and baselined.

The assessment must be done from the perspective of the six primary components of the enterprise, namely, organization structure, process, people, technology, governance, and customer, and the two foundational blocks, namely, mindset and culture, and leadership.

The following are typical variables that should be examined:

♦ **Structure**: This includes the extent to which teams are empowered, cross-functional, and self-organizing; the alignment between teams on outcomes, the effectiveness of feedback loops, the role of middle managers in enabling value creation, and the effectiveness of knowledge sharing.

♦ **Process**: This includes rigidity, work prioritization, delivery cadence, the extent of hands-offs and waiting times, the management of dependencies and blockers, the extent of work in process, and to what extent quality is built in throughout the process, are all the relevant Agile practices being followed. Also to be considered are barriers to communication and collaboration, visibility, and transparency of the process.

♦ **People**: This includes how well is the understanding of and focus on outcomes, the ratio of people in roles within teams, morale and motivation, the performance appraisal process, drivers of reward and recognition, the hiring process, the process for identifying capability development needs and building them, engagement and happiness levels, and the focus on continuous improvement. Also important are the fear of failure, conduciveness of the work environment, and tools for communication and collaboration.

♦ **Technology**: This includes responsiveness to change, continuous delivery capability, DevOps capability, ability to evolve architecture, collaboration with business and alignment to business outcomes, maturity of development practices, and alignment with technology partners on ways of working.

♦ **Governance**: This includes the alignment of current initiatives to strategy, idea prioritization, people being able to connect their work with the desired strategic outcomes, the extent to which decision-making is delegated, adaptive planning, the extent of change control, budgeting and funding, and the ability to gather and act on external feedback. Also should be examined are enabling experimentation and innovation, the extent of bureaucracy and its impact on the ability to create value, and metrics being tracked and their impact on people's behaviors.

♦ **Customer**: This includes robustness, that is, end-to-end coverage of customer journeys and the handling of "non-happy path" scenarios, alongside consistent user experience. Also important to examine are the skills and motivation of customer-facing people, including those in customer support, the nature of customer complaints and their root causes, and effectiveness of getting and acting on feedback.

♦ **Leadership**: This includes alignment on purpose and strategies, connecting with teams and customers, how failures are treated, evidence of systems thinking, and the success criteria of performance.

♦ **Mindset and culture**: This includes behaviors, willingness to discuss challenges, and the working environment.

The preceding lists of variables should be treated as guidelines, as the context of the enterprise will determine the specific nature of the variables that need to be assessed. Many variables may have their subset of additional variables, which may need to be assessed further, for example, for the idea prioritization variable in the governance component, some of the aspects to be examined include: what is/are the source/s of new ideas? How are ideas selected and validated for market acceptance and feasibility? What is the basis of prioritizing ideas? What is the role of the technology function is selecting and prioritizing ideas?

The techniques used for collecting information include workshops (for example, retrospectives), interviews with employees and customers, observation of meetings and team-level practices (for example, demos and estimation meetings), examination of artefacts created by teams (for example, plans and requirements documentation), corporate policies and metrics at team, program and enterprise levels. Niche techniques are used such as **value stream mapping** (**VSM**) [xiv], a technique to identify the efficiency of the value stream/process and the **Agile Maturity Model** (**AMM**) [xv], a model to assess and guide improvements.

The outcomes of this phase should be the identification of strengths / what is working well, and the identification of root causes of challenges / pain points and data for **key performance indicators** (**KPIs**), which are intended to be tracked.

Envision the future

An enterprise must have a vision for its future, as that sets the direction and focus for the business. The vision for the future enables the company to set appropriate strategies, which are aligned with the purpose, and allocate resources and capabilities most effectively to meet the strategic objectives.

The future state must be defined not only for the enterprise as a whole but also for its foundational blocks and its primary components. The future state for the company is reflected in its vision statement, which should not be confused with the purpose/mission statement.

According to Mark Watson, a senior advisor at Effective Governance, a corporate governance advisory firm:

> *"The vision statement describes what the organization will look like in the future. It serves as a guiding beacon that depicts the kind of future to which the organization aspires. It also provides direction to everyone in the organization as they focus their efforts on achieving the vision. A mission statement, on the other hand, describes what an organization does and for whom. In addition, it can also state the benefit or benefits provided by the organization." [xvi]*

He goes on to refer to the BBC's mission statement, which is "to enrich people's lives with programmes and services that inform, educate and entertain" and its vision statement, which is "to be the most creative organisation in the world."

An enterprise may choose to define the vision based on time horizons, such as the following:

◆ **Short term**: To protect the existing customer base

◆ **Medium term**: To grow the customer base by targeting untapped market segments

◆ **Long term**: To delight customers through innovative offerings by leveraging technology

The vision statements should be treated as a direction toward which the organization should be steered, and as a guideline to prioritize initiatives and to align the capabilities and resources to the prioritized initiatives. Treating the vision as a fixed state is likely to make the enterprise more inwardly focused and thereby less sensitive to changes in the external environment. It is imperative that the vision be aligned with the purpose of the company. Furthermore, each foundation block and component of the enterprise should have its own vision, which should align with the overall vision of the organization.

For example, the technology function could define its vision as follows:

◆ **Short term**: Invest in building capabilities of Agile ways of working and platform infrastructure

◆ **Medium term**: Mature the core capabilities and align technology strategy to business strategy

◆ **Long term**: Enhance the technology platform and Agile capabilities to enable innovation and responsiveness

The vision for the customer component could be to put the customer at the center, supported by the following themes:

◆ Design digital channels to provide a consistent and seamless user experience

◆ Design customer experiences to cater to the functional and emotional needs of the customer

The use of trade-off sliders, while defining vision statements and the future state, can help to uncover the underlying assumptions and create alignment among the stakeholders about the level of criticality of decision parameters, which can be used as guidelines for important, as well as day-to-day, decisions.

Some trade-offs may not be obvious, but it is important to uncover them and get alignment. For example, if lowering cycle time is important, then maximizing capacity utilization automatically assumes lower importance, as cycle time is a function of the amount of work that is in process and maximizing capacity utilization often leads to increased work in process. Trade-off decisions also can have an impact on important decisions related to architecture and budgeting. For example, the following could be a trade-off slider for a future state that is about quickly getting new ideas to market, to gauge customer response:

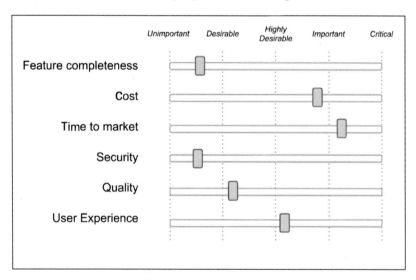

Figure 14.2: Trade-off sliders

In this diagram, it is clear that time to market and keeping costs to the minimum are the two most important variables, while feature completeness and security are the least important variables.

Once the vision statements / future states are defined, the relevance of the agility capabilities identified for the purpose must be validated against the vision statements and future states of the enterprise, the foundational blocks and the components. It may emerge that some capabilities may not be relevant or additional capabilities may be needed, for example, innovativeness as a capability may be associated with the enterprise purpose and vision but may not be relevant for the process component. The process component may instead need efficiency as an additional capability. The outcome of this phase is a vision statement and/or a future state defined for the enterprise and its foundation blocks and components, and capabilities of agility, which are linked to the vision statement and future state.

It is critical that people who are directly creating and delivering value are involved in shaping the vision. This will help to not only factor in the ground level realities, and also create a greater sense of ownership of the vision across the enterprise.

Plan the change

This phase is about creating a plan for change, to steer the business toward the defined vision, by enabling the components and foundational blocks to move toward the future state. For many enterprises, the change will be highly transformational in nature. The nature of change will span tangible changes, such as structure of teams and ways of working, and intangible and relatively more difficult changes, such as leadership style and mindset and culture. In order to treat the enterprise like a living system, it must be seen as a whole, and not just as a sum of its blocks and components. Hence, while changes may be introduced at component level, their impact will almost always be felt across multiple components and often at the company level as well.

For example, if the biggest impediment for the enterprise is assessed to be the matrix organization structure, and the business wants to introduce the pattern of flat organization structure, as discussed in *Chapter 6, Organization Structure* the key factors to consider are as follows:

♦ Should the structure be changed for the enterprise or, to begin with, should the change be limited to only one product?

♦ What roles will the middle managers, who would no longer fit into a flat structure take, and how should they be prepared to take on the new roles?

♦ What is the impact of change in structure on the performance appraisal process?

♦ How can the business help people to move from an individual-driven to a team-driven culture and how should teams be supported to become self-organizing?

♦ What is the implication of the change in organization structure on team, program, and enterprise-level governance?

Change can be approached in either of the following two ways:

♦ A **big bang approach**, in which most of the identified actions for enabling change are introduced simultaneously. While success stories of the big bang approach exist, for example, PayPal's Agile transformation [xvii], this approach is highly risky. This approach assumes that the relationship between the actions and expected outcomes is linear and that the impact of those actions will be localized and not be systemic. Such an assumption has a very high probability of being proven wrong in a CAS, which every single enterprise is.

◆ A **roadmap-driven approach**, in which actions are introduced in a phased manner. Under most circumstances, it is better to take the roadmap-driven approach for the following reasons:

   ○ The approach allows time to "test and learn," thereby providing flexibility to refine the map, based on the emergence of outcomes

   ○ It provides an opportunity to create the appetite for change in people, through celebrating stories of early successes

   ○ It helps to create a culture of continuous change, which is an imperative for enterprises, given the fast-changing external environment

   ○ It helps toward aligning resources and capabilities, where the greatest need is at a given point in time, rather than spreading them thinly across the entire enterprise

Since emergence is a core property of a CAS, the outcomes of measures for bringing change cannot be predicted accurately. These measures, therefore, by default become mere hypotheses, and whether the hypotheses about the intended outcomes are proved or not can only be accurately assessed in hindsight.

According to Steve Denning, author of *The Age of Agile*:

> *"The change idea itself will steadily evolve. This is not a matter of crafting a vision and then rolling it out across the organization. It's not a mechanical eight-step program. It's about continuously adapting the idea to the evolving circumstances of the organization. As the organization and everyone in it adapts the story of change to their own context, each individual comes to own it." [xviii]*

The first step toward creating a change roadmap is to identify the actions needed to introduce change. For each foundation block, component and blind spot, and for every capability associated with agility, the inhibitors that impede that capability and the enablers that enhance that capability must be identified. The findings from the current state assessment and the agility capabilities should be the primary basis for deriving the actions. Action items should be identified for each foundational block and component separately. It is important to note that the need for additional actions or to drop some action items may emerge based on how the enterprise reacts to the change.

While defining the actions, the level of optimal agility, which was discussed in *Chapter 2, From Agile to Agility* should be kept in mind. Essentially, optimal agility is that level of agility that has a favorable cost-benefit balance, for example, a global online retailer is releasing software code at an average of 11 seconds per release, whereas a bank may not need such a sophisticated continuous delivery [xix] capability.

The list of action items is likely to be quite large, not only at the enterprise level but also for some of the components as well. Given this, it is critical to prioritize the action items. The two primary variables that can be considered for determining priority are: a) effort/complexity involved and b) value/impact of the action. Needless to say, the values assigned to these variables are based on the prevailing circumstances at a point in time and hence, must be revisited as often as needed to validate the prioritization, and change it if needed.

The matrix shown in the following diagram can be used for doing the first level of prioritization:

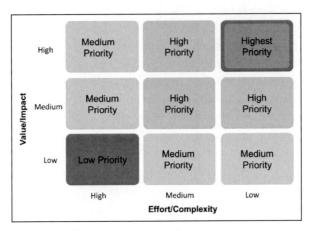

Figure 14.3: The prioritization matrix

The preceding diagram depicts that actions that fall in the quadrant of low complexity-high value should get highest priority, while those falling in the high complexity-low value quadrant should get low priority, and other actions will be prioritized between these two levels. This prioritization should be refined based on dependencies between actions, that is, the impact of some actions may depend on some other action being done as a prerequisite for example, actions for implementing DevOps can be taken only when teams implement basic software engineering practices.

Prioritization based on a matrix is not meant to oversimplify issues. Rather, matrices should be used as the initial guidelines for prioritization, and the basis of prioritization must be refined based on emergent circumstances, as needed. The journey toward achieving a sustainable level of agility can take years, and hence it is important to have milestones along the journey, to ensure that the focus is maintained on the actions that are relevant for the respective stages of the journey.

The following diagram depicts an example of staging the journey:

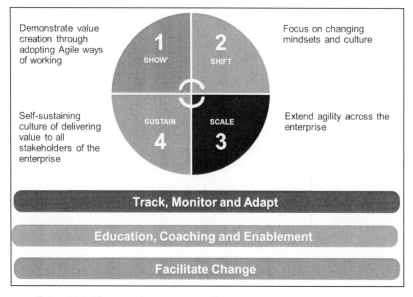

Figure 14.4: Phases in the journey to achieving a sustainable level of agility

The preceding diagram depicts that this phase is divided into four broad stages, namely show, shift, scale, and sustain. Each stage has a theme associated with it, which indicates the primary focus area of change in that stage. The diagram also depicts that the entire journey across all four stages is supported by three continuous streams of work: track, monitor, and adapt. This stream is about measuring the progress of the journey, as well as the impact on the strategic outcomes, and adapting the journey based on the insights gained from these measurements. For example, in the current state assessment, it was found that the frequency of releasing features into production was six months.

If the envisioned state is to be able to release on a daily basis, and if the frequency has improved to monthly releases, it may be a good point to ascertain whether the envisaged outcomes arising from the increased frequency are being realized, and, if so, whether it is still worthwhile aiming for a daily frequency, considering the incremental costs and benefits.

The education, coaching, and enablement stream is about building new capabilities and adopting new ways of working. The journey will involve acquiring new capabilities and learning new ways of working for most people in the enterprise. The capability building and learning needs to be enabled by appropriate training, followed by coaching and, where necessary, enabling the learning by pairing the coach with the team members. The facilitating change stream is discussed at length in *Chapter 15, Facilitating Change*. Regardless of how the journey is phased, it is highly recommended that you have these three streams as an integral part of the change journey.

Some other examples of staging the journey are as follows:

♦ Example 1:

     ○ **Foundation**: Demonstrate improvements

     ○ **Growth**: Drive organizational change

     ○ **Sustenance**: Commit to change

♦ Example 2:

     ○ **Phase 1**: Create value-driven culture

     ○ **Phase 2**: Expand value-driven culture

     ○ **Phase 3**: Optimize value-driven culture

     ○ **Phase 4**: Sustain value-driven culture

The following are some of the key factors that should be considered while defining the scope and themes of the stages:

- ◆ Business priorities and drivers for organizational change
- ◆ Current pain areas
- ◆ Severity of organizational/systemic constraints
- ◆ Appetite of the organization for digesting disruption, without putting the business as a whole at undue risk
- ◆ Dependencies between actions

It is important to always keep in mind that these stages are not watertight and, therefore, overlaps between stages are to be expected. However, each stage must also have clear outcomes, which can be used as a guideline to shift the focus to the next stage, for example, for the show phase, as shown in the preceding *Figure 14.4*, the theme is to demonstrate value creation through Agile ways of working. The primary outcome of this phase can be that the **minimum viable product (MVP)** for a strategically critical business stream is delivered through Agile ways of working and is creating value for customers. Having said this, the phases should not be treated as hard gates, otherwise the risk of slowing down or even derailing the journey is very high. Moreover, the approach to achieving the outcomes should be iterative, for example, the MVP, as stated here, should be delivered in an iterative way, that is, by refining it based on emergent feedback.

Some organizations make the mistake of taking a pause between phases and this is usually a death knell for the change journey, particularly if done so after the initial/foundation phase. This is because until the change, and consequently agility, gets deeply rooted, the *organization inertia* [xx] will remain strong and the risk of the enterprise regressing to its original state is very high.

Another critical decision, which needs to be made in the planning phase, is to decide the scope of the first stage of the execution phase, that is, which team/s should be the "early adopters/exemplars." The rule of thumb approach might be to select the same teams / value streams that were selected for current state assessment. However, teams / value streams should be validated for their potential to deliver meaningful business outcomes and for representing the typical nature of work that happens in the business. In addition to this, co-located teams and teams who want to lead the change should be preferred in this phase, as the challenges of distributed teams can drag the speed of change, which is crucial in the initial phase of the journey. It is also critical to provide all the required support needed to these teams, such that they can create a success story, with positive outcomes for the business and the customers.

The change program office should also be established prior to commencing the execute phase. The objective of creating a change program is to facilitate alignment of change initiatives across the organization and ensure that adequate support and empowerment is provided to execute these initiatives.

Gary Hamel and Michele Zanini, co-founders of Management Innovation eXchange, have aptly said:

> *"What's needed is a real-time, socially constructed approach to change, so that the leader's job isn't to design a change program but to build a change platform — one that allows anyone to initiate change, recruit confederates, suggest solutions, and launch experiments." [xxi]*

This office must be headed up by the executive sponsor of the program, who must be a senior leader who has influence across the enterprise. The influencing skills are critical from the perspective of removing impediments and blockers, especially those at the systemic level, and prioritizing change-related actions over **business as usual (BAU)** work.

This office must also have a program manager, who, among other things, will manage the backlog of actions, reprioritize the backlog based on emergent feedback, track progress, and communicate and build and maintain alignment with stakeholders across the enterprise. The program governance team must include the executive sponsor, program manager and two-to-three senior leaders who head critical functions such as business, technology, and operations.

Ram Charan, author of multiple book, including *Boards That Deliver*, highlights the criticality of senior executive involvement in transformation initiatives. He says:

> *"Transforming a company for the digital age cannot be delegated, outsourced, or done piecemeal. Rather, it involves many steps that are interconnected. The CEO should spend at least 50% of the time on the transition to transformation. The CEO must have the imagination to conceive the reconstituted business and the scope to manage the broad range of elements in and outside the organization that must change." [xxii]*

The governance team must also include representatives of teams that are leading/undergoing the change. This is critical to ensure that governance is inclusive of stakeholders who are most impacted by the change. Their inclusion will significantly improve the effectiveness of the feedback loops between the change program and the teams that are spearheading the change. The change program should not be run as a traditional PMO, which is based on a "top-down" approach, but as an enabler of initiatives and experiments, which can spur organic change on the ground and across the organization.

Execute the plan

The following learnings can help to improve the effectiveness of the execution phase.

Don't copy frameworks blindly

As discussed earlier, the context and circumstances of each enterprise are unique. Hence, what has supposedly worked in one business may not be suitable for another. This means that companies must avoid the "cookie-cutter" approach while adopting anything from a practice or a framework.

According to Christopher Handscomb, a partner at McKinsey, and others:

> *"Too often, companies end up shifting the focus of an Agile transformation away from minimizing processes and changing mindsets and behaviors to enable innovation, toward putting in place the right framework. While frameworks can be valuable in providing structure to the transformation, it is important not to be rigid in their adoption, and to always think of how they can be adapted to suit the needs of the organization. After all, one of the pillars of the original Agile manifesto was to favor "individuals and interactions over processes and tools.""* [xxiii]

According to Scrum [xxiv], which is one of the more popular Agile mythologies, the team size should be seven people, with a variation permitted of + or − two people. Now, if the size of the team is 11 people, and if the disadvantages of breaking this team into two teams outweigh the benefits, Scrum can still work for this team. Sure, there will be some extra overheads related to communication, but if that is best option under the circumstances, then it is absolutely pragmatic to make this deviation.

Moreover, combining appropriate practices across methodologies and frameworks may often produce better outcomes, for example, a team may be primarily using Scrum practices, but may find it useful to put in limits on work in process items, which is a practice in Kanban methodology.

Balance evolution and execution

While executing the actions as per the roadmap to enhance agility, care must be taken to balance emergent evolution and planned execution. Given the lack of a linear relationship between cause and effect, the journey toward greater agility is unlikely to move in a straight line. The journey is more likely to resemble a trajectory as shown in the following diagram:

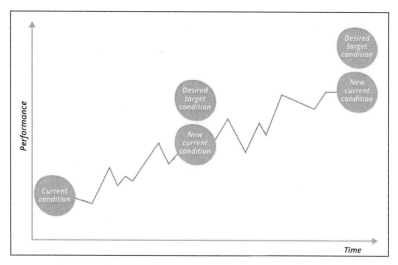

Figure 14.5: The likely path of an agility enhancement journey

The preceding figure depicts that the journey toward the desired target condition has peaks and troughs. It also depicts that the time taken to reach the first desired target condition was the time that was planned to reach the second desired target condition. While it is important to remain alert during troughs, what is most critical is the trajectory of change.

In this journey, which involves changes not only in ways of working but also in mindset and culture, the direction of change is more important than the quantum of change. Enterprises must therefore be steered in the direction of the desired target state and the "driving" must factor in the emergent circumstances, including a "bumpy road."

Regression in periods of crisis

In the initial stage of the journey, when the new mindset and culture in the enterprise are perhaps still fragile, it is critical spot to signs of regression to the original state, especially during crisis situations. For many people, including leaders, the extent of change in both practices and mindset can be unnerving and as dysfunctional as the situation may have been prior to commencing the journey, it will remain a comfort zone for many people until the new mindset and culture become part of "muscle memory." Generally, people have the tendency to look for comfort in a crisis and hence the chance of people reverting quickly to old practices and behaviors is very high. The problem gets aggravated even more when people see their leaders reverting to the comfort of command and control behaviors. Leaders must be extremely mindful of their behaviors during a crisis and must also actively support and work with people going through the crisis to overcome it.

Keep teams stable

A common dysfunction in low agility organizations is that the star performers are specially picked to tackle crisis and "firefighting" types of situations. These people are often unilaterally and suddenly "yanked" away from the teams they belong to. Such a knee-jerk reaction can be quite destabilizing for the concerned team, and can upset their rhythm, especially when the team is still learning to adopt new ways of working.

Moreover, it can demoralize the other team members, as someone had the privilege of being handpicked, but the others did not. While such ad hoc measures may give some short-term benefits, their systemic impact can create a drag on agility.

Leverage ways of working using propagation techniques

For most enterprises, the journey to enhancing agility will involve adopting Agile practices and processes. If the business follows the path of starting the journey with early adopters, it is important to propagate the practices that they have adopted with the learnings thereof.

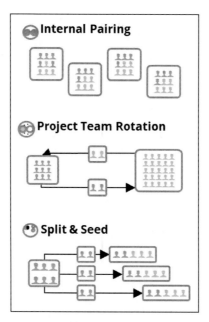

Figure 14.6: Propagation models

The preceding diagram depicts the three propagation models:

♦ **Pairing**: The coaches/experts pair with team members to enable them to adopt the new ways of working

♦ **Project team rotation**: The core team members are intact, but others come into the team and move out when they have passed on the ways of working

♦ **Split and seed**: A team that has learned the ways of working is split and team members are then seeded in other teams

Adopting the appropriate strategy for propagating ways of working can improve the effectiveness and efficiency of the agility enhancement journey. Propagating ways of working should not be confused with scaling agility. If scaling agility is about having agility across the enterprise, then the way to approach it is to have teams that deliver value through outcomes that are linked to strategy, and which are supported by the foundational blocks and components of the enterprise, as discussed in the book.

As Peter Merel, CEO of XSCALE Alliance says:

"An Agile organization is a pod of dolphins, not a dancing elephant. It isn't scaling Agile to the organization; it's de-scaling the organization to Agile." [xxv]

Agility as a journey and not a destination

Just like good health needs maintenance after achieving it, enterprises need to be able to sustain agility after achieving optimal agility. Moreover, given that the pace of change is expected to increase further, the state of sustenance may only be transient. To add to this, the ecosystem around businesses is a CAS, which will continue to evolve. This may mean that the enterprise may need new capabilities that are underlying agility or may have to further enhance the existing capabilities.

Complacency in adding or enhancing capabilities can result in enterprises facing the sustainability gap, which was discussed in *Chapter 3, Enterprise as a Living System*. Agility is, therefore, not a destination but a journey that does not have an end.

Summary

In this chapter, we learned that because an enterprise is a CAS, each one is a distinctly different entity. The combination of strategy, systems, people, capabilities, leadership, and culture create a context that is unique to that enterprise. Hence, while good practices and patterns can be used as guidelines, the action plan for enhancing agility must be based on the specific circumstances of the enterprise.

The approach to enhancing agility must be holistic and systemic, from validating and, if necessary, redefining the purpose of the enterprise to creating a milestone-driven action plan. Taking a systemic approach also implies that all foundational blocks and components of the enterprise must be included in the scope of the agility enhancement journey. Moreover, since emergence is an integral property of a CAS, the plan must balance emergent evolution and planned execution. Finally, the fact that agility is a perpetual journey and not a destination implies that enterprises need to constantly strive to enhance and sustain agility.

The next and final chapter is about learnings that can help in facilitating change across the enterprise.

References

[i] https://www.mckinsey.com/business-functions/
organization/our-insights/how-to-mess-up-your-agile-
transformation-in-seven-easy-missteps?cid=other-eml-
alt-mip-mck-oth-1804&hlkid=8e6aa95b232a4ba09b900ae62
e9da335&hctky=9719866&hdpid=9a62de33-9c77-4300-bbb9-
bdcb3109ef73

[ii] https://www.inc.com/simon-sinek/leadership-how-to-identify-your-companys-purpose.html

[iii] https://www.ft.com/content/294ff1f2-0f27-11de-ba10-0000779fd2ac

[iv] https://www.theguardian.com/sustainable-business/blog/maximising-shareholder-value-irony

[v] https://www.johnkay.com/2004/01/17/obliquity/

[vi] https://www.forbes.com/sites/karlmoore/2014/10/02/millennials-work-for-purpose-not-paycheck/#2186fba36a51

[vii] https://www.babylonhealth.com/about

[viii] https://blog.hubspot.com/marketing/inspiring-company-mission-statements

[ix] https://blog.hubspot.com/marketing/inspiring-company-mission-statements

[x] https://www.google.com/about/our-company/

[xi] https://startwithwhy.com/find-your-why/

[xii] https://www.mckinsey.com/business-functions/organization/our-insights/agility-it-rhymes-with-stability

[xiii] http://www.businessdictionary.com/definition/cycle-time.html

[xiv] https://en.wikipedia.org/wiki/Value_stream_mapping

[xv] https://info.thoughtworks.com/rs/thoughtworks2/images/agile_maturity_model.pdf

[xvi] https://www.effectivegovernance.com.au/vision-mission-and-purpose-statements-what-is-the-difference/

[xvii] https://searchcio.techtarget.com/feature/Four-pillars-of-PayPals-big-bang-Agile-transformation

[xviii] https://www.forbes.com/sites/
stevedenning/2018/02/26/ten-steps-to-launch-your-
agile-transformation/#467be49927a2

[xix] https://en.wikipedia.org/wiki/Continuous_delivery

[xx] https://www.researchgate.net/post/What_is_
organizational_inertia

[xxi] https://www.mckinsey.com/business-functions/
organization/our-insights/build-a-change-platform-
not-a-change-program

[xxii] https://hbr.org/2016/02/how-to-transform-a-
traditional-giant-into-a-digital-one

[xxiii] https://www.mckinsey.com/business-functions/
organization/our-insights/how-to-mess-up-your-agile-
transformation-in-seven-easy-missteps

[xxiv] https://www.google.co.in/search?q=what+is+scrum
&oq=what+is+scrum&aqs=chrome..69i57j0l5.2486j1j8&sour
ceid=chrome&ie=UTF-8

[xxv] http://xscalealliance.org

15

FACILITATING CHANGE

Many enterprises will need to start significantly reinventing themselves, in order to enhance their agility. The change needed is tectonic in nature, as it encompasses not only the extrinsic and tangible elements of a business, like people, process, and governance, but also, and more importantly, the intrinsic and intangible elements like mindset and culture.

This chapter is about key learnings related to facilitating change at the company level, based on the author's experience. The takeaways from these learnings will help to alleviate pain and disruption, which are often side effects of enterprise-level change.

The chapter will explore the following topics:

♦ The significance of change for an enterprise
♦ Learnings related to facilitating change

Significance

The biggest challenge that organizations are facing today is how to adapt and evolve at the frenetic speed at which the external environment is changing. Most organizations find change difficult due to the disruptions caused by it, which generally result in people having to step out of their comfort zone, thereby creating feelings of uncertainty and fear. Moreover, leaders need to demonstrate courage, conviction, empathy, and patience to manage the turbulence arising from change.

Robin Sharma, author of multiple books on leadership topics, has so aptly said:

"Change is hard at the beginning, messy in the middle and gorgeous at the end." [i]

What makes matters even more complicated is that this change cycle, as stated by Robin Sharma, is a continuous cycle in today's era and the pace of the rollover of the cycle will only get faster going forward. What is not encouraging is that the success rate of major change initiatives is quite low. John Kotter, author of the international bestseller, *Leading Change*, whose research was published in 1996, concluded that only 30% of change programs succeed. A subsequent survey of over 3000 executives, by McKinsey in 2008, found, similar to Kotter, that the success rate is merely one in three. [ii] The numbers are dismal.

While these numbers are no indication of how things are going to pan out in the future, clearly how change is introduced and scaled in enterprises needs careful handling. Given the pressing need for change, and also the huge breadth and depth of change that companies are likely to undertake, failure to change can be disastrous for an enterprise's agility.

Learnings

The following are the key takeaways gained from experience in facilitating enterprise-level change.

People do not resist change

A commonly held belief is that, in general, people's instinct is to resist change. What is supposedly seen as resistance is actually people's reaction to the potentially negative impact of change on them. It is therefore obvious that if people believe that the change is beneficial for them, they will not react negatively toward it.

It can thus be concluded that resistance to change is a myth. It can also be inferred that the so-called resistance is just a symptom of an underlying problem.

Some of the causes of resistance include the following:

- Disappointment and resentment about not having a voice in shaping the nature of change

- Processing information about the change selectively, influenced by past bad experiences and mental models

- Uncertainty, leading to insecurity, about how the change will impact them

- Realization that the change will expose their incompetence

- Fear of the unknown

For each of these causes, there needs to be a specific way of preventing and/or overcoming them. For example, for the first point, opportunities should be provided to people to have their voice heard about shaping the change, before rolling the change out formally. For the third point, it will be a combination of communication regarding the benefits of change for the people involved and individual counseling.

The key takeaway about resistance is that it should be viewed as valuable feedback. The feedback, as a response to change, could be that the message about the change is not properly understood, the impact of the change is perceived as negative by some individuals, or a group of individuals, or just that some people are resisting change simply due to a bad attitude. Depending on what the resistance is actually translating into, corrective actions can be determined. It is therefore critical that resistance is not ignored or, even worse, quashed.

Things will get worse before they get better

In a book published in 2015, German authors Klaus Leopold and Siegfried Kaltenecker noted that the dip in performance in the change curve occurs when the change necessitates that the people in the organization have to unlearn old behaviors, processes, and systems and learn new ways of doing things. [iii]

One thing that all change models depict is the *Valley of Despair*. The Satir model [iv], as shown in the following diagram, depicts this trough. The Valley of Despair reflects that things usually will get worse before they get better with respect to any change. In this phase, individuals experience negative emotions, like anxiety and fear, and the organization experiences a slowdown in throughput and responsiveness. There is a lot of uncertainty, and sometimes even chaos, in this phase, as both the organization as a whole and the individuals are grappling with eliminating behaviors, processes, and practices and simultaneously adopting new behaviors, processes, and so on.

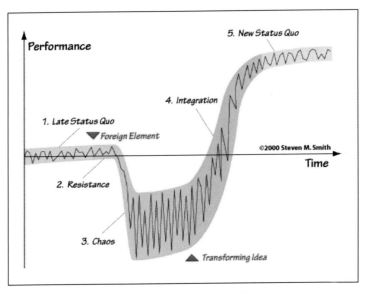

Figure 15.1: The Satir model of change

The Valley of Despair phase has multiple implications:

- The investment of both time and effort to get out of this phase will be high

- It is difficult to climb out of the valley if it gets too steep

- Facilitating change can become the highest priority for the organization, overriding even business priorities

- It is as good an opportunity as it gets to weed out and modify what does not seem to be working well

- Learnings from dealing with this phase should help to modify the rollout of change across the wider organization

Continuous adaptation should be the norm

According to Jim Highsmith, one of the creators of the Agile Manifesto:

> *"We tend to think of change management, perhaps better called adaptation management, as managing the exceptions— the deviations from the norm. But maybe we should view adaptation as the normal and steady state as the exception— it sure seems that way in today's business environment."* [v]

Considering the extent and pace of change in the external environment, to which an adaptive organization will need to be responsive to, it is futile to envision a precise "end state" for any change that impacts the organization as a whole. Hence change/adaptation should be continuous in nature, where the states post change are merely transitory. In line with the principle of emergence, there will be multiple flips to achieve wider and deeper changes, but the fact is that the change of state is in the present and not in the distant future. Hence, if change is not continuous, that needs to be seen as an exception and handled accordingly.

Employee engagement is a prerequisite for extrinsic enablers to have impact

Employee engagement is the emotional attachment and commitment that an employee has toward the business. This means that the employee truly cares about their work, their colleagues, and the organization. Employees are truly engaged when they can identify with the mission and vision of the enterprise, find meaning in their work, and have alignment between their aspirations and the goals of the company. These drivers of engagement are intrinsic in nature. Increasing employee engagement through extrinsic employee wellbeing measures can be achieved only when the employee has already achieved a certain threshold of engagement through intrinsic drivers. Introducing extrinsic employee wellbeing measures is likely to be misused. For example, measures like the flexibility to play table tennis anytime during working hours, not monitoring time in office, and so on are more likely to be misused if introduced when the employee engagement is low. Hence, such changes aimed toward employee wellbeing should not be rushed into and should be introduced only after the employee engagement has reached a certain level of maturity.

Need to slow down to go faster

As mentioned earlier, any change, especially of the intrinsic type, will involve a learning curve and simultaneously a phase of negative emotions like insecurity, anxiety, fear, and so on. Hence, during this period, a slowdown in performance and throughput is inevitable. Expecting people to maintain the same level of performance/throughput and adopt major changes at the same time will put tremendous stress not only on employees, but on processes and structure as well. Hence, a slowdown should be anticipated and planned for accordingly. Care should be taken to factor this in when conducting performance appraisals.

Another important reason to plan for slowing down is to allow sufficient time for inquiry and discovery. In an adaptive organization, the way forward in progressing change should be decided by the network of *agents* and that should be based on emergence. Collaboration, exploration, and learning should always get precedence over speed. Slowing down is in fact necessary to see patterns and to be able to distinguish symptoms from problems. If these basics are in place, not only will speed be a natural outcome, but so will effectiveness and sustainability of the change be.

Watch out for change fatigue

Most people find it difficult to deal with change, at least in the initial period, as it entails people stepping out of their comfort zone. This is especially true when the change is intrinsic in nature. Moreover, change can be stressful, as it can create insecurity about the job and the role and also self-doubt about adapting to the changed circumstances. On top of this, change can be slow and gradual, resulting in people not being able to see the "light at the end of the tunnel." All of this can result in "change fatigue" for individuals and teams, and if this fatigue becomes widespread at the organization level, it can negatively impact the adaptiveness of the organization.

Some fatigue at individual and team level will be unavoidable, especially if the change is significant at the enterprise level. What is important is to spot the fatigue early and implement measures to contain it. Visible signs of change fatigue include symptoms of continuous stress and anxiety, increase in absenteeism, cynicism in conversations, and increased apathy in meetings and group discussions.

The following are some measures to avoid/contain change fatigue:

- Provide outlets for people to express their feelings, especially negative ones. Providing access to internal and/or external counsellors, anonymized qualitative surveys and "all hands" meetings can help people to bring out their feelings into the open and also provide valuable feedback to the leadership team.

- Celebrate successes. These could be in terms of milestones, business impact, behaviors, and so on.

- Ensure that "innovators" and "early adopters" continue to maintain and radiate their enthusiasm through closer participation in leadership meetings, providing opportunities to drive communication and messaging around change in the wider organization, and so on. Since these people are usually "opinion leaders," any change fatigue in them will have a cascading impact on the wider organization.

- Avoid starting too many big changes at the same time. Spreading the start of some initiatives over a few weeks may make a marginal difference strategically but can be key in avoiding fatigue.

- Avoid communication overload, particularly which comes from the "top." Choice of timing and a balanced mix of formal and informal communication can ensure that "noise," which can cause fatigue, is avoided.

According to Arun Arora, a digital partner at McKinsey, and others:

> *"Teams can become overwhelmed by the sheer scale and complexity of the change. Effective leaders, therefore, design small projects with frequent milestones so that teams feel a sense of accomplishment.*

They also focus on keeping things simple, for example by limiting the number of KPIs. One consumer business chose three: amount and source of traffic to digital assets, quality of traffic, and conversion rates." [vi]

Don't "steamroll" the "laggards"

The technology adoption life cycle [vii], as depicted here, also applies to intrinsic change:

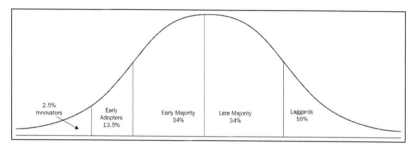

Figure 15.2: Technology adoption life cycle

In any adoption initiative, including change, every organization will have people falling into each of these five categories, but the curve will not necessarily be bell-shaped. Laggards are those who are most resistant to adopting change. In this state, they will adopt change only as a last resort, that is, only when non-adoption threatens their survival or identity. It is quite easy for this group to not be noticed in the initial stages, as their resistance may not be overt right away. Someone can be a laggard primarily due to either feelings of fear and insecurity arising from change or a bad attitude. It is important to identify which of these is the case, as the treatment will be different for each.

It may be tempting to overlook this group of people, as they appear to be a small minority. However, doing so carries a huge risk that many of these people, particularly those with a bad attitude, can turn into a "bad apple."

The impact of being a bad apple is not limited to just that person but has a negative impact at a much wider level, and therefore identifying and dealing with the negative attitudes and behaviors at the earliest possible moment is essential.

While a bad attitude may need a tough stand, fears and insecurities need to be treated with sensitivity and patience. Laggards can provide perspectives on roadblocks and challenges, both current and potential, which might be completely overlooked by the vast majority. Hence, the group of laggards deserves as much attention as the innovators, who are on the other extreme of the adoption curve.

Don't "shoot the enablers"

This is borrowed from the "shoot the messenger" metaphor. Moving to an adaptive state can cause underlying problems to surface very early, particularly when adopting Agile, for example, after implementing **continuous integration** (**CI**), the feedback on whether a check-in has broken the build will be known immediately. This fast feedback should actually encourage the developers to check-in code frequently. However, if the developers are measured based on the number of successful and failed check-ins, CI may actually discourage the developers from performing a check-in frequently. The problem is not the change from no CI to having CI or the behavior post the change. Introducing CI is actually pointing toward at least two underlying problems: measurement which punishes the right behavior and lack of safety nets for developers, such as **test-driven development** (**TDD**), which encourages the right behaviors. In this instance, rolling back the CI implementation would be a grave mistake, as it is an enabler that has exposed the problems which, if resolved, will increase the organization's agility.

Sense of purpose over sense of urgency

Many traditional change models advocate creating a sense of urgency as the first step in the change process. The primary intent is right: to help people to see the need for change. The belief also is that by doing this, change can be sped up. However, there are several problems with urgency being the primary driver, some of the key ones being:

♦ People are inclined to take shortcuts

♦ It discourages creativity and holistic thinking, as the focus is on "just getting it done"

♦ It can create a sense of panic, leading to knee-jerk reactions

♦ Urgency implies a need to be always busy and hence people become keener to be "seen" as busy, which has potential to introduce behavioral anti-patterns

♦ It can lead to a blame game

A better first step is to have a sense of purpose as the primary driver for change. This will help employees to understand the need for change even better, as it will provide a better understanding of the expected outcomes and behaviors. The intrinsic motivation and therefore the ownership of change will be higher, as purpose is more likely to resonate with people, rather than urgency.

Reaching a consensus on the problem statement is the first step toward creating a sense of purpose. This may not be as straightforward, as people's perception of the nature and gravity of the problem often differs considerably. Many times, investing in workshops to get to a common understanding of the problem becomes an absolute necessity.

Focusing on purpose does not imply losing sight of what is currently wrong. Focusing purely on purpose that involves imagining a better future has the risk of inadequate engagement and momentum. This is because, as human beings, we are more willing to take risks to avoid losing something, rather than to gain something more. Hence, the messaging about change must have the appropriate balance of purpose and urgency, to evoke concern about what is wrong and excitement about what the future holds in store.

Clarity on "what's in it for me?"

Intrinsic-driven changes are meaningful and sustainable at an organization level when every impacted individual in the organization can clearly answer this question: "What's in it for me?" Conviction about the change and true buy-in for the change will come only when an individual can answer the question unambiguously.

Answering this question, especially for major changes like culture and structure, is a matter of both perception and reality. For example, regarding learning new skills, some may see this as a dilution of their core skills, while others may see it as an addition to their existing skills. Unless the individual is able to see the potential gains of the change as higher than the potential to lose their skills, intrinsic change within the individual is unlikely to happen. For individuals to truly buy into the change and align themselves fully to make it happen, the change has to appeal to both the head and the heart.

Quite often, leaders assume that what motivated them to undergo change will also motivate everyone else in the enterprise. In reality, the motivations of different groups of people may vary and some may not be motivated at all. Understanding the difference in motivators will help in coming up with ways and means to make the change relevant for people across the business.

A combination of organization, team, and individual-level two-way communication is needed to achieve this. The proportion of investment in individual communication and counselling will depend on which group in the adoption curve the individual belongs to, and generally the investment will be higher as the employee moves toward the right on the curve.

Primary focus on outcomes over means

While initiating change, there must be clarity and alignment about the outcomes that are expected to be influenced by the change. While guidelines and recommendations should be provided on better ways to achieve the intended outcomes, people must be given enough space and freedom to figure out what works best to achieve the outcomes.

This is important from two perspectives. Firstly, the suggested ways of achieving the outcomes, be it in the form of procedures, practices, or policies, are mere hypotheses in a scenario when change is happening constantly. Hence, enforcing "one right way" of doing things will impede a culture of learning and bring rigidity to the system. Secondly, and perhaps more importantly, people value freedom and if their perception of freedom is impacted in a negative way, it will result in rebellious behaviors. The rebellion arising from the perceived loss of freedom has been explained by the reactance theory, which is propounded by Jack Brehm, a professor at the University of Kansas. [viii] The theory has two guiding principles:

♦ The more important the person's freedom is perceived to be, the larger the reaction will be to the removal of it. In other words, if the freedom being threatened is perceived as very important to the individual, they will react on a larger scale than if the freedom is seen as not so important. The stronger the feeling of freedom, the larger the resistance to the limitations.

♦ When several freedoms are threatened, the reaction is greater.

While people may figure out the best way of doing things, and often do so through trial and error, the non-negotiable boundaries must be specified and agreed upon. These include any behaviors that do not align with the values of the enterprise and any shortcuts that compromise on safety and create unacceptable risks.

Small gestures of appreciation can have disproportionate positive impact

As discussed in *Chapter 3, The Enterprise as a Living System*, **lever points**, that is, small measures that have potential for a disproportionate higher impact, can be leveraged to facilitate change. One such lever point is for the leaders to express their appreciation toward employees when the change begins to influence the intended outcome and on special and festive occasions.

For example, Gordon M. Bethune, the former CEO of Continental Airlines, while turning around the airline, sent an unexpected $65 cheque to every employee when Continental made it to the top five for on-time airlines. John McFarlane, the former CEO of ANZ Bank, sent a bottle of champagne to every employee for Christmas, with a card thanking them for their work on the company's "perform, grow and breakout" change program. [ix]

In rational terms, these gestures may appear insignificant. However, human beings are often irrational and such gestures of appreciation are usually remembered by people for months and even years. Such measures, which are unexpected and timed right, can have a much higher impact than direct monetary incentives like commissions and bonuses.

Upgrade skills

Change initiatives often necessitate people to upgrade their skills or even acquire new skills. In the flurry of activities leading to and arising from change, the need to upgrade skills may appear like a low priority item or the need may not be felt at all until it is too late.

For example, a bank decided that its loan underwriters should directly interact with potential loan applicants, with the objective of improving customer-centricity and achieving better risk assessment. It changed its processes accordingly to mandate the interactions. However, after a certain period of time, it was noted that there was no impact on customer-centricity or risk assessment but the morale of the underwriters was distinctly low. On investigating the root cause, it was found that the underwriters had got used to working behind the scenes, dealing with paperwork and computer screens. Given the nature of the work, the underwriters were not hired for or trained for customer-facing skills. The sudden exposure to facing customers directly left the underwriters feeling very nervous and tense.

Respect the hard constraints

Enterprises often imagine being in a utopian state post a change. Quite often, the utopian state is imagined based on idolizing another business. For example, a company might say, "We want to have a culture like Google," or "We want to have a structure like Spotify." While it is fine to draw inspiration from other organizations, blindly wanting to be a copy of them is a highly unrealistic expectation. Each company's context is different and each will have a unique combination of strengths, weaknesses, constraints, and capabilities. Enterprises must be realistic about the extent of change that the firm can handle at a given point in time and based on emergent feedback, the constraints and weaknesses that can be influenced at that point in time must be appropriately addressed.

The analogy of a human body will bring this point to life. Each human body is unique and has positives and weaknesses, and, while bringing change to the body, the constraints prevailing currently must be respected. Take the example of a highly obese person, who is struggling to walk beyond 100 steps at a time but has aspirations to become a champion sportsperson. It will be unrealistic to begin changing them toward becoming a highly physically fit person right away. At that stage, it will be absolutely absurd to put them through any kind of rigorous training meant for athletes. This could pose a serious threat to that person's life. What might be more appropriate in their current state might be to focus on helping them to lose weight through a combination of upper body exercise, diet change and physical therapy. Once they get into slightly better shape, interventions appropriate at that time can be introduced. Once they get into a reasonably good shape, there might be a realization that their knees are not good enough to support running but given their structure and strength in the upper body, they could aim to excel in a sport like javelin.

According to Paul Taylor, a social innovation consultant:

"Maybe we need to accept that not all problems are there to be fixed. That our organizations are flawed. They always have been and always will be.

Perhaps we need:

♦ Reflection and contemplation rather than lots of management activity

♦ Devolving resources and influence to those closest to the problem

♦ Changing little and fast through small-scale experimentation

♦ Not rolling out anything until we have evidence that it works" [x]

Don't manage change, facilitate it

For the business to be able to at least keep up with, if not outpace, the rate of change in the external environment, change has to happen organically, that is, it must be owned and driven by people across the company.

The words manage and change do not go well together, if change needs to happen organically. Manage implies, among other things, thinker-doer separation, upfront planning, and adherence to processes created to minimize uncertainty and variation. When change is managed in this way, people feel like it is imposed on them.

In this context, it is important to remember that **complex adaptive systems (CAS)**, which enterprises are, can be externally guided toward change by nudging or "disturbing" them through appropriate interventions. The interventions will influence the interactions and behaviors of the people, that is, agents in CAS terminology, which will move the organization from the current to the new state. If early feedback indicates that the interventions are not leading to the desired outcome, the nature and extent of interventions may need to be modified. The role of leaders is thus to facilitate the change through appropriate interventions and not to manage the change.

Summary

In this chapter, we learned that change is hard and time-consuming. However, for an organization to enhance agility, change is not only inevitable but it also needs to be continuous and fast enough to keep pace with the changes in the environment. Hence, change deserves strategic importance and should be treated as on a par with the importance of any major initiative.

References

[i] http://www.aleanjourney.com/2015/07/lean-quote-change-is-hard-at-beginning.html

[ii] https://www.mckinsey.com/business-functions/organization/our-insights/the-irrational-side-of-change-management

[iii] http://www.oxford-review.com/blog/is-the-change-curve-real

[iv] https://stevenmsmith.com/ar-satir-change-model/

[v] https://assets.thoughtworks.com/articles/adaptive-leadership-accelerating-enterprise-agility-jim-highsmith-thoughtworks.pdf

[vi] https://www.mckinsey.com/business-functions/digital-mckinsey/our-insights/a-ceo-guide-for-avoiding-the-ten-traps-that-derail-digital-transformations?cid=other-eml-alt-mip-mck-oth-1712

[vii] https://en.wikipedia.org/wiki/Technology_adoption_life_cycle

[viii] https://study.com/academy/lesson/brehms-reactance-theory-definition-lesson-quiz.html

[ix] https://www.mckinsey.com/business-functions/organization/our-insights/the-irrational-side-of-change-management

[x] https://paulitaylor.com/2018/02/12/the-big-problem-with-change-programmes/amp/

SUMMARY

In this era of fast-paced change, enterprises have a choice: to treat the disruptions arising from change as a threat or as an opportunity. If it is the latter, businesses must have the necessary agility to enable them to leverage change for delighting customers and creating competitive advantage.

Organizations are **complex adaptive systems (CAS)** and must be treated as living systems. Businesses that are modeled to optimize on predictability and certainty will struggle to deliver value to their stakeholders in an environment characterized by **volatility, uncertainty, complexity**, and **ambiguity (VUCA)**.

The implication of being a CAS is that the company as a whole is greater than the sum of its foundational blocks and components. This necessitates that the approach to enhancing and sustaining agility is holistic. The capabilities underlying agility will be specific to each enterprise and must be identified and defined considering its own context and that of its ecosystem. The journey to enhancing and sustaining agility, which is perpetual, must balance emergence and planned execution. The ideas and suggestions presented in this book should be treated as guidelines and must be customized to suit the unique circumstances of every business.

OTHER BOOKS YOU MAY ENJOY

If you enjoyed this book, you may be interested in these other books by Packt:

Lean Product Management

Mangalam Nandakumar

ISBN: 978-1-78883-117-8

- ♦ How do you execute ideas that matter?
- ♦ How can you define the right success metrics?
- ♦ How can you plan for product success?
- ♦ How do you capture qualitative and quantitative insights about the product?
- ♦ How do you know whether your product aligns to desired business goals?
- ♦ What processes are slowing you down?

Understanding Software

Max Kanat-Alexander

ISBN: 978-1-78862-881-5

- ♦ See how to bring simplicity and success to your programming world
- ♦ Clues to complexity - and how to build excellent software
- ♦ Simplicity and software design
- ♦ Principles for programmers
- ♦ The secrets of rockstar programmers
- ♦ Max's views and interpretation of the Software industry
- ♦ Why Programmers suck and how to suck less as a programmer
- ♦ Software design in two sentences
- ♦ What is a bug? Go deep into debugging

Leave a review – let other readers know what you think

Please share your thoughts on this book with others by leaving a review on the site that you bought it from. If you purchased the book from Amazon, please leave us an honest review on this book's Amazon page. This is vital so that other potential readers can see and use your unbiased opinion to make purchasing decisions, we can understand what our customers think about our products, and our authors can see your feedback on the title that they have worked with Packt to create. It will only take a few minutes of your time, but is valuable to other potential customers, our authors, and Packt. Thank you!

Index

O

Offshore Development Centers (ODCs) 244
optimal agility 36
organization culture
ownership transfer (OT) 375

P

PBD (privacy by design) 305
people
  agility enablers 222
  agility impediments 210-222
people agility 113
personal traits 115-122
preceding diagram
  about 413
  pairing 414
  project team rotation 414
  split and seed 414
processes
  agility inhibitors 186
  aiming for 100% utilization 189-191
  capacity, determining based on
    throughput 206
  enablers for enhancing
    agility 193-205
  estimation and capacity
    planning 192
product owner (PO) 174
Professional Development Units (PDUs) 236
projection bias 124
project management office (PMO) 260, 284, 393
purpose of enterprise
  redefining 385-389
  validating 385-389

R

request for proposal (RFP) 310
results agility 114
rigid processes
  agility inhibitors 189

S

self-awareness 114
self-organizing teams
  characteristics 163
service-level agreement (SLA) 278
stability bias 125
subject matter experts (SMEs) 310

T

**Taylor's scientific management
    theory** 43-48
technology
  agility enablers 254
  agility inhibitors 243-251
technology partners
  agility inhibitors 353-357
  enablers for enhancing agility 357
time and materials (T&M) 360

U

unique selling proposition (USP) 253
user acceptance testing (UAT) 311

V

values
  aligning, to agility 90
value stream mapping (VSM) 396

W